Warfare in History

SWEIN FORKBEARD'S INVASIONS AND THE DANISH CONQUEST OF ENGLAND 991–1017

Warfare in History

General Editor: Matthew Bennett
ISSN 1358–779X

Previously published volumes in this series
are listed at the back of this book

SWEIN FORKBEARD'S INVASIONS AND THE DANISH CONQUEST OF ENGLAND 991–1017

Ian Howard

THE BOYDELL PRESS

First published 2003
The Boydell Press, Woodbridge

ISBN 0 85115 928 1

The Boydell Press is an imprint of Boydell & Brewer Ltd
PO Box 9, Woodbridge, Suffolk IP12 3DF, UK
and of Boydell & Brewer Inc.
PO Box 41026, Rochester, NY 14604–4126, USA
website: www.boydell.co.uk

A catalogue record for this book is available
from the British Library

Library of Congress Cataloging-in-Publication Data
Howard, Ian, 1941–
  Swein Forkbeard's invasions and the Danish conquest of England,
991–1017 / Ian Howard.
    p. cm. – (Warfare in history)
Includes bibliographical references and index.
  ISBN 0–85115–928–1 (Hardback : alk. paper)
1. Sweyn, King of Denmark, d. 1014.   2. Great Britain – History –
Ethelred II, 979–1016.   3. Ethelred II, King of England, 968?– 1016.
4. Danes – England – History – To 1500.   5. Great Britain – History –
Invasions.   I. Title.   II. Series.
DA159 .H69 2003
942.01'74 – dc21   2002152574

This publication is printed on acid-free paper

Printed in Great Britain by
St Edmundsbury Press Ltd, Bury St Edmunds, Suffolk

Contents

List of figures   vi

General Editor's Preface   vii

Acknowledgements   xi

Abbreviations   xii

Introduction   xiii

1. Propaganda and legend: Accounts of the invasions and conquest of England   1

2. Hindsight: Features explaining the invasions and conquest   12

3. Swein Forkbeard's first invasion   31

4. Swein Forkbeard's second invasion   54

5. The invasion in 1006   72

6. Swein Forkbeard's third invasion   99

7. Thorkell the Tall and the English succession   124

Conclusion   144

Appendices
1. *Heimskringla*   147
2. The *Anglo-Saxon Chronicle*: A reconstruction of the annal for the year 1008   163

Bibliography   169

Index   179

List of Figures

1. The *Anglo-Saxon Chronicle*: schematic   4
2. Swein Forkbeard: family tree   10
3. Æthelred II: family tree   15
4. Expenditure causing high taxation from 991   20
5. Scandinavian itinerary: 991–992   41
6. Scandinavian itinerary: 992–994   45
7. Scandinavian itinerary: 1003–1005   65
8. Ealdorman Ælfhelm's family connections   69
9. The English fleet: 1008–1009   80
10. Scandinavian itinerary: 1009–spring 1010   87
11. Scandinavian itinerary: 1010   89
12. Territories that recognised Swein's authority in August 1013   105
13. Initial stages of King Swein's campaign route   112
14. King Swein's campaign route: 1013   114

General Editor's Preface

Everyone has heard of the invasion and conquest of 1066–72, popularly called the 'Norman Conquest'; few have ever encountered the Danish conquest, completed with the accession of Cnut in 1016, but based upon campaigns over the preceding decade and earlier. In this volume Dr Howard provides an account of the Scandinavian attacks, the English response, the course of events and their later interpretation by the historical sources at our disposal, which leads to a revision of previous views on an important and neglected subject.

One point to emerge is how different the nature of operations conducted by Swein was from the Viking attacks of Alfred's reign. His was a centralised and powerful monarchy in contrast to the more 'private enterprise' activities of the ninth century. Indeed, even to use the word Viking to describe the invasion forces of the early eleventh century is a lazy construct. If it took the Danish king a decade to establish his authority over a country as large as England, this is hardly surprising. William the Conqueror's campaigns took five years, and that with the advantage of knocking out his chief rival at the very beginning.

This ties in with another of Dr Howard's themes on the relative durability of Aethelred II's regime. Although much criticised by English sources in the wake of the conquest, the author's careful scrutiny of all the materials available brings out how much the king did to maintain his rule. The 'Unready' slur has been dismissed by historians of late, and this book provides ample further evidence of the doggedness of English resistance. In part, this was made possible by the wealth of the nation and the ability of the Old English state to tap into it. The knotty issue of 'Danegeld' and just how much it was really worth in financial terms is also thoroughly explored. A modern readership can easily forget that both Alfred and William paid tribute to Scandinavian fleets when the occasion demanded.

From the point of view of straight military history (which of course includes naval activity: Swein and his contemporaries would not have made any distinction between them), Dr Howard provides a detailed and revised analysis of the three phases of invasion which he describes. A common theme throughout (especially in the chapter devoted to Thorkell the Tall), is the importance of mercenary forces in the period. Although the word has negative connotations to modern ears, it is anachronistic to consider that they were regarded in the same way by contemporaries then. Indeed, Thorkell's defence of London in 1013 in support of Aethelred certainly delayed Swein's conquest; and if he changed horses again, this is hardly surprising for so did the country at large. This is not to say that mercenary forces did not have their disadvantages, and it was Aethelred's eagerness to rid himself of some which prompted the St Brice's Day Massacre in 1002, the fall-out from which was to haunt him all his days.

The legacy of nineteenth-century nationalism is still with us, and has distorted many earlier attempts to interpret events at the turn of the first millennium. It is not the least of the virtues of this book that it takes a very balanced view of the who, why, how and what of the Danish invasion and tries to look through the eyes of participants rather than repeat old assumptions about motives and behaviours. A military conquest is necessarily a traumatic event, although the damage to the economy and wider society may be much less than the more recent experience of twentieth-century wars suggests. The change of dynasty in 1016 did not mean a change of social structures or ideology; that was half-a-century in the future.

Matthew Bennett
Royal Military Academy Sandhurst
December 2002

For Mary, Sara and John

Acknowledgements

This book is based, in part, on my doctoral thesis. Whilst researching my thesis I was very fortunate in receiving guidance from many people who found time in a busy schedule of activities to help me. I should like to thank all those who have given me general and specific guidance, including in some instances copies of their published and unpublished work. These include, in alphabetical order, Dr Keith Briffa, Professor Alan Harding, Dr Nick Higham, Professor Simon Keynes, Professor Niels Lund, Mr Stewart Lyon, Dr Alexander Rumble, Professor Donald Scragg and Dr Diana Whaley. I should also like to thank Caroline Palmer, of Boydell & Brewer, for her encouragement and help during the production of this book and the General Editor of the series, Matthew Bennett, for reading and commenting on the draft.

I count myself fortunate in having the excellent resources of the John Rylands University Library of Manchester available to me. I am also grateful to Dr Michelle Brown and Dr Andrew Prescott of the British Library for their help, which included providing me with access to the MS D (Cotton, Tiberius B iv) version of the *Anglo-Saxon Chronicle*.

Last but far from least, I am very happy to acknowledge my considerable debt to my wife, Mary, for her unfailing support and practical advice.

Despite these grateful acknowledgements, the views expressed in this book are my own as are any errors.

Abbreviations

ÆE	*The Æthelredian Exemplar*
ASC (A, B, etc.)	*Anglo-Saxon Chronicle* (MSS A, B, etc.)
ASE	*Anglo-Saxon England*
BL	British Library, London
Brut y Tywysogion	J. Williams ab Ithel (ed.), *Brut y Tywysogion or The Chronicle of the Princes*, Rolls Series, London: Longman, Green, Longman, and Roberts, 1860
EHR	*English Historical Review*
Encomium	A. Campbell (ed.), *Encomium Emmae Reginae*, Camden 3rd series, vol. LXXII, London: Royal Historical Society, 1949
JW	R. R. Darlington and P. McGurk (eds), *The Chronicle of John of Worcester*, Volume II, *The Annals from 450 to 1066*, Oxford: Clarendon Press, 1995
MGH	*Monumenta Germaniae Historica*
S. (+ number)	P. H. Sawyer, *Anglo-Saxon Charters: An Annotated List and Bibliography*, London: Royal Historical Society, 1968 (by number)
TRHS	*Transactions of the Royal Historical Society*
Whitelock, *EHD*	D. Whitelock (ed.), *English Historical Documents*, vol. I, *c. 500–1042*, London: Eyre & Spottiswoode, 1955

Introduction

This book deals with the Scandinavian invasions of England during the reign of King Æthelred II (the Unready), starting with an invasion leading to the battle of Maldon in 991 and concluding with the Danish conquest of England more than twenty years later. Swein Forkbeard, king of Denmark, played a significant part in the invasions of England until his death in February 1014. The conquest was completed by his son, King Cnut the Great, who was acknowledged as king of all England at the beginning of 1017.

Attention is focused upon the activities of Swein Forkbeard and, after his death, the Danish warlord, Thorkell the Tall. Both were outstanding warriors and political leaders of what is sometimes termed 'The Second Viking Age'. A focus upon the invasions and conquest from the Scandinavian viewpoint provides new insight into events in England during this period. In particular, it reveals the complexity of the political and economic relationship between the leaders of Scandinavian *lið*s,[1] or armies, and the English establishment.

English wealth was an important factor in attracting the attention of the Scandinavian *lið*s that invaded England. Most commentators have focused on the payment of *gafol*, or tribute, during this period, but, whilst acknowledging its significant cost to the English and its value to the invaders, this book also describes the evidence of other costs arising as a result of the invasions which, together, created an economic impact on an annual basis. This economic impact is investigated and it is shown that the invasions had the effect of stimulating trade and the economy for much of the period. An important distinction between English and continental military technology is also described and evidence is considered supporting the deduction that it was this distinction that made England a target for Scandinavian invasions in preference to countries nearer home.

This account of the invasions is based on research undertaken during preparations for the author's doctoral thesis.[2] A study of British, Flemish, Scandinavian and North German source material, coupled with a chronological analysis of events and tracing the itineraries of Scandinavian armies provided a fresh and exciting insight into the events of the period, demonstrating that the relationship between the Scandinavian invaders and the English establishment was far more complex than has been supposed and that events in England had a significant impact upon the development of the Scandinavian kingdoms.

One of the early invaders was Olaf Tryggvason, a Norwegian adventurer who had campaigned successfully in Slav countries along the Baltic coast. He and his followers joined a Scandinavian invasion of England, then he made a peace agreement with King Æthelred whereby he campaigned against

---

1 For an explanation of the Scandinavian *lið* see Chapter 3, pp. 31–2.
2 Howard, 'Swein Forkbeard's Invasions of England'.

Æthelred's enemies on the Irish Sea coasts as one of the commanders of the king's mercenary army. Æthelred and Olaf became friends and allies and the English king provided encouragement and assistance to Olaf when he undertook the expedition that resulted in him becoming king of Norway.[3]

After Olaf's departure, the mercenary army in England became less reliable and Æthelred lost patience with his mercenaries when one of the army leaders, Pallig, decided to rebel. Responding to treachery with treachery, King Æthelred ordered the notorious St Brice's Day massacre. Æthelred's objective was a surprise attack on mercenary forces billeted in the south-west of England but the massacre was also extended to include Danish traders in some other parts of the country. The king of Denmark, Swein Forkbeard, had once served Æthelred as a mercenary but, from the time of the massacre, he became his implacable enemy. In exploring these and the subsequent events, which led to the Danish conquest, the importance of Scandinavian leaders such as Tostig, Heming, Eglaf, St Olaf and Erik of Lade, will be explained.

The source research included chronological analyses, revealing that the timing of and relationship between events differs from what has previously been supposed. An important consequence of this approach is the recognition that Olaf Tryggvason probably led an attack on London in September 993, not, as previously thought, in September 994. This revised dating resolves the problem of what happened to a Scandinavian army that attacked Bamburgh in 993; allows time for Archbishop Sigeric to participate in drawing up the peace agreement, known as _II Æthelred_, before he died; and allows time for Olaf Tryggvason to carry out the terms of the agreement before leaving England to become king of Norway.

The chronological analyses also suggest that, in the period 1013 to 1023, Scandinavian and North German sources have been unnecessarily discounted or amended in analysing events in England. A significant explanation for this has been the inability of historians to align events in these sources with events recorded in the various versions of the _Anglo-Saxon Chronicle_. A summary of a chronological analysis of _Heimskringla_ and _Knytlinga saga_ is provided as Appendix 1 to this book. This analysis resolves many problems of alignment with the _Anglo-Saxon Chronicle_ and, consequently, justifies the use of Scandinavian and North German sources to help explain events in England in the decade following Swein Forkbeard's death. This leads to a significant reinterpretation of the events which culminated in the recognition of Swein Forkbeard's son, Cnut, as king of all England.

This study shows that members of the English establishment, and King Æthelred in particular, were not so much the victims of events as used to be supposed and it becomes increasingly apparent that the generally accepted view of Æthelred's reign and English reaction to the invasions need reassessment.[4]

---

[3]   The agreement is numbered amongst the Laws as _II Æthelred. ASC_ C D E _s.a._ 994 refers to the agreement and the cordial relations between Olaf and Æthelred. See also, Andersson, 'The Viking Policy of Ethelred the Unready' and Sawyer, 'Ethelred II, Olaf Tryggvason, and the Conversion of Norway'.

[4]   A task which I am undertaking in _The Reign of Æthelred II (the Unready)_, forthcoming.

1

Propaganda and Legend:
Accounts of the Invasions and Conquest of England

Manuscript Sources

We are fortunate in having a number of documentary sources for events in this period, some of which focus directly on the invasions. The manuscript sources include annals from the various versions of the *Anglo-Saxon Chronicle* (*ASC*)[1] that are contemporary, or nearly contemporary, with events. A related source is the *Chronicle of John of Worcester* (*JW*)[2] which, though written about one hundred years after the events, draws upon the *ASC* and some other early sources that are no longer otherwise extant. The *Encomium Emmae Reginae* (*Encomium*)[3] is a source dating from the mid-eleventh century, containing information about Swein Forkbeard's final invasion of England and Cnut's conquest. Much of the information in the *Encomium* came directly or indirectly from contemporary witnesses who were themselves leading participants in those events. There are other documentary sources that will be referred to, as they become relevant.

At the outset, it should be acknowledged that a detailed critical analysis of the manuscript sources leads inevitably to doubts about their reliability. Fortunately, advances made in our knowledge of the late Anglo-Saxon period have been extensive and exciting. Dating techniques, such as dendrochronology, have been developed and used to good effect. We have a better understanding of climate and weather conditions and their impact on events. Archaeological research has been extensive, opening up new perspectives on the age, as has the study of numismatics. Palaeographical research and the careful analysis of diplomas have added greatly to our knowledge. Aided by developments in other research disciplines, historians have established a clearer understanding of economic, social and political changes. Because of the increase in background knowledge, it is now easier to undertake a reasoned criticism of the written

---

[1] There are several translations of the *ASC*, including: Whitelock, *English Historical Documents*, vol. I, *c. 500–1042*; Garmonsway, *The Anglo-Saxon Chronicle*; Swanton, *The Anglo-Saxon Chronicle*.
[2] Darlington and McGurk, *The Chronicle of John of Worcester*, vol. II, *The Annals from 450 to 1066*.
[3] Campbell, *Encomium Emmae Reginae*. This book has been reissued with a supplementary introduction by Simon Keynes, Cambridge: Cambridge University Press, 1998.

sources that have so dominated our knowledge of this period. Not surprisingly, we find that they are sometimes biased, evasive, contradictory or deliberately misleading. Yet the written sources remain a most valuable asset as we attempt to unravel the story of the past and this justifies a critical approach to them aimed at gleaning a better understanding of events.

To appreciate the significance of manuscript sources, such as the *ASC*, the *Encomium* and *JW*, we should consider their contemporary use as vehicles for political messages. From the mid-tenth century, when Northumbria became part of it, the kingdom of England had boundaries similar to those of today. The population of England at the turn of the tenth and eleventh centuries was probably no more than two million and could have been much less. Domesday Book provides information about population levels at the end of the eleventh century, and one hundred years earlier the population might have been less if allowance is made for the positive effects on population growth of economic expansion in the intervening period.[4] The English economy was largely agrarian and its social structure hierarchical. The existence of a strong centralised monarchy, based in southern England is evidence that road, river and coastal trading routes were sufficient for government communication and control purposes throughout most of the kingdom.

The subject of communication is an important one. If a government cannot communicate readily and frequently with a region it cannot exercise political control over it. The king's council comprised the most important clerical and lay leaders of the whole country, though it usually met in the south at various places in the Thames valley. There, important matters of state were debated and policy and law were developed. Although Latin was the common language of communication throughout Western Europe, it is apparent that the king's councillors preferred to speak and hear the vernacular language: Old English. This was so even on semi-formal occasions, if we may trust the evidence of the laws, homilies and annals written in Old English and the translations of important secular and religious works from Latin into Old English.

Communication was through the spoken word and manuscripts were evidently produced, amongst other reasons, to facilitate spoken communication. A simple example of the communication process will help to explain how the system worked. The king held a formal council, which lasted for several days. During the course of the council there would be occasions when the assembly would listen to formal readings: homilies containing religious messages, laws to remind members of the assembly of their legal responsibilities, annalistic material containing political messages. Assuming that at least 125 important leaders of society heard the messages, that they each returned to their own regions and convened local meetings at which they repeated what they had heard to 75 local leaders of society, that each of the latter communicated the message to 25 other people, then more than 10% of the population would have heard the

---

4   Darby, *Domesday England*, provides analyses of the population of England at the end of the eleventh century.

messages from the king's assembly at first, second or third hand.[5] In a hierarchical society, such as Anglo-Saxon England, few people of any consequence could have missed these royal communications.

Propaganda

One of the reasons why we have so much manuscript material for this period of Scandinavian invasions is that one of King Æthelred's leading ministers, Archbishop Wulfstan of York, believed very strongly in the value of maintaining a written record of the laws, homilies and annals which were probably used at important assemblies. He was a prolific writer and the different versions of his laws and homilies demonstrate that the written word was not sacrosanct as in, say, modern statute law. The written word was there to facilitate spoken communication and was slightly variable according to changing circumstances.[6]

In the confused political situation that followed King Æthelred's death in April 1016, Archbishop Wulfstan tried to rally support for Æthelred's eldest surviving son, Edmund (Ironside). King Edmund was in difficulties because England was being invaded by a Scandinavian army led by Cnut and because his succession to the English throne was disputed by his step-mother, Queen Emma, and the Ealdorman of Mercia, Eadric, who wanted Emma's son, Edward, to be king. Edward was the elder of Emma's two sons by Æthelred.[7]

As part of a propaganda campaign supporting King Edmund, Archbishop Wulfstan instructed his scribes to prepare an updated version of the *ASC*. This version of the *ASC*, which will be referred to as the *Æthelredian Exemplar* (*ÆE*), drew upon earlier versions of the *ASC* and other sources for early annals. Then annals covering the reigns of King Æthelred and King Edmund were added by one man.[8] The scribes were probably based at Worcester, a see that Wulfstan held in plurality with York. Version D[9] of the *ASC* is possibly a fair copy of this updated version up to and including part of the annal for the year 1016. The annals covering the reigns of King Æthelred and King Edmund in versions C and E of the *ASC* are derived from the same source.[10] Figure 1, p. 4,

---

[5] i.e. 125 councillors x 75 local leaders = 9,375 people. 9,375 x 25 = 234,375 people, or 11.7% of a total population of 2,000,000 people.

[6] For Wulfstan's involvement in the written laws of the period, see Wormald, 'Æthelred the Lawmaker', pp. 47–80; and Wormald, *The Making of English Law*. For Wulfstan's homilies, see Bethurum, *The Homilies of Wulfstan*.

[7] Keynes, *The Diplomas of King Æthelred 'the Unready'*, p. 187, n. 116 and 'Table I: Subscriptions of the Athelings, 993–1015'. Edward eventually succeeded to the throne in 1042 and became known as Edward the Confessor.

[8] Wulfstan and the annals added to *ASC ÆE* are considered in Howard, 'Swein Forkbeard's Invasions of England', pp. 61–89 and 94–101.

[9] BL MS Cotton Tiberius, B iv.

[10] C: BL MS Cotton Tiberius B i. E: Oxford, Bodleian Library MS Laud 636. *ASC* versions C and E are copied from exemplars to which had been added the *ÆE* annals for the period covering the reigns of Æthelred and Edmund.

Figure 1. The *Anglo-Saxon Chronicle*: schematic

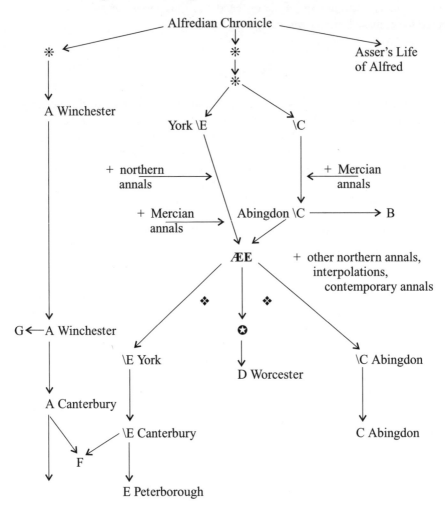

* = Intermediate exemplars
\E = Exemplar of E   \C = Exemplar of C
ÆE = Æthelredian Exemplar
❖ = \E and \C were updated with ÆE annals for King Æthelred's reign
✪ = D was a fair copy of ÆE

provides a schematic illustration of how various versions of the *ASC* were inter-related.[11]

The hero of the new annals was King Edmund. There is a marked contrast in the annals between English resistance to invasion under Edmund's energetic direction and that offered by the English leadership during the reign of King

[11] Discussed in more detail in Howard, 'Swein Forkbeard's Invasions of England', with schematics, Figures 5 and 6, on pp. 53–4.

Æthelred. To emphasise this contrast, the annals concentrate on the Scandinavian invasions during the reigns of Æthelred and Edmund; this has caused Professor Keynes to remark:

> By concentrating on the Danish invasions the chronicler has telescoped the reign, and has created the impression that the invasions were the only theme worthy of attention and that the country suffered continuously under them.[12]

The annals indicate that the English suffered defeat because God was punishing them for the murder of King Edward the Martyr, King Æthelred's half-brother and predecessor, whose death had never been properly explained and avenged:

> No worse deed for the English race was done than this was, since they first sought out the land of Britain. Men murdered him, but God glorified him. In life he was an earthly king; he is now, after death, a heavenly saint. His earthly kinsmen would not avenge him, but his Heavenly Father has greatly avenged him.[13]

The passage continues in similar vein and the words may originate from the hand of Archbishop Wulfstan himself. English mistakes and indecisiveness were also blamed on the king's ineffective council or were directly attributed to the treachery of some of the king's ministers, especially Ealdorman Eadric of Mercia, King Edmund's enemy. However, Wulfstan took care that there was no direct criticism of King Æthelred, Edmund's father, because he did not want the people to be concerned by the biblical warning that the sins of the father would be visited on the sons. Despite this, the clear contrast between the two reigns and Edmund's energetic leadership implied a criticism of King Æthelred, which later writers were to embellish.

In chronological order our next important source is the *Encomium*. One of the propaganda objectives of the *Encomium* was to glorify the Danish conquest of England. It made Cnut's struggle and eventual success more praiseworthy by enhancing the heroic attributes of his opponent, King Edmund. Although it did not mention King Æthelred directly, the enhanced praise of King Edmund served to give added emphasis to the perceived failure of his predecessor. The *Encomium* also condemned Edmund's enemy and opponent, Ealdorman Eadric of Mercia, as a treacherous villain. This served the dual purpose of explaining Edmund's downfall and of justifying Cnut's treatment of Eadric: after at first befriending Ealdorman Eadric, Cnut had taken an early opportunity to betray him and have him killed.

The next of our sources is *JW*. This shows an awareness of the *ASC ÆE* annals, and some annals which were removed from *ASC* D. It also contains quotations from what is probably a lost life of King Edmund, which was written in the mid-eleventh century as propaganda supporting Edmund's exiled son as

---

[12] Keynes, 'Declining Reputation', p. 233.
[13] Translation of *ASC* D: BL Cotton Tiberius B iv, *s.a.* 979. I discussed the murder and the development of the cult of King Edward the Martyr in a paper for the Manchester Centre for Anglo-Saxon Studies (April 2002). Much of the information from this paper will be incorporated into my forthcoming book, *The Reign of Æthelred II (the Unready)*.

successor to the childless King Edward the Confessor. Edmund was the hero of the 'life' and was given the by-name 'Ironside'. Ealdorman Eadric of Mercia was the villain and was given the by-name 'Streona', which may be translated as 'acquisitive' or 'grasping'. Since Eadric had been King Æthelred's leading ealdorman and advisor, there was again an implied criticism of Æthelred.

In practice, Edmund was never recognised as king by the whole of England and his six-month reign was no more than a postscript to the exceptionally long reign of his father. However, so much favourable propaganda was written about him in these sources that Edmund Ironside has been long-remembered as one of the great hero kings of Anglo-Saxon times,[14] whilst his father has been denigrated as one of the most ineffective kings ever to have ruled England.

Legendary Accretion

There was much legendary accretion to the stories of the invasions. In particular, later writers developed the story of the murder of King Edward, King Æthelred's half-brother and predecessor. They accused Æthelred's mother of instigating the murder of her stepson so that her own son could succeed to the throne. In the legends, Æthelred and his mother are condemned by no less a person than St Dunstan, who forecast that the country would suffer from invasions following his, Dunstan's, death and that Æthelred would suffer directly because he had benefited from his brother's murder. These legends were pleasing to the political establishment following the Norman Conquest because they explained why God had allowed the Anglo-Saxon monarchy to be overthrown and England to be conquered, first by a Danish king and then by a Norman duke.

Professor Keynes recognised the progressive nature of the stories about Æthelred and the conquest and provided detailed commentary on the phenomenon, in 1978, a thousand years after Æthelred's accession.[15] The legendary accretion is to be found in many sources, including various lives of St Dunstan, the chronicles of Henry of Huntingdon and the chronicles of William of Malmesbury. The following extract from Eadmer provides an example of what was being written in the late eleventh and twelfth centuries:

> This Ethelred, because he had grasped the throne by the shedding of his brother's blood, was sternly denounced by Dunstan who declared that Ethelred himself would live in blood, that he would suffer invasions of foreign foes and all their horrible oppression and that the Kingdom itself was to be worn again and again by bloody devastations.[16]

---

14 Edmund's reputation and these sources are discussed in I. Howard, 'Sources for the Life of Edmund Ironside', an unpublished paper read at the Leeds International Medieval Congress on 13 July 2000.
15 Keynes, 'Declining Reputation', pp. 227–53.
16 Bosanquet (trans.), *Eadmer's History of Recent Events in England*, pp. 3–4.

Because King Æthelred ruled peacefully for many years, the legends agreed that God protected England until His saint, Dunstan, had died. Disaster then struck. Eadmer describes what happened:

> The indolence of the King became known round about and the greed of those outside her borders, aiming rather at the wealth than the lives of the English, invaded the country by sea at one point after another and laid waste at first the villages and cities next the coast, then those further inland and in the end the whole province, driving the inhabitants in wretchedness from their homes. The king instead of meeting them in arms panic-stricken shamelessly offered them money sueing for peace; where-upon they accepted the price and retired to their homes, only to return in still greater numbers and still more ruthless, from renewed invasion to receive increased rewards.[17]

This is the account of the Scandinavian invasions and the English reaction that has survived over the centuries and may still be found in some historical accounts of the period today. However, following the itineraries of the Scandinavian invasions it becomes apparent that the truth is less simple and probably a lot more exciting.

Swein Forkbeard

It is by focusing upon the activities of this king of Denmark that it has been possible to establish a new understanding of the Scandinavian invasions from 991 onwards, invasions which culminated in the Danish conquest of England.

Essentially, Swein Forkbeard was a competent military commander, politician and diplomat, attributes, which will become apparent as this study unfolds and which, together, contributed to making Swein a formidable and successful king. Although Swein was one of the most influential men of his age, surprisingly little is known about him. There is propaganda, legend and saga; the chroniclers who mention him are partisan. The following synopsis of his life is based upon a detailed analysis of the available sources. Some of our available written evidence is in Snorri Sturluson's great history of the kings of Norway, which is generally known as *Heimskringla*.[18] Although it was written in the thirteenth century, it evidently draws upon the work of earlier writers. Snorri was also an avid collector of skaldic verses that were created by men who were contemporaries of, and were often acquainted with, the kings. Snorri uses and explains many of these verses in his work. For Swein Forkbeard's life, particular reference should be made to that part of *Heimskringla* known as Olaf Tryggvason's saga.[19] There are other Scandinavian sources, such as Knytlinga

---

[17] *Ibid.* p. 4.
[18] See Appendix 1, below.
[19] Jónsson (ed.), *Heimskringla*, contains the variant readings as well as a separate analysis of the skaldic verses. There are English translations of *Heimskringla*. One that is often recommended is Hollander, *Heimskringla*. Other translations are to be found in Monsen, *Heimskringla*; Laing, *Heimskringla, the Norse King Sagas*; Laing, *Heimskringla, the Olaf Sagas; and Hearn, The Sagas of Olaf Tryggvason and of Harald the Tyrant*.

saga, the saga of the Jomsvikings, Danish 'king lists', the writings of Saxo Grammaticus and Sven Aggesen, which are referred to as appropriate. Because of the nature of the sources, they are subject to various interpretations: some of these interpretations are discussed, here and in later chapters.

Swein was born c. 960, a date with a probable accuracy of +/– two years. His father was Harald Bluetooth, king of the Danes. Harald's realm included the Jutland peninsula, the Danish islands such as Fyn and Sjæland, and the coastal regions of Halland, Skåne, Bleking, Agder, Grenland, Vestfold, Vingulmark and Raumariki. His influence over the Norwegian regions varied considerably and towards the end of his reign the Norwegian leader, Earl Hákon of Lade, was openly defying him. Harald had alliances with the Slavs on the southern Baltic coast and some influence on Scandinavian enclaves on that coast, Jomsborg being an important example. Inevitably, there was conflict between Harald and the rulers of Sweden as they disputed control over the central and western Baltic.

Swein's mother was not of noble birth: she was later described as a servant girl.[20] Harald never recognised his son as a potential successor to his kingdom. However, in c. 987, there was a rebellion against Harald in which Swein was involved. Harald's forces appear to have got the better of the conflict but, in the fighting, King Harald received wounds from which he subsequently died. His legitimate sons had pre-deceased him and, in these circumstances, Swein was able to make himself king of the Danes.

As king, Swein continued his father's policies. The manner of his accession had weakened the Danish alliances with the Slavs on the southern coast of the Baltic. It is possible that Swein led an expedition against the Slavs and suffered setbacks, since there is a story in Adam of Bremen's *History of the Archbishops of Hamburg-Bremen* that he was captured by the Slavs.[21] This story was later subject to much legendary accretion and is to be found in a greatly embellished form in the Saga of the Jomsvikings.[22] The outcome of his dealings with the Slavs was that Swein re-established his alliances by a marriage to the sister of King Boleslav. Swein had already been married and had a daughter, Gytha, who was born c. 980. Swein's new wife took on the Scandinavian name Gunnhild when she married. She was probably the mother of his son, Cnut the Great, who eventually succeeded Swein as king of Denmark and England.[23] This marriage

---

[20] Blake, *The Saga of the Jomsvikings*, c. 10, pp. 11 and 12: she is named as 'Saum-Æsa' and described as 'a poor woman' but 'by no means ignorant'. See also Olaf Tryggvason's saga, in Jónsson, *Heimskringla*, K. 12: 'Haraldr konungr er nú gamall mjok, en hann á þann einn son, er hann ann lítit ok frilluson er.'

[21] Tschan, *Adam of Bremen*, p. 75, c. xxix (27); see also, Lappenberg, *Mag. Adami*, Bk 2, c. 27.

[22] Blake, *The Saga of the Jomsvikings*, pp. 25–7, c. 25.

[23] Jónsson, *Heimskringla*, Olaf Tryggvason saga, K 34; also, Trillmich, *Thietmari Merseburgensis*, Bk 7, c. 39 (28). There is a confusing reference in Adam of Bremen's history of this period, which says that Cnut was Swein's son by a later marriage to the Swedish queen, Sigrid. See Lappenberg, *Mag. Adami*, Bk 2, c. 37. Some historians have accepted this statement at face-value; others have suggested that Gunnhild and Sigrid were one and the same person: see, for instance, the footnotes to Lappenberg, *Mag. Adami*, Bk 2, c. 37, and the footnotes to Trillmich, *Thietmari Merseburgensis*, Bk 7, c. 39 (28). Cnut's parentage and date of

also made Swein the brother-in-law of Sigvaldi, the Danish ruler of Jomsborg, who had previously married a sister of King Boleslav.

Early in his reign he sent an expedition to attack Earl Hákon of Lade in Norway. His forces were reinforced by Danish allies from Jomsborg on the southern Baltic coast. Later legends state that the expedition was led by the commander of the Jomsborg contingent, Sigvaldi, who was accompanied by his younger brother, Thorkell the Tall, a man who was to have a significant influence on Scandinavian and English history. The attempted invasion of Norway was a failure and the Danish fleet suffered considerable losses, although Sigvaldi and Thorkell were able to escape. The history of Swein Forkbeard, the Jomsborg Vikings and the expedition against Norway was subject to much legendary accretion.[24] Despite a comment in the chronicle of Thietmar of Merseburg to the effect that Swein was captured by Norwegians,[25] it is unlikely that he took part personally in the campaign against Norway.

For some time the Danes had not been seriously troubled by the Swedes because of internal disputes. However, at about this time Erik the Victorious became the undisputed ruler of the Swedes and turned his attention to expanding his influence westwards. There is no reliable evidence for what happened other than that King Swein was driven into exile in c. 990. His wife, Gunnhild, was also driven into exile, probably in Pomerania on the southern Baltic coast, where she subsequently died.[26] Denmark appears to have fallen under Swedish influence whilst Swein was travelling abroad.

Swein's travels and successful invasion of England are described in Chapter 3, below. In 995, following the death of Erik the Victorious and other events that weakened Swedish influence, Swein was able to return to Denmark. His return was opposed and there is some evidence of fighting around Hedeby.[27] According to the chronicle of Adam of Bremen, Swein suffered military setbacks at this time. However, he overcame his difficulties by arranging a marriage to the Swedish dowager queen, Sigrid.[28] Swein's new marriage alliance, coupled with a marriage alliance between his daughter, Gytha, and Erik Hákonarson of Lade brought him a potential hegemony over the whole of

birth were explored in I. Howard, 'The Anglo-Saxon Chronicle *s.a.* 1013 and Some Problems of Chronology', a Paper read at the Leeds International Medieval Congress on 13 July 1998.

[24] See Blake, *The Saga of the Jomsvikings*.

[25] 'a Northmannis insurgentibus captus': Trillmich, *Thietmari Merseburgensis*, p. 392, c. 36 (26). Thietmar's Chronicle is also in Lappenberg, *Thietmari Chronicon*, pp. 723–871.

[26] Jónsson, *Heimskringla*, Olaf Tryggvason saga, K 91. See also, Trillmich, *Thietmari Merseburgensis*, Bk vii, p. 396, c. 39 (28): note that Thietmar's 'quae a viro suimet diu depulsa' may be translated to read that she 'was exiled for a long time *from* her husband' rather than '*by* her husband' as it is usually translated. The story in the *Encomium* that she was brought back from exile by her sons after Swein's death has been rejected here. It appears to owe much to Queen Emma's imagination and is there as a contrast to her own return from exile with her sons after the troubles that followed King Cnut's death.

[27] The evidence is the inscriptions on the famous Hedeby Stones: see Lund, 'The Danish Perspective', pp. 127–8 and plates 6.6 and 6.7.

[28] Jónsson, *Heimskringla*, Olaf Tryggvason saga, K 91. See also, Tschan, *Adam of Bremen*, p. 81, c. xxxix (37). The passage is confused and includes some information that is unlikely to be correct.

Figure 2. Swein Forkbeard: family tree

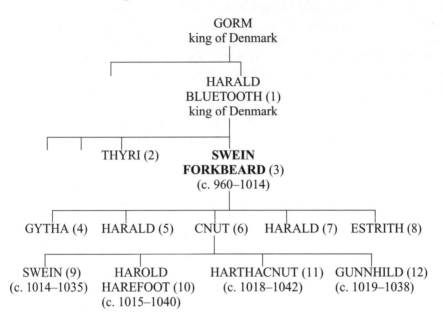

(1)   There is rune stone evidence (DRI no. 55) that Harald Bluetooth married a Slav princess named TOVA
(2)   Harald's daughter, though it is not certain whether she was Tova's daughter. Harald may have married more than once and also had liaisons.
(3)   Jónsson *Heimskringla*, Olaf Tryggvason saga K. 12, and Blake, *Jomsviking Saga* c. 10, indicate that Swein was the son of a servant girl, named SAUM-ÆSA. Harald Bluetooth's sons, other than Swein, appear to have pre-deceased him. He may have been survived by daughters other than Thyri.
(4)   Mother unknown. Gytha married Earl ERIK HAKONARSON in c. 997. Her son was Earl HAKON ERIKSSON (998–1030).
(5)   Full brother of Cnut. Died before his father.
(6)   Mother GUNNHILD (?) / SIGRID (?). Born c. 990 or c. 999; died 1035. King of England, Denmark and Norway. Married ÆLFGIFU of Northampton in 1013. Married Queen EMMA (Ælfgifu) in 1017.
(7)   Younger half brother or full brother of Cnut.
(8)   Half sister or full sister of Cnut. Married ULF THORGILSSON. Her son was SWEIN ESTRITHSSON (or 'ULFSSON'), who became king of Denmark.
(9)   King of Norway.   (10) King of England.   (11) King of Denmark and England.
(12) Queen of Germany through her marriage to HENRY (later Emperor Henry III).

Scandinavia. This position was consolidated when Swein, in alliance with the Swedes and Erik of Lade's Norwegians, defeated Olaf Tryggvason, king of Norway, at the sea battle of Svold, in c. 1000. It is not known when Sigrid died but she had a daughter, Estrith, and probably a son, Harald, by Swein. Harald, as was normal practice, was named after Swein's father. There is some confusion in our sources because Swein appears to have had more than one son named Harald, possibly because he was following the custom of replacing the name of a dead child. The first 'Harald' was Cnut's elder full brother, the son of Gunnhild, and he pre-deceased his father. The name 'Harald' was later given to another of Swein's sons, probably by Queen Sigrid. There are references to Cnut having a younger brother of this name in our sources, including an English 'notice of confraternity'.[29] There are various interpretations of Swein's marital arrangements and the status of his children: see Figure 2, opposite, for his family tree.

Events in England, which are described in Chapter 4, led to Swein's second invasion of that country during the years 1003 to 1005. Subsequently, Swein encouraged Scandinavian armies to invade and remain in England. Amongst other advantages, a suitable venue with potentially rich pickings distracted adventurers, who might otherwise have been a disruptive influence in Scandinavia. By 1012, however, circumstances in England were changing such that Swein felt that it was necessary to lead an invasion of that country personally. It was not until the late summer of 1013 that Swein's preparations were completed. The successful invasion of England and the campaign that culminated in the exile of King Æthelred and the recognition of Swein as king of England are described in Chapter 6.

Scandinavians

It will be observed that the word 'Scandinavian' is often used in this book rather than 'Viking' or a national designation. Scandinavian adventurers of this period were sometimes raiders, sometimes traders, sometimes mercenaries, and sometimes settlers. The same group of Scandinavians might perform different functions at different times or in different places. There is no one portmanteau word that can account for a complex social, military and political phenomenon but the term 'Scandinavian' is often less misleading than 'Viking' which may be deemed too restrictive to imply all these possibilities.[30] Nor is it realistic to give the forces that invaded England a national designation. They were formed of adventurers from many regions of the modern Scandinavian countries and there is circumstantial evidence that they included other nationalities such as Slavs from the southern Baltic states and Celts from Ireland.

[29] N. R. Ker, *Catalogue of Manuscripts Containing Anglo-Saxon*, p. 317. See also references to Cnut's younger brother, Harald, in Campbell, *Encomium*, Bk I, c. 3; Bk II, c. 2.
[30] For a more detailed consideration of the word 'Viking' see Niels Lund, 'Viking Age'.

2

Hindsight: Features Explaining the Invasions and Conquest

The Invasions

The invasions show how the objectives of Swein Forkbeard and his Scandinavian followers changed, over time, from raiding and tribute seeking to a conquest that must have seemed impossible in 991 but was achieved with comparative ease in 1013–14. More than the objectives may have changed during the period of Swein's invasions. Professor Niels Lund has pondered the question of whether the 'Viking armies' were transformed from privately raised forces (*lið*) to 'state armies recruited on the basis of a Public obligation' (*leding*). Professor Lund concludes that:

> there can be little doubt that the armies involved were bigger and probably drawn from a wider area, indeed from most of Scandinavia, than Viking armies had previously been. This does not mean, however, that they were different in principle from those armies with which the west was already familiar.[1]

During this period the powerful centralised monarchy, or more correctly 'oligarchy', that controlled England was forced to change its attitude to the Scandinavian invaders several times and was eventually forced to relinquish power. One consequence was the long and successful reign of King Cnut the Great, Swein Forkbeard's son.[2]

In the ninth century, Scandinavian invaders had threatened to overwhelm the Anglo-Saxon kingdoms of England. They established a permanent presence in eastern England in territory that became known as the Danelaw. They also established a significant presence in lands bordering the Irish Sea including north-western England. During the tenth century the Anglo-Saxons recovered control of England and by the mid-tenth century the country, including the Danelaw and Northumbria, was united under the rule of the West Saxon kings. King Æthelred's father, King Edgar, was known as 'the Peaceable' because there is no record of significant invasions during his reign and the country as a whole enjoyed a period of peace and increasing economic prosperity. A renewal of the

---

[1] Lund, 'Armies'.
[2] Figure 2, p. 10, above.

Scandinavian invasions of England towards the end of the tenth century eventually threatened this prosperity.[3]

Swein Forkbeard succeeded his father as king of Denmark in about 987 after taking part in an uprising in which his father was wounded and subsequently died.[4] Swein took part in three invasions of England. He participated in a large-scale invasion in the closing decade of the tenth century, but not as supreme commander. Although he had succeeded his father as king of Denmark, some sources say that he was in exile at the time:

> For indeed, abandoning his sovereignty at that time to foreign enemies, he exchanged safety for roving, peace for warfare, a kingdom for exile[5]

His contribution to the Scandinavian army at that time seems to have been as an important commander of a band of adventurers.

Following the St Brice's Day massacre which, from a Danish viewpoint, was a treacherous attack on Scandinavians who were settled in parts of England, and which was sanctioned by King Æthelred, Swein Forkbeard took personal command of an army and invaded England for a second time in 1003. Following this attack a state of war existed between invading Scandinavians and the Anglo-Saxons, which was fought in England for several years.

In 1012 an agreement between King Æthelred and an invading Scandinavian army encouraged the direct intervention of King Swein of Denmark in English affairs for a third time. This invasion was one of conquest. On his arrival, in the late summer of 1013, the peoples of Northumbria and the Danelaw immediately submitted and reinforced the invading army. With this support, Swein undertook a campaign that brought about the submission of most of England south of Watling Street in a period of a few weeks. King Æthelred then went into exile and London and the south-east were the final areas of the country to submit to King Swein.

Underlying the English history of this period are two important factors. One is England's wealth, which attracted the attention of Scandinavian adventurers. The other is England's military weakness in response to the Scandinavian invasions.

---

3   See Fellows-Jensen, 'The Vikings in England', for an explanation of the debate about the manner and extent of the early Scandinavian settlements. The classic description of events in England during the ninth and tenth centuries remains Stenton, *Anglo-Saxon England*, pp. 239–76, 'The Age of Alfred', and pp. 320–63, 'The Conquest of Scandinavian England'. For a more recent appreciation of events, see Stafford, *Unification and Conquest*, pp. 24–44, 'Edward to Eadred, 899 to 955', and pp. 45–68, 'Eadwig to Æthelred II, 955 to 1016'.
4   Sawyer, 'Swein Forkbeard and the Historians', pp. 36–7. Lund, 'Cnut's Danish Kingdom', p. 27 and n. 2 quoting an article by N. Refskou in *Kirkehistoriske Samlinger*, 1985, pp. 19–33. See also Figure 2, p. 10, above.
5   A translation of Thietmar's Chronicle, Bk VII, c. 36 (26): Trillmich, *Thietmari Merseburgensis*. Stories of 'exile' are also in the work of Adam of Bremen, Bk II, cc. 30, 34. For discussion of Adam's account see Sawyer, 'Cnut's Scandinavian Empire', p. 14; also, Lund, 'The Danish Perspective', pp. 137–8. It will be argued in this book, Chapter 3, pp. 32–4, that Swein Forkbeard was not exercising royal authority in Denmark during a period of some five years when he was campaigning in Saxony, Frisia and the British Isles.

English Wealth

For an appreciation of the economic situation that made England so attractive to the Scandinavian invaders, it is necessary to start with a brief consideration of the reign of Æthelred's father, King Edgar.[6] Following upon the costly but successful military exploits of his predecessors, from 959 Edgar ruled a kingdom with boundaries similar to present day England. More importantly, he inherited a period of peace during which the Anglo-Saxons were able to reap the benefits of the previous military expansion and a respite from significant Scandinavian invasions.

During this period of peace there was a reduction in taxation and military activity.[7] Consequently, the Anglo-Saxon nobility enjoyed greater economic prosperity. The Church also prospered as king and nobility endowed it with landed property and silver.[8] The enlarged kingdom provided a larger market and, because of links with Scandinavia and northern Europe, there was an increase in external trade as well as internal.[9]

Economic expansion and increasing trade would have led to an increase in the use of coins and this probably encouraged King Edgar and his ministers to undertake a major reform of the currency. Professor Sawyer says:

> We are, therefore, entitled to think of England in the eleventh century as a land richly endowed with a silver currency which was well regulated and was widely dispersed throughout the country among many classes and types of people.[10]

The reform was probably implemented about 973 and was taking effect at the end of Edgar's reign. It was a further stimulus to trade, as English currency became more readily acceptable abroad.[11]

Economic growth meant that the Church and nobility, having satisfied their primary economic needs, could accumulate wealth in the form of silver plate, bullion, or, when possible, in the acquisition of further landed property rights.[12]

---

[6]   Figure 3, p. 15.

[7]   Only a 'reduction' because there is evidence that Edgar maintained a fleet (*ASC* D and E *s.a.* 972), that there were problems in some provinces (*ASC* D E F *s.a.* 966), and that he raised armed forces (*ASC* D E F *s.a.* 969). In addition, events such as his coronation as king of all the English must have been costly and there was raiding activity along the Irish Sea coast that threatened English interests.

[8]   See Stafford, 'Reign', p. 17, for the wealth of the nobility and 'their massive benefactions to the Church'.

[9]   One source of increasing trade and wealth was wool; see Sawyer, 'The Wealth of England'.

[10] Sawyer, 'The Wealth of England', pp. 155–6.

[11] Dolley, 'An Introduction to the Coinage of Æthelred II', p. 117. Also, Jonsson, 'Coinage of Cnut', pp. 195–7.

[12] Commenting on the great wealth of the churches and monasteries in the final decade of the tenth century, Hart quotes the words of Hugh Candidus: 'nec sufficit eius ut solummodo Burch uocaretur, quin pocius terris, auro et argento diuersisque rebus in tantum ditauerunt ut

Figure 3. Æthelred II: family tree

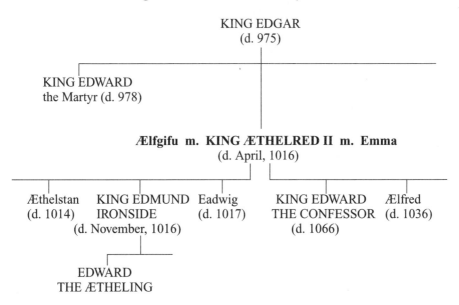

KING EDGAR
(d. 975)

KING EDWARD
the Martyr (d. 978)

Ælfgifu m. KING ÆTHELRED II m. Emma
(d. April, 1016)

Æthelstan   KING EDMUND Eadwig   KING EDWARD   Ælfred
(d. 1014)   IRONSIDE   (d. 1017)   THE CONFESSOR   (d. 1036)
              (d. November, 1016)   (d. 1066)

EDWARD
THE ÆTHELING

Thus, the value of land and silver appreciated, more land was brought into production and the population grew. This was a further stimulus to trade and a benign economic cycle was achieved. It existed over many years because it was in the best interests of the government to maintain the intrinsic value of the currency. Certain land dues were assessed in monetary terms and other dues were assessed in terms of animals or produce that had a fixed monetary value. Thus the laws of Æthelstan[13] gave monetary values to certain animals, values that were presumably not 'market values', which would have varied according to the quality of the animal as well as the economic dictates of supply and demand. If the currency were devalued, commutations in coin to the king and to his nobles would have been worth less in real terms. Another important factor helping to maintain the intrinsic value of the currency was that the economy was firmly based on traditional asset-values such as land and silver and so was less volatile than our present day multi-faceted economy.[14]

eum merito Gylden [*sic, recte* 'Gyldene'] burch, id est auream ciuitatem, uocarent': it was inadequate to name it only Burch [the monastery at Peterborough], they had enriched it so much with land, gold, silver and divers other possessions that it was deservedly called 'Golden Burch', that is 'golden city' (my translation). Hart, *The Danelaw*, p. 549. Also Mellows, *The Chronicle of Hugh Candidus*, p. 38.

[13] *VI Æthelstan.*

[14] Jonsson, 'Coinage of Cnut', table 11.2. The table shows that King Æthelred and his ministers maintained the intrinsic value of the coinage. Variations in coin weight may be explained by several factors including manipulation to encourage the availability of silver bullion and plate for coin production during periods of high demand, e.g. for payment of tribute. However, it should be noted that there was a devaluation of the currency early in Cnut's reign, which may also be evidenced from the table. These matters are explored in I. Howard, 'The Fiduciary Element in English Silver Coins in the Late Tenth and Early Eleventh Centuries',

A disputed succession, which followed King Edgar's death, had some short-term effects but no longer-term economic consequences. Following the murder of King Edward the Martyr, Edgar's economic policy seems to have been continued under the direction of Æthelred's mother and existing ministers.[15] There was a period of stability and economic growth during the final years of Edgar's reign, Æthelred's minority and the early years of Æthelred's personal reign. However, as in our own times, economic growth would have lost impetus without a further stimulus.

It might be expected that the invasions during Æthelred's reign would cause a major setback to economic activity. In parts of the country this happened, but only to a limited extent and after 1006 when England was invaded by a particularly large army. Commenting on King Æthelred's reign, Professor Loyn wrote:

> and indeed all was not gloom. In the financial and legal fields solid advance was made. England enjoyed the benefit of a stable and strictly regulated coinage. The courts of the shires, hundreds and wapentakes were well organized, and the royal role as the source of law-codes applicable to the whole community heavily emphasized. This was a great age of vernacular scholarship with Ælfric and Wulfstan the outstanding scholars. Benedictine monasticism flourished in spite of the barbarian raids.[16]

An economic model of the known facts could show the activities of the invaders providing an important stimulus to the economy. There now exists sufficient information about the period of King Æthelred's reign for a detailed study to be undertaken, starting with a consideration of the money supply and the consequences of central manipulation of the economy. However, this is beyond the scope of the present study, which simply seeks to highlight the considerations that made English wealth a continuing attraction to Scandinavian adventurers during three decades. The economic stimulus helps to explain the attitude of the English government towards invading armies and its willingness to employ them as mercenary forces.[17] It also helps to explain the political stability that England enjoyed for most of Æthelred's reign.

The activities of Scandinavian invaders began to have an economic impact during the final decade of the tenth century. Even then, by comparison with England's neighbours in northern Europe and Ireland, there was comparative peace. Disturbances in England during this period were as nothing by comparison with the wars between countries, between provinces, between town and country, between families and within families, which are a feature of the history of its neighbours at that time.[18]

---

an unpublished paper read at the Leeds International Medieval Congress on 15 July 1999. See also the reference to this paper in n. 29, below.

[15] Keynes, *Diplomas*, p. 175: 'there are no signs of an upheaval in the composition of the king's council'. See also, Stafford, 'Reign', pp. 24–6.

[16] Loyn, *The Vikings in Britain*, pp. 65–6. He added: 'But the general suffering over a period of some twenty years was great.'

[17] For example, see the discussion of the law, *II Æthelred*, in Chapter 3, pp. 46–9, below.

[18] The classic descriptions of the situation in northern Europe are to be found in F. Lot, *Les Derniers Carolingiens*, and in Holtzmann, *Geschichte der sächsischen Kaiserzeit*. See also,

By the commencement of the final decade of the tenth century England had enjoyed economic growth for twenty years. It was a mature economy and, although the country was significantly more prosperous than it had been twenty years earlier, it would have been becoming increasingly difficult for the economy to maintain a significant percentage increase in gross domestic product.[19] The escalation in the Scandinavian invasions of England from early in the final decade of the tenth century had an economic impact. One result was that the English government raised vast quantities of silver and increased the coinage in circulation.[20]

In the period 991 to 1002, Scandinavians came as raiders and many remained as mercenaries, settlers and traders. Some remained in England for considerable periods and were given 'peace land'.[21] Such arrangements were not unique to England. At the turn of the tenth century, Erik of Lade's followers were provided with similar facilities in Sweden, St Olaf's in Normandy and various Scandinavian forces in Russia and Byzantium. In England, mercenary forces were used to discourage further invasions and to campaign in the Irish Sea and bordering coasts. This feature of the Scandinavian invasions is described in Chapter 3. As a direct consequence of the Scandinavian invasions enormous sums of money were raised in taxation and were re-circulated, directly or indirectly, within the English economy. The requirement for vast quantities of provisions for native armies and for invading armies, during periods of truce, created resource and logistical problems that had a significant economic impact. Money and provisions were raised in most years between 991 and the early years of King Cnut's reign for one or other of the following: (1) *landfyrd* (2) *scypfyrd* (3) *gafol 7 metsung* (4) *heregeld*. The following paragraphs explain this expenditure.

Landfyrd. In order to restrict the activities of the armies of Scandinavian invaders, the Anglo-Saxons mobilised the *landfyrd*. This was a militia that was sometimes mobilised on a local basis, sometimes from several shires, sometimes on a national basis, depending upon the perception of the threat. The *landfyrd* had to be equipped and provisioned, so there was an economic cost in terms of money, equipment and supplies. There are references to *landfyrd*, or *fyrd* or *þeodscipe*, meaning 'national army', in *ASC* C D E, in annal years 991, 993, 998, 999, 1001, 1003, 1004, 1006, 1009, 1010, 1014, 1015 and 1016 and in

---

Whitton, 'The Society of Northern Europe in the High Middle Ages', pp. 160–72, on 'The Kingdom of France'; Bates, *Normandy before 1066*, pp. 46–93 on 'Normandy and its Neighbours'; and Davis, *A History of Medieval Europe*, pp. 210–31, on 'The Saxon Empire'.

[19] This is a normal occurrence in economic terms. Also, see Metcalf, 'The Ranking of the Boroughs', p. 180, on the subject of 'a balance of payments surplus'. Metcalf discussed the final decade of the tenth century and the early eleventh century when there was no economic downturn and growth had not lost impetus, but he did not review the reasons.

[20] For coinage, see Metcalf, 'The Ranking of the Boroughs', p. 180, table K.

[21] The law *II Æthelred* contains clauses indicating that Scandinavian forces were billeted on the land when they were not campaigning. *ASC* A *s.a.* 1001 complains that Pallig deserted King Æthelred despite gifts that included 'estates'. Lund, 'The Danish Perspective', p. 116, explains Æthelred's arrangements with Scandinavian forces in a wider context. See also the introductory remarks in Ann Williams, ' "Cockles Amongst the Wheat" ', pp. 1–2.

the annal year 1000 there is reference to the king taking his army into 'Cumberland'.[22]

Scipfyrd. The Anglo-Saxons deployed fleets to protect the country from invaders. Sometimes they employed a Scandinavian fleet for this purpose. There are references to *scipfyrd* or '*scipu*', in *ASC* C D E, in annal years 992, 999, 1000, 1008, 1009, 1012, 1013, 1015 and 1018.[23]

Gafol 7 metsunge. At the end of a campaigning season, the Anglo-Saxon *fyrd* went home and thus it was often necessary to come to terms with an invading army. *Gafol* may be translated as 'tribute' and was a payment made to gain agreement to a truce during which the invading army ceased harrying. The invading army could not survive without provisions and if they were not to harry for them, the Anglo-Saxons had to provide them, hence *metsunge*, which may be translated as 'feeding' or 'provisioning'. The provisioning of a Scandinavian army in winter quarters must have been difficult, since provisions would have to be brought in from a wide area. It was, therefore, an expensive undertaking. The *ASC* provides figures for some of the *gafol* payments and, if they are to be believed, they were very large. There has been much debate on the subject of these payments and conflicting arguments are to be found in articles submitted to *English Historical Review* by John Gillingham and M. K. Lawson.[24] There are references to *gafol* or *metsunge* in *ASC* C D E, 991 (10,000 pounds), 994 (16,000 pounds), 1002 (24,000 pounds), 1006, 1007 (36,000 pounds), 1009 (3,000 pounds), 1011, 1012 (48,000 pounds), 1013 and 1018 (72,000 pounds plus 10,500 pounds).[25]

---

[22] 991: 'Byrihtnoð ealdorman ofslagan æt Meldune' ('landfyrde' implied); 993: 'mycle fyrde'; 998: '7 man oft fyrde ongean hi gadrede'; 999: 'Centisce fyrd'; 'landfyrde'; 1000: 'se cyning ferde into Cumberlande'; 1001: 'ormæte fyrde'; 1003: 'micle fyrde'; 1004: 'fyrde'; 1006: 'ealne þeodscipe of Westseaxum 7 of Myrcum'; 'fyrd gesomned æt Cynestan'; 1009: 'ealne þeodscipe'; 'fyrd æt Lundenne'; 1010: 'Ulfcytel mid his fyrde'; 'þonne ferde seo fyrd ham'; 1014: 'mid fulre fyrde'; 1015: 'fyrde'; 1016: 'fyrde'. Quotations are from BL MS Cotton Tiberius B iv. *ASC* A also makes reference to 'landfyrde' during this period, mostly duplicating the references in *ASC* C D E.

[23] 992: 'gegadere ealle þa scipu'; 999: 'mid scypfyrde'; 1000: 'his scypu'; 1008: 'man sceolde ofer eall Angelcyn scypu fæstlice wyrcan'; 1009: 'wurdon þa scypo gearwe'; 1012: 'fif 7 feowertig scype'; 1013: 'se cyning wende þa fram þam flotan'; 1015: '7 Eadric ealdorman aspeon ða feowertig scipa fram þam cyninge'; 1018: 'xl scypa belifon mid þam cynge Cnut'. Quotations are from BL MS Cotton Tiberius B iv.

[24] Gillingham, ' "The Most Precious Jewel in the English Crown" ', pp. 373–84; Lawson, ' "Those Stories Look True" ', pp. 385–406; Gillingham, 'Chronicles and Coins', pp. 939–50; Lawson, 'Danegeld and Heregeld Once More', pp 951–61.

[25] 991: 'gafol'; 'x. þusend punda'; 994: 'gafol 7 metsunge'; 'xvi þusend punda'; 1002: 'hi to metsunge fengon. 7 to gafole'; 'xxiiii þusend punda'; 1006: 'gaful 7 metsunge'; 1007: 'gafol'; 'xxxvi þusend punda'; 1009: 'frið' ('peace'); 'þreo þusend punda'; 1011: 'gafol 7 metsunge'; 1012: 'þæt gafol'; 'ehta 7 feowertig þusend punda'; 1013: 'Bead þa Swegen ful gyld ['tax'/'tribute'] 7 metsunge to his hære þone winter. Þurcyl bead þ ylce to þam here þe læg æt Grenawic.'; 1018: 'gafol'; 'twa 7 hundseofonti þusend punda'; 'Lunden ----- endlifte healf þusend punda'. Quotations are from BL MS Cotton Tiberius B iv (but here and elsewhere in this book the letter *w* has been substituted for wynn).

Heregeld. The Anglo-Saxons distinguished between their native army (*fyrd*), and an invading army (*here*). One means of dealing with an invading force was to pay it as a mercenary army that could fight the king's enemies and discourage other invaders. There is a copy of a treaty for such an arrangement, numbered in the Laws as *II Æthelred*. This treaty is discussed in Chapter 3, pp. 46–9, below. Such an arrangement could be expensive because the *here* required provisions and payment for their services. The payment was known as *heregeld* and this word was later used to describe the tax that the king raised to pay for his mercenary fleet, an arrangement that became a permanent feature of English taxation until it was abolished by Edward the Confessor in 1051.[26] Although it will be argued in this study that King Æthelred made many such payments, only two are clearly recorded. There is a payment of 22,000 pounds referred to in the Law, *II Æthelred*, and a payment of 21,000 pounds referred to in *ASC* C D E *s.a.* 1014.

The extent of the payments required to meet this expenditure may be judged from the analysis in Figure 4, p. 20. As a result, enormous amounts of silver, in bullion, plate and coin, were raised on the authority of the *witan* and new coins were minted.[27] The official moneyers must have been over-worked and greatly enriched as they endeavoured to meet the demand for coins. Minting coins was a major economic activity judging from the number of mints in England, a number that increased significantly during the latter part of Æthelred's reign.[28]

Billeting Scandinavian forces upon the land would have increased the value of land, as would the demand for provisions for native and foreign forces. Paying them geld, whether by way of tribute or for their mercenary activities, forced the government, the nobility and the Church to bring back huge amounts of stored silver into circulation as coin and it also drew silver into England from abroad. The English government seems to have had a fiscal mechanism that encouraged people to bring silver to official moneyers for coin production when there was an urgent requirement.[29] The recipients of the payments were keen to acquire land, goods and services, and, even when the silver coins were taken back to Scandinavia, they served to benefit trade because they could be returned to England in exchange for manufactured goods and other produce, such as wheat, woollens, tin and honey.[30] There was an encouragement to trade with

[26] *ASC* D *s.a.* 1052 (*recte* 1051). This and Darlington and McGurk, *John of Worcester s.a.* 1051 indicate that the official periodic tax commenced about the time of King Æthelred's agreement with Thorkell (*ASC* C D E *s.a.* 1012). This does not preclude the possibility that *heregeld* was raised and paid by Æthelred on an intermittent basis prior to this.

[27] For bullion being drawn into the coinage, see Lawson, ' "These Stories Look True" ', pp. 402–3.

[28] Jonsson, 'Coinage of Cnut', pp. 195–7 and figure 11.1.

[29] This mechanism was discussed in Howard, 'The Fiduciary Element in English Silver Coins'. An extract from this paper will be included as an appendix to my forthcoming book, *The Reign of Æthelred II (the Unready)* to support an explanation of economic developments during King Æthelred's reign.

[30] See J. D. Richards, *English Heritage Book of Viking Age England*, p. 88, illustration 52. See also Sawyer, 'The Wealth of England', pp. 161 and 163, for the importance of wool as an export in exchange for silver.

Figure 4. Expenditure causing high taxation from 991

Year	(1) Landfyrd	(2) Scipfyrd	(3) Gafol 7 Metsunge	(4) Heregeld	Reference	
991	☆		10,000		*ASC* CDE	
992		☆			*ASC* CDE	
993	☆				*ASC* CDE	
994			16,000	22,000	*ASC* CDE / II Æ	*
995						**
996						**
997						
998	☆				*ASC* CDE	
999	☆	☆			*ASC* CDE	
1000	☆	☆			*ASC* CDE	**
1001	☆				*ASC* CDE	
1002			24,000		*ASC* CDE	
1003	☆				*ASC* CDE	
1004	☆				*ASC* CDE	
1005						
1006	☆		☆		*ASC* CDE	
1007			36,000		*ASC* CDE	
1008		☆			*ASC* CDE	
1009	☆	☆	3,000		*ASC* CDE	
1010	☆				*ASC* CDE	
1011			☆		*ASC* CDE	
1012		☆	48,000		*ASC* CDE	
1013		☆	☆		*ASC* CDE	**
1014	☆			21,000	*ASC* CDE	
1015	☆	☆			*ASC* CDE	
1016	☆				*ASC* CDE	
1017						
1018		☆	72,000}		*ASC* CDE	
			10,500}			
1019 ↓						** ↓ **

☆ Costs not specified. Numbers quoted are in pounds.
* The gafol of 16,000 pounds was paid in the winter/spring 993/4. The heregeld of 22,000 pounds was probably paid in summer/autumn 995.
** Heregeld may have been paid in some or all of these years, but there are no specific references.

(1) army levy; (2) naval levy; (3) tribute and provisions; (4) payment to mercenaries.

England because the coinage had a fiduciary element and was worth more than its intrinsic silver content in England.

This provided a stimulus to the economy, and internal[31] and external trade[32] must have flourished as a result. So, just as the expansion in Gross Domestic Product might have been expected to level, there was an unforeseen and exceptional boost to the economy, which was triggered by the Scandinavian invasions.[33]

It should be remembered that the population of England and Europe was only a small fraction of that of today. Exact figures are not available but, as a very approximate guide, the population of England was probably less than two million; the discussion of 'Domesday' population figures by Darby shows the complexity of this subject.[34] Also, communities were more self-sufficient. In our present age a home would have little by way of food, furniture and implements that had been produced within a ten miles radius, but at the turn of the tenth and eleventh centuries there would have been little that had not been produced within that radius. What might be considered an insignificant volume of trade in an insignificant tonnage of shipping was very large in terms of the tenth-century English economy.[35] Percentage growths would be such as we presently see only in so-called 'tiger economies'.

However, the stimulus was not evenly distributed in England. It was greatest in the east and the south-east. Consequently, there would have been a shift in comparative economic wealth and power from Wessex and English Mercia to the Danelaw, London and the south-east. We are fortunate in having Domesday Book to provide evidence of the population and wealth of the eastern and south-eastern regions of the country and a comparison with Wessex towards the end of the eleventh century. Unfortunately, there is no similar comparison for the mid-tenth century. It follows that any shift in comparative economic wealth must be deduced from economic models. The 'resultant' comparison between the more heavily populated eastern counties and the less heavily populated counties of Wessex and English Mercia is well evidenced.[36] The economic strength of London and the east may also be illustrated by the comparative size

[31] Metcalf, 'The Ranking of the Boroughs', p. 171, discusses 'the pervasiveness of the money economy' and the evidence of extensive movements of goods and coins as an indicator of commercial activity.
[32] See Metcalf, 'The Ranking of the Boroughs', p. 180, for favourable English balance of payments and the wealth of England's trading partners in Scandinavia and northern continental Europe. See Sawyer, 'Swein Forkbeard and the Historians', p. 31, for the economic prosperity and development of towns in Scandinavia during Swein Forkbeard's reign in Denmark.
[33] Economic prosperity can have a reciprocal benefit on the economies of trading partners. The export of wool from England to the Continent benefited the woollen manufacturers (see n. 30 above). It has been suggested that Swein Forkbeard used English wealth to revive Denmark's economy after the excessive expenditure on public works by his father: Wilson, 'Danish Kings and England', pp. 188–96, particularly, pp. 188 and 195.
[34] Darby, *Domesday England*, ch. III, pp. 57–94.
[35] Richards, *English Heritage Book of Viking Age England*, pp. 87–96, provides evidence of trade and comments upon its paucity, though without explaining its *relative* significance.
[36] Darby, *Domesday England*, figures 34 to 36 on pp. 90–3.

of mints in terms of numbers of moneyers at each mint. London ranked first, Lincoln second, York third, Thetford sixth, Stamford eighth, Canterbury ninth, and Norwich tenth.[37]

In Chapter 4, p. 54 and n. 3, reference is made to Scandinavian mercenary forces being settled in the south-west in the final decade of the tenth century. Estimating those forces at, say, between 2,000 and 4,000 men, would amount to between 0.1% and 0.2% of the total population of England, which is not significant. However, in the south-west region a *concentration* of numbers of this order might amount to between 1% and 10% of the total population depending upon the definition of 'region'. Also, it is evident that people of Scandinavian extraction were moving into English Mercia. For instance, there is charter evidence of a significant community of 'Danes' in Oxford at the time of the St Brice's Day massacre in 1002.[38]

In essence, it is possible that the economic impact of a Scandinavian military presence in England during the last decade of the tenth century and the early decades of the eleventh century was to increase the coinage in circulation, stimulate demand for land, food and implements, redistribute wealth, and enhance the economic prosperity of London and the eastern shires.[39]

The *ASC* specifies the payment of very large sums of money to Scandinavian forces. Whether or not the figures are symbolic and exaggerated we cannot be sure. What seems certain is that there was great expenditure over and above that mentioned in the *ASC*.[40] There has been much comment about the payments as a proportion of the coinage in circulation.[41] An obvious explanation, in economic terms, is that the silver coinage must have been circulated rapidly.[42] Although the economic picture may appear complex, it can readily be appreciated that Scandinavian adventurers were attracted to England by its wealth. It is ironic that the economic impact of their presence was to help put England in a position to sustain large payments to them over several decades and so undermine the political establishment.

[37] See Hill, 'Trends in the Development of Towns', p. 216, illustration 9.2. The other mints in the top ten were Winchester fourth, Chester fifth, Exeter seventh. For present purposes this ranking is indicative only: it ignores the fact that York and Chester, in particular, were remote from other mints and that there was a concentration of mints in the Bath/Shaftesbury area; features which are shown *ibid.* p. 221, illustration 9.4.

[38] See the reference to the burning of St Frideswide's Church, probably during the massacre of 1002, when Danes sought refuge there, in Whitelock *EHD*, no. 127, pp. 545–7. See also, Williams, ' "Cockles amongst the Wheat" ', pp. 1–2. Æthelred's charter to St Frideswide's Church is no. 909 in Sawyer, *Anglo-Saxon Charters*.

[39] See Keynes, *Diplomas*, pp. 108–9 including note 73, and pp. 202–3 including note 182, for evidence of land sales. See Whitelock, *EHD*, pp. 527–9, for a sale of land by the archbishop of Canterbury to meet the pressing demands of Scandinavian raiders. Hinton, 'Late Saxon Treasure and Bullion', p. 142, comments on the redistribution of wealth and the adverse effect of this on the Church.

[40] Figure 4, p. 20.

[41] Metcalf, 'The Ranking of the Boroughs', p. 181, table L. See also the debate between Lawson and Gillingham in *EHR* 1989 and 1990.

[42] This 'velocity of circulation' factor is described and explained in Howard, 'The Fiduciary Element in English Silver Coins'. See n. 29, above.

English Military Weakness

During the last decade of the tenth century and the first two decades of the eleventh century England was the destination of many Scandinavian adventurers, arriving in comparatively large numbers on almost an annual basis. 'Comparatively large numbers' is a relative term and it should be borne in mind that a major city of the time might number less than 5,000 people[43] and that a body of 2,000 men was a 'large' army. Darby, in *Domesday England*, discusses views about the total population of England, including the northern counties and concludes that:

> there can hardly have been less than one million people in England in 1086, and that there may well have been substantially more. An estimate around 1.5 million may be not far from the truth.[44]

Of course, nearly a hundred years earlier the population could have been less since the influx of settlers and the economic expansion discussed above should have had the effect of increasing numbers over the intervening years. The expansion of Gross Domestic Product should be considered in the context of Darby's remarks, as should the debate about the size of Scandinavian armies and the density of the ninth century settlements which was initiated by Peter Sawyer's article in the *University of Birmingham Historical Journal*, in 1958.[45]

Often Scandinavians arrived from the Baltic on a route that took them along the coasts of Saxony and Frisia. The saga of Olaf Tryggvason provides an illustration of the westerly movement of Scandinavian adventurers.[46] Olaf was the leader of King Valdamar of Garda's host in what is now Russia, maintaining a warrior band on estates allotted to him by the king. He left Garda in the penultimate decade of the tenth century and campaigned in the Baltic, Slavia and, eventually, the British Isles. It is a feature of the Scandinavian invasions during this period that they chose to concentrate their attention on England rather than on continental Europe. There were exceptions to this general observation, particularly the invasion of Saxony in 994, which is discussed in this section.

---

[43] Darby, *Domesday England*, p. 303, explains that the evidence for London and Winchester is lacking and continues 'Of the other boroughs, we can only conjecture from the unsatisfactory Domesday evidence that the following had at least 4,000, and maybe over 5,000, inhabitants each in 1086: York, Lincoln, Norwich and possibly Thetford. To this group Oxford had belonged in 1066, but twenty years later it appears to have been in a very reduced position.' Darby, p. 307, says that Leicester and Nottingham 'may have had 2,000 inhabitants or more' and Chester, Cambridge, Huntingdon and Northampton 'in 1086 cannot have been less than 1,500'. On p. 308, Ipswich and Maldon are given as examples of places with 'between 1,000 and 2,000' inhabitants. The population numbers would have been different in the last decade of the tenth century but not materially so for the purposes of the comparison that is being made in this passage.

[44] Darby, *Domesday England*, pp. 87–91.

[45] Sawyer, 'The Density of the Danish Settlement in England', pp. 1–17.

[46] Jónsson, *Heimskringla*, 'Olaf Tryggvason saga', K 21 to K 32.

Obviously, English wealth was a great attraction but that is not sufficient in itself to explain why Scandinavians tended to avoid major expeditions into a western continental Europe which was closer to their homeland and had plenty of wealth to be looted or extracted as tribute. The explanation is to be found in a significant development in military technology, a development that centred upon the deployment of mounted horsemen in battle.

Armies had used horses throughout the Dark Ages and the early Middle Ages in northern Europe as a means of transporting men and equipment. Battles had been fought on foot. In these circumstances, the Scandinavian invaders of Europe in the ninth century enjoyed an advantage over local forces. Using their ships they could invade unexpectedly, capture horses locally and travel great distances as easily as a native army.[47] When a battle took place, invaders and native defenders fought on foot. There is evidence that the Anglo-Saxons used horses for transport purposes but invariably fought their battles on foot.[48] Horses were small, sure footed and carried a large weight in relation to their own body weight. Davis says:

> In North-West Europe, where mounted knights were to be found earlier and in greater numbers than in any other part of the medieval world, the indigenous horse was no larger than a Shetland pony. By the eleventh century, if not before, someone had somehow discovered how to produce large numbers of horses which were bigger.[49]

The breeding of a larger horse was not an obviously advantageous development. A Shetland pony can carry a comparatively heavy load over ground that it might be unsafe to travel with a large horse.[50] Yet the development was undertaken and by the middle of the tenth century western Europeans had horses on which they were able to deploy mounted warriors in battle to great advantage. Whitton says that 'trained knights proved an effective response to the Magyar attacks in the tenth century'.[51] Otto the Great's victory at the battle of Lechfeld in 955 ended the threat from the Magyars, expert horsemen who threatened to

---

[47] Clapham commented on this feature in 'The Horsing of the Danes', pp. 287–93, especially pp. 291–3.

[48] R. A. Brown, *The Norman Conquest*, Documents of Medieval History 5, London: Edward Arnold, 1984, p. 93; also, Abels, *Lordship and Military Obligation*, p. 140. Abels also shows a photograph of the Canterbury Hexateuch, BL MS Cotton Claudius B iv, f. 25r, and says of it: 'The early eleventh-century illustrator of the Canterbury Hexateuch depicted Abram's men pursuing Lot's captors on horseback but engaging them on foot,' *ibid.* p. 268 n. 73. In *ibid.* p. 268, n.74, Abels writes: 'The early eighth-century *Vita Wilfridi* implies that the early Northumbrian fyrds rode to battle and fought on foot.' *Life of Wilfrid*, chap. 19, ed. Colgrave, pp. 40–42.

[49] R. H. C. Davis, *The Medieval Warhorse*, p. 6. In imagining 'bigger' horses during this period, the reader should think in terms of a heavy weight cob, of no more than 15.2 hands, rather than a shire horse. See Bennett, 'The Medieval Warhorse Reconsidered', pp. 19–40.

[50] Ponies and small horses generally have a greater life expectancy than large horses. However, the longevity of a horse is dependent upon many factors: see M. Horace Hayes, *Veterinary Notes for Horse Owners*, London: Stanley Paul, 1877, revised P. D. Rossdale, 1987, pp. 686–7.

[51] Whitton, 'The Society of Northern Europe in the High Middle Ages', p. 123.

overrun Europe. Interestingly, R. H. C. Davis does not comment on the importance of 'trained knights' at the battle of Lechfeld in his important assessment of 'the Saxon Empire'.[52] He had, however, already explained that Henry the Fowler had deployed trained knights against the Hungarians to gain his victory at Unstrut in 933. Davis recognised the significance of this development in Europe and was amongst the first to recognise that it could not have happened unless suitable horses had been bred first in a painstaking manner.[53] However, the breeding of warhorses and the training of horses and men was extraordinarily expensive[54] and could only be justified where the need was fairly constant.

Although continental Europe, like England, was increasingly prosperous it was far from peaceful. The annals of this period do not dwell on problems with Scandinavian invaders, except in the year 994. They deal rather with internal warfare, incursions by Slavs and retaliatory expeditions.[55] Because warfare was a common feature of life, it was relatively easy to bring together a fighting force to combat any piratical coastal raids that did not employ 'hit and run' tactics.

In the year 994, the people of Saxony were surprised by a Scandinavian invasion on an unusually large scale. At first they overran the land and took hostages. Then they demanded tribute and, when there was a failure to accede to their demands, they mutilated their hostages.[56] It is likely that this invasion was directed at Saxony because of events in England where a defensive treaty had been agreed with a Scandinavian army led by Olaf Tryggvason and others. The possible relationship between these events has not previously been recognised because of a misunderstanding about chronology in the *ASC* as it deals with events leading up to the treaty arrangement. Chapter 3, pp. 42–3, below, explains that an attack on London, led by Olaf Tryggvason and Swein Forkbeard, described in *ASC* CDE *s.a.* 994, took place in September 993. Because historians previously believed that it took place in September 994, it was thought that the attack on Saxony preceded it.[57] Whatever had precipitated

---

[52] Davis, *History of Medieval Europe*, pp. 210–31. Davis considers Henry the Fowler's breeding and training strategy in his book, *The Medieval Warhorse*, p. 54.

[53] Davis' Introduction in *The Medieval Warhorse*, pp. 6–9.

[54] A point made by Davis. However, for a better appreciation of the cost, see the chapter on 'The Army Horse' in Fillis, *Breaking and Riding*, pp. 213–35. Fillis was an Englishman, born in 1834, who taught horsemanship in France and Russia and whose example and writings have influenced international riders to the present day.

[55] The Magyar threat had been overcome by the mid-tenth century. For subsequent warfare see Lappenberg, *Thietmari Chronicon*; Pertz, *Annales Corbienses*, pp. 1–18, *Annales Hildesheimenses* and *Annales Quedlinburgenses*, pp. 52–98.

[56] Trillmich, *Thietmari Merseburgensis* Bk IV, 23(16)–25(16); Pertz, *Annales Corbienses*, *s.a.* 994, *Annales Hildesheimenses*, *s.a.* 994.

[57] Thus Christiansen, in *Saxo Grammaticus*, vol. I, p. 179, n. 64, describes a 'protracted viking raid – probably starting in June 994 with a savage attack on Saxony'. He suggests that Olaf Tryggvason and Swein Forkbeard were involved in the attack on Saxony. Peter Sawyer, in 'Swein Forkbeard and the Historians', p. 34 and n. 36, mentions this suggestion of Swein's involvement and says it 'seems unlikely'. Following the revised chronology of events, Olaf and Swein were already campaigning in the British Isles in 993 and remained there in 994, so they could not have participated in the raid on Saxony and Olaf's treaty agreement with King Æthelred may well have instigated the raid.

the attack, the Saxons soon raised an army against the invaders who were attacked and defeated.[58] Many were killed and there are no records of major incursions on this scale in subsequent years.

Although it was relatively easy for the Saxons to raise an army of experienced armed men, it was their superior military technology which made it impossible for an invading army to maintain itself far inland. Because of their endemic need for armed forces, it was economically practical to maintain trained armed horsemen in northern Europe. It was this technology which Henry the Fowler and Otto the Great used to good effect in defeating the Magyars, and the Saxons used it thereafter in their warfare against the Slavs.[59] Further west, the letters of Gerbert reveal that Hugh Capet was able to muster 600 knights in 985.[60] The Slavs developed the technology later and the battle of Listven in 1024 demonstrated the superiority of mobile cavalry forces over Scandinavian foot soldiers.[61]

The word 'trained' is important. For a warrior to be able to deploy a horse successfully in battle required that he and his horse should spend many hours a week, on almost a daily basis, in training.[62] Even though many Scandinavians were experienced horsemen, they did not have the means to transport a significant number of trained horses on their overseas expeditions.[63] So, if they ventured far inland and were forced to fight a battle in Saxony they ran the risk of being out-flanked by mounted warriors. Those same mounted warriors could pursue them most effectively as they fled.

It has been suggested that Scandinavians transported horses by ship on their raiding expeditions to the British Isles. Gillian Fellows-Jensen notes that 'Bertil Almgren has stressed the importance of Viking ships and horses for the success of the raids.'[64] Dr Fellows-Jensen continues:

A further advantage of the Viking ships was that it was comparatively easy to land horses from them and this was important for the later raids on England,

---

58 Lappenberg, *Mag. Adami*, pp. 267–389, Bk II, cc. 29–30.
59 Whitton, 'The Society of Northern Europe in the High Middle Ages', pp. 122–4. See p. 124 for the evolution of knights to combat 'the Viking threat'.
60 Lattin, *The Letters of Gerbert*, pp. 106–7, Letter 65.
61 Noonan, 'The Scandinavians in European Russia', p. 155.
62 For an example of a training regime for a military horse, see Fillis, *Breaking and Riding*, pp. 226–30.
63 Transporting horses overseas was a very difficult logistical exercise. In the poem *Beowulf*, King Hrothgar rewards the hero with gifts that include eight horses ('eahta mearas'). In context Alexander realistically translates this as 'eight war-horses' and the poet has no difficulty with the concept that Beowulf can transport them home in his ship. On returning home, Beowulf presented four of the horses to King Hygelac. See Alexander, *Beowulf: A Verse Translation*, pp. 83 and 119. Sawyer states that raiders did sometimes travel with their horses but that it severely restricted the number of men that could be transported as well: he says that in '1142 it took fifty-two ships to carry a force of less than 400 mounted knights across the Channel'. See Sawyer, *Kings and Vikings*, p. 93; and P. Sawyer, *The Age of the Vikings*, 2nd edition, London, 1971, p. 127. This suggests an average of eight horses to a ship. By the late thirteenth century, Charles of Anjou, King of Sicily, had special transport ships that could carry about forty horses. See Davis, *The Medieval Warhorse*, p. 62.
64 Fellows-Jensen, 'The Vikings in England', pp. 186–7.

when the Danes landed with a well-trained, heavily armed professional cavalry that was capable of over-running the boroughs which the English had fortified against Viking attack.

Cavalry would have been of limited use against well-fortified positions and it is difficult to imagine Scandinavian invaders being able to transport a significant number of horses and sufficient fodder on long sea journeys, and doing so whilst maintaining their fitness for immediate deployment. During the period covered by this study, the *ASC* does not support the view that the invaders brought horses with them, but it does record how the invaders acquired horses in England.[65] The *Encomium Emmae Reginae* does not suggest that Swein and Cnut invaded with horses although there are fulsome descriptions of the ships and men making up their invasion fleets. The *Encomium* makes specific reference to the invaders fighting, initially, on foot and states that Cnut's men were so fleet of foot that they scorned the speed of horsemen.[66] However, the encomiast assumed that the invading forces acquired horses because when Cnut attacked London, he wrote: 'Et quia hoc pedites equitesque nequibant explere.'[67] This aligns the *Encomium* with the *ASC*.

The evidence of the *ASC* shows that Scandinavian forces in England made frequent use of horses.[68] This greatly increased their mobility on inland expeditions.[69] Because of such references, it is sometimes assumed that Scandinavian invaders were able to deploy mounted men in battle on their overseas raids.[70] There is a need for a study of the psychology of the horse and its training to

---

[65] *ASC* D *s.a.*
> 994 '7 æt neaxtan namon him hors; 7 ridon swa wide swa hi woldon.'
> 999 '7 namon þa horsan. 7 ridon swa wide swa hi sylf woldon.'
> 1010 '7 þær wurdon gehorsode. 7 syþþan ahton east engla geweald.'
> 1013 'Syþþan he ['Swegen'] undergeat þ eall folc him to gebogen wæs. þa bed he þ mon sceolde his here mettian. 7 horsian.'
> 1014 '7 þæt folc on lindesige anes þ he hine horsian sceoldon 7 wið þan ealle ætgædere faran 7 hergian.'
> 1015 '7 wæst seaxe bugon. 7 gislodon. 7 horsedon þone here.'

The above quotations are from BL Cotton Tiberius B iv. The *ASC* does refer to a Danish army transporting horses by sea on one occasion. After being defeated at the battle of the river Dyle, the army retired on Boulogne and from there went to England in 250 ships, 'horses and all'. This was in 892 and the *ASC* used the phrase to indicate that this army had abandoned continental Europe completely.

[66] Campbell, *Encomium*, Bk I, c. 4, 'Denique relictis nauibus regii milites ad terram exeunt, et pedestri pugnae intrepidi sese accingunt'; and Bk II, c. 4 'omnes tantae uelocitatis, ut despectui eis essent equitantium pernicitates'.

[67] Campbell, *Encomium*, Bk. II, c. 7. 'And because infantry and cavalry could not accomplish this [i.e. capture London]'.

[68] *ASC* D *s.aa.* 994, 999, 1010, 1013, 1014, 1015.

[69] Griffith, *The Viking Art of War*, pp. 102–3.

[70] Griffith, *The Viking Art of War*, p. 103. His analogy with mounted police is erroneous. It ignores the need to train a police horse to overcome its natural instinct for self-preservation: flight! This is an action that may be preceded by rearing and kicking. There is a similarity between the training of the police horse for crowd control and a military horse: for the special training see Fillis, *Breaking and Riding*, pp. 228 and 230.

participate in battle, to be read alongside R. H. C. Davis' masterly exposition on the importance of horse breeding.[71] There is an element in a horse's psychology that makes a highly trained animal obedient in the tumult of battle and, provided there are sufficient highly trained horses in a group of mounted warriors, the herd instinct can be relied upon to keep less experienced horses together during a charge.[72]

The chances of Scandinavian invaders finding horses locally which were trained to ignore the noise and tumult of battle must have been small. So were the chances of the riders being able to achieve an instant rapport with horses such that they could be controlled almost entirely from the leg, leaving the hands free to carry weapons and shield.

After many years of relative peace, the evidence suggests that King Æthelred's armies did not have the benefit of such military technology.[73] In these circumstances, although an English king might expect his forces to be mounted, he could not expect to be able to deploy mounted men in battle, no more than could the Scandinavian invaders. Also, the English forces were relatively inexperienced to the extent that many of them may have lacked body armour in the early fighting.[74] In border areas, where fighting took place most frequently, there is evidence that the English had deployed 'foreign' mercenaries since the time of King Edgar.[75] England, therefore, was one of the few places in western Europe where Scandinavian armies could have a reasonable expectation of military success over a period of months, or years, since King Æthelred and his *witan* seemed unwilling to take a long term view and develop continental military technology until matters had gone beyond their control. It was probably during its exile in Normandy that the English Court began to gain a true appreciation of the value of mounted warriors in battle.[76]

It is an interesting comment on the comparatively peaceful state of England that armed mounted warriors do not appear to have been available to King Harold, for use in battle, in 1066. The speed with which he moved his army about the country demonstrates that many horses were used for transport

---

[71] Much has been written about horse psychology and horse breeding. It is the historical perspective, supplied by Davis with regard to breeding, that is lacking.

[72] Although Fillis discusses the training of an army horse, he does not discuss the psychology of the horse in relation to battle: he takes it for granted that the horse can be trained to ignore its natural instincts. However, see his footnote, *ibid.* pp. 230–2, concerning the horse and deep water. Wätjen expressed the importance of understanding horse psychology when he wrote, 'Take the trouble to find your way into your horse's mind without trying to make it human. Only those can become experts who are in tune and as one with their horses both physically and mentally': Wätjen, *Dressage Riding*.

[73] Abels, 'English Tactics and Military Organization', pp. 148–9 and n. 26 on p. 154. Also, Brown, *Norman Conquest*, p. 93.

[74] Brooks, 'Weapons and Armour', pp. 216–17.

[75] The complaint in *ASC* D E F *s.a.* 959, in the style of Archbishop Wulfstan, that King Edgar 'attracted hither foreigners and enticed harmful people to this country', read in context, may be a reference to the use of foreign mercenaries and the practice of giving them land and provisions to sustain them and their families.

[76] For the importance of horses to the Normans, see Davis, 'The Warhorses of the Normans', pp. 67–82.

purposes. Yet he did not deploy trained horsemen in battle, preferring to take up a position at the battle of Hastings that would counter or reduce the effectiveness of his opponents' mounted warriors.[77] At Hastings, William the Conqueror did deploy mounted warriors and the Bayeux Tapestry is an important record of that fact. In the tapestry William's forces are to be seen crossing the Channel with their trained horses and then deploying them very effectively in battle. These circumstances suggest that, some decades earlier, Æthelred's reticence in developing mounted forces for battle was understandable, though it was detrimental to his cause.

Before concluding this section on England's military weakness, some consideration should be given to ships and naval technology. To return to Gillian Fellows-Jensen's article, which was mentioned above, she has more to add about the ships of the Scandinavian invaders:

> The rather surprising ease with which this success was achieved must have been in large part due to the fact that the shallow draught of the Viking ships gave them several advantages. They were fast sailing, they could use oars as complement to sails and they made it possible for the Vikings to use islets in shallow estuaries as landing-places and winter strongholds, since the ships of the English drew too much water for them to be able to land there.

This explanation for Viking successes in England is evidenced in *ASC* A s.a. 896, where English ships which had been made, apparently, to King Alfred's own design ran aground when in pursuit of six Viking ships. Alfred Smyth is particularly scathing about the performance of these ships.[78] However, it may be observed that conceptually they were many decades in advance of their time. English warships of similar size were built at the end of the tenth century[79] and *Heimskringla* records that Olaf Tryggvason's great warships, which were at the battle of Svold, were of similar size.[80] An equivalent construction technology was available to all the maritime nations of the north. Scandinavian ships were made of pine or oak, depending to some extent on the availability of timber and they were built to different shapes and sizes according to their destined usage.[81] A Scandinavian fleet was made up of a variety of ships, including transport ships as well as the long and high-sided warships. The fleets of their English opponents were made up in similar manner. In 992 the English fleet was made

---

[77] At the battle of Stamford Bridge, Harold and his opponents fought on foot. Brooks, 'Arms, Status and Warfare in Late-Saxon England', argues that the English could not deploy cavalry, using the Bayeux Tapestry as evidence. He says, 'The continental knight fought on horseback; the Anglo-Saxon thegn on foot, and we have seen his byrnie to have been distinctly designed for infantry warfare' *ibid.* p. 97.

[78] Smyth, *King Alfred the Great*, pp. 111–13.

[79] Whitelock, *EHD*, no. 122, pp. 536–7, Old English will of Bishop Ælfwold of Crediton (997–1012). Also, Sawyer, *Anglo-Saxon Charters*, no. 1492.

[80] Jónsson, *Heimskringla*, K 72, K 78 (see K 80 for the change of name for this ship), K 88.

[81] There are many books on Viking Age ships. Ole Crumlin-Pedersen, 'Ships, Navigation and Routes', provides an overview and a bibliography. See also, Binns, 'Ships and Shipbuilding'.

up of the ships available, but in 1008 ships were specially constructed.[82] *Heimskringla*'s description of naval battles depicts them as land battles fought at sea.[83] The objective was to capture ships, not sink them. In open water a large, heavily armed and manned ship with high sides would have had a great advantage. Smaller vessels might escape into shallower water. Transport vessels were needed to carry provisions and booty. During the period of this study, the English were able to acquire shipbuilding technology and build ships on a grand scale,[84] so naval technology does not seem to have been a major factor in explaining why Scandinavian invaders were successful in penetrating into England and not elsewhere. The English, Frisians and others had the requisite technology, although the English did not deploy it very well.

[82] *ASC* C D E *s.aa.* 992 and 1008.
[83] Jónsson, *Heimskringla*, K 101–12.
[84] For the construction of large ships by the English, see reference to the reconstruction of the annal for 1008 in Chapter 5, p. 78 and Appendix 2, below.

3

Swein Forkbeard's First Invasion

Leding or *Lið*

In 1986, Professor Niels Lund published an important paper that discussed:

> the organisation of those Viking armies which under the leadership of Swein
> Forkbeard and his son Cnut succeeded in conquering England in the second
> decade of the eleventh century: were the forces of these kings privately orga-
> nized, like the ones operating in the ninth century, or were they state armies
> recruited on the basis of a public obligation on all free men to serve the king in
> war?[1]

Professor Lund's paper explains that this question 'has an important bearing on
the problem of the formation of the state of Denmark', and he has continued to
develop his views on this subject over subsequent years.[2] A privately organised
army was a *lið*; a state army was a *leding*.[3] In this book, it is intended to use the
terms *leding* and *lið* solely in relation to developments in England. In this
context, the conclusion of Lund's paper is important:

> The conquests of England accomplished first by Swein Forkbeard and then by
> his son Cnut undoubtedly belong to the most spectacular achievements of the
> whole Viking age, and there can be little doubt that the armies involved were
> bigger and probably drawn from a wider area, indeed from most of Scandina-
> via, than Viking armies had previously been. This does not mean, however,
> that they were different in principle from those armies with which the west
> was already familiar. The distinction between the two Viking ages of Britain
> does not lie in state organization in the sense that in the second of these ages
> the kings of Denmark were able to draw on resources not available to their pre-
> decessors in the ninth century; it lies in a difference of purpose and determina-
> tion and perhaps in their greater ability to control the magnates within their
> empire, reflecting the growth of royal power between Horik I and Swein
> Forkbeard.[4]

---

[1] N. Lund, 'Armies', pp. 105–18.
[2] Most recently in: *Lið, Leding og Landeværn*.
[3] *Ibid.* Lund wrote: 'what is known in the Scandinavian countries as *leding, ledung* or
leiðangr, a system by which the king's subjects put a great number of manned and armed
ships at his disposal.'
[4] Lund, 'Armies', p. 118. Horik I was a king of Denmark who died in 854.

By way of contrast, the English king, Æthelred II, had the resources of an organised state at his disposal and he, with his *witan*, could command local or 'national' armies to be gathered. Similarly, he could command the provision of a fleet. This does not mean, of course, that there were no limitations to the availability of the English *fyrd* and *scipfyrd*; there were. However, the contrast between the power and authority of the kings of England and Denmark – between the facility of *lið* and *leding* – further emphasises the spectacular nature of the achievements of Swein Forkbeard and his son, Cnut.

As Lund indicates, power is not static; it develops. This is why events associated with Swein Forkbeard's invasions may be used to show how the leadership of raiding forces developed over time and how the organisational purpose of those forces developed from coastal raiding on a large scale to one of total conquest. Swein's status as leader of invading armies developed also during the period 990 to 1014, and, whilst Lund has explained why Swein's army in 1013 could not be described as *leding*, there can be little doubt that the gathering of Swein's army and its organisation for his final invasion of England differed markedly from that of his first army, which may be regarded as a typical *lið*.

Swein Forkbeard's Departure from Denmark

The general reasons for the invasion of England by bands of Scandinavian adventurers at this time have been discussed in Chapter Two. Swein Forkbeard's personal motivation for leading an army of adventurers, or *lið*, out of his kingdom of Denmark deserves some further consideration.

Chapter 1, pp. 7–11, describes a version of his birth and his relationship with his father, King Harald Bluetooth (Gormsson). Whether or not that version is correct, there was a rebellion in Denmark against Harald Bluetooth in about 987. Harald fled from Denmark and died of wounds received during the rebellion. He was succeeded as king of Denmark by Swein Forkbeard.

The history of Scandinavia in the period 990 to 995 is confused. Adam of Bremen says that Swein was driven into exile.[5] His account is supported by the chronicle of Thietmar of Merseburg who was a contemporary witness to events.[6] There is documentary evidence that Swein spent many years in the west leading a raiding force or *lið*. *Heimskringla* says that after Harald Bluetooth's death, Swein went to war in Saxony, Frisia, and finally also in England.[7] His exploits in England are recorded in the *Anglo-Saxon Chronicle* (*ASC*),[8] and there is documentary evidence of his presence in Essex.[9] There is a reference in the Welsh Annals to his activities in the Irish Sea.[10] Adam also provides an

---

5   Lappenberg, '*Mag. Adami*', Bk II, c. 28.
6   Trillmich, *Thietmari Merseburgensis*, Bk 7, c. 36 (26).
7   Jónsson, *Heimskringla*, Olaf Tryggvason saga, K 53.
8   *ASC* C D E *s.a.* 994.
9   S.939. Also, 'Old English Charter of King Ethelred Confirming the Will of Æthelric of Bocking' in Whitelock, *Anglo-Saxon Wills*, pp. 42–6.
10 Keynes, 'The Historical Context of the Battle of Maldon', pp. 81–113, at p. 92. Also, Williams ab Ithel, *Brut Y Tywysogion*, pp. 32–3, *s.a.* 994.

account of Swein's activities in the British Isles,[11] which lends general support to the other evidence of Swein's movements.

An assertion in the *Encomium Emmae Reginae*, that Swein ruled Denmark undisturbed for many years after his father's death, is contradicted by evidence that Swein was absent from Denmark throughout most of the six-year period, 990 to 995. It is clear that the writer of the *Encomium* is being selective in his information in that he makes no reference to Swein's foreign adventures until the expedition in which he conquered England in 1013.[12]

There is a gap in our knowledge of the political control over Denmark during the years 990 to 995. Initially, it seems to be agreed by our sources that Swein succeeded Harald Bluetooth as king in about 987. Scandinavian and North German sources indicate that he suffered considerable setbacks in his dealings with the Slavs and the Norwegians. Whilst Scandinavian sources refer to Swein's campaigns in the west, in Saxony, Frisia and eventually in the British Isles,[13] they give no indication that he ceased to exercise royal authority in Denmark. Adam of Bremen and Thietmar of Merseburg, on the other hand, say that he was driven into exile,[14] indicating that he did not exercise royal authority for a number of years. This is supported by documentary and chronicle evidence that Swein was active in the British Isles on a continuous basis from about 991 until 995. Allowing time for campaigns in Saxony and Frisia, it seems likely that he was absent from Denmark from about 990 until 995. For most, if not all, of this time, his absence must have been on a continuous basis. Whether Swein would have agreed with Adam that he was 'in exile' does not really matter; it seems unlikely that he was exercising royal authority in Denmark either directly or indirectly during this period.

It should be observed that, in 1991, Professor Lund expressed a different view about Swein Forkbeard's situation and activities during this period. He wrote that a case could be made for Swein's participation in the Maldon campaign in 991,[15] that he may have participated in the great Scandinavian raid on Saxony in 994,[16] and that Swein was:

> no adventurer leading what forces he could gather from one event to the next; he was king of Denmark and probably the first ruler of a Scandinavian country who was able to take his army abroad on a viking expedition without, apparently, having to fear for his position at home.[17]

Support for Lund's view may be found in a paper written by Professor Sawyer, in 1991, who concluded that previously held views about Swein's early failures as ruler of Denmark should be questioned and wrote:

[11] Lappenberg, *Mag. Adami*, Bk 2, cc. 26 and 32.
[12] Campbell, *Encomium*, Bk 1.
[13] Jónsson, *Heimskringla*, Olaf Tryggvason saga, K 53.
[14] Lappenberg, *Mag. Adami*, Bk 2, c. 28. Trillmich, *Thietmari Merseburgensis*, Bk 7, c. 36 (26).
[15] Lund, 'The Danish Perspective', pp. 114–42.
[16] *Ibid.* p. 138. But see Chapter 2, pp. 25–6, above.
[17] *Ibid.* p. 133.

The more favourable comments in the *Encomium Emmae Reginae* have been dismissed as biased. In discussing that text Dorothy Whitelock posed the rhetorical question 'what are we to think of the reliability of a writer who can describe Swein Forkbeard as a generous and religious king, whose end was happy "from both the spiritual and the worldly point of view"?' The evidence discussed here suggests that the answer is that we should take him seriously; his judgement was sounder than Thietmar's, and he was better informed than Adam.[18]

Lund's view, which seems to require that Swein returned to Denmark from time to time during this period, is undermined by the chronological evidence that Swein was in England from 993 to 995. This would have precluded his participation in the raid on Saxony in 994, which is, in any event, questionable, as Lund himself pointed out, since Thietmar makes no mention of Swein, and Thietmar and his family were involved in events to an extent that should have informed them of King Swein's presence. If we exclude him from the raid on Saxony, there remains no positive evidence that Swein returned to Denmark before 995, whilst there is evidence to account for his activities outside Denmark during the period 990 to 995 on a continuous basis.

Since there is no evidence of Swein's presence in Denmark during this period, there may be some substance in the implication in the chronicle of Adam of Bremen that Erik the Victorious, king of Sweden, took advantage of the situation in Denmark to establish Swedish hegemony over much of Scandinavia during this period. Swedish influence in Denmark may have continued after King Erik's death,[19] and, for a time, after Swein's return to Denmark in 995 because it appears that Swein had to capture Hedeby. The evidence is the inscriptions on two stones at Hedeby, one of which commemorates a follower of King Swein who had been west with him and had then lost his life at Hedeby, the other commemorates a man who served under one of Swein's followers and who lost his life during a siege of Hedeby. The reference to 'west' suggests that 'King Swein' is Swein Forkbeard and that the siege took place on his return from his adventures in the British Isles.[20]

When Swein left Denmark in c. 990/991, he and the force he led formed a typical *lið*. His political status would not necessarily have affected his ability to gather a band of warriors around him. Lund explains that:

> it was not only kings and emperors who had liðs; anybody would [*sic* ?'who'] could afford it could gather a lið around him, and the runic inscriptions, both Swedish and Danish, offer many examples of such private military bodies serving otherwise known as well as otherwise unknown magnates.[21]

[18] Sawyer, 'Swein Forkbeard and the Historians', pp. 27–40 at p. 39.
[19] Adam of Bremen's Chronicle suggests that Eric died in c. 994. Lappenberg, *Mag. Adami*, Bk II, c. 36–7.
[20] There are photographs of the stones, and a description indicating their significance, in Lund, 'The Danish Perspective', pp. 127–8.
[21] Lund, 'Armies', p. 110.

A raiding expedition touching Saxony and Frisia and eventually reaching England represented a relatively easy coastal route for Swein and his companions. Ole Crumlin-Pedersen has provided a detailed analysis of a voyage from Kaupang in southern Norway to Hedeby at the southern end of the Jutland peninsula,[22] estimating that it took five days to travel about 400 nautical miles.[23] On this basis, Scandinavian ships could sail along the coast to northern France, cross the Channel and then sail up the coast to Sandwich within a month, given favourable wind and general weather conditions and depending upon whether they set out from Limfjord or southern Jutland. This coastal route was used by traders and was subject to piratical raids from time to time.

Whilst there is evidence of raiding activity in Saxony and Frisia, there are no specific references to Swein Forkbeard.[24] His *lið* was one of several that were raiding in a westerly direction at that time. For instance, Olaf Tryggvason's *lið* probably followed a similar route in the final stages of his passage from the Baltic. Swein's route would bring him off the south-east coast of England, giving him the choice of an expedition along the south coast or against the south-eastern shires of Kent and Essex.[25]

According to the sagas, Olaf Tryggvason and his *lið* commenced their journey to the British Isles from Garda in present day Russia. Sagas in *Heimskringla* provide valuable evidence of the movement and typical activities of a *lið* at this time, although the specific detail of the history of the individuals concerned may be debatable. Reference to a Norwegian, Jostein, in the law, *II Æthelred*, may be taken as evidence of the presence in England of *lið*s from Norway during this period.

The Battle of Maldon

The battle of Maldon took place in August 991. The *ASC* informs us that:

> Ipswich was ravaged, and very soon afterwards Ealdorman Brihtnoth was killed at Maldon.[26]

We have an account of the battle in a contemporary, or nearly contemporary, poem, which describes how Ealdorman Byrhtnoth gathered an army to fight the

---

[22] Crumlin-Pedersen, 'Ships, Navigation and Routes', pp. 33–9.

[23] A nautical mile, 6080 feet, is about 15% further than a British standard mile.

[24] The *Annales Hildesheimenses* for the year 991 say: 'Piratae etiam Staverun depredando vastaverunt, aliaque in litore loca perdiderunt.' Staverun is in Frisia. The time of year is not indicated, so it is possible that the raiders' ships engaged in this attack took part in the campaign leading to the battle of Maldon later in the year.

[25] *ASC* A *s.a.* 993, an annal which confuses events in 991 and 993, indicates that the Scandinavian forces that fought at Maldon in 991 crossed to Folkestone, and sailed to Sandwich and Ipswich before turning on Maldon.

[26] In *ASC* C D E *s.a.* 991. The translation is from Whitelock *EHD*. The ealdorman's name is given as 'Brihtnoð' in *ASC* C E F and as 'Byrihtnoð' in *ASC* D. The spelling 'Byrhtnoth' (for Byrhtnoð) is now generally accepted and follows the text of the poem about the battle of Maldon: see, for instance line 16 of the facsimile in Scragg, *Maldon*, p. 3.

invaders. The two armies were separated by tidal water but, as the tide went out, a land bridge was formed between the two armies. Then, Ealdorman Byrhtnoth allowed the Scandinavians to cross this land bridge and form up in battle order. Battle was then joined and many of the Anglo-Saxons were driven from the battlefield, but Ealdorman Byrhtnoth refused to accept defeat and remained on the field. Byrhtnoth received a mortal wound and his retainers, refusing to abandon him, died with him. It was a heroic event and a significant defeat for the Anglo-Saxons.[27]

Although they may have been in England in 991, it is unlikely that Swein Forkbeard and Olaf Tryggvason took part in the battle of Maldon in August of that year because, according to the *Chronicle of John of Worcester* (*JW*), the Scandinavian leaders at Maldon were Justin and Guthmund.[28] The fact that John of Worcester appears to have had access to a copy of *II Æthelred*, which names Olaf as a leader along with Justin and Guthmund, indicates that the omission of Olaf's name from his account of the battle of Maldon was deliberate.[29] It is possible that Olaf and Swein were already in England but were not with the contingent of forces that fought at Maldon. Given the nature of the battle and style of fighting, later accounts make the reasonable assumption that the Scandinavians at Maldon suffered heavy losses.[30] Yet, after the battle, their activities were such that the English felt obliged to pay tribute,[31] so it is probable that only a part of their army was involved at the battle of Maldon and there were contingents (*liðs*) that had not participated.

Professor Lund, citing charter evidence,[32] suggests that Swein Forkbeard was in England early in the final decade of the tenth century and was in Essex at that time and concludes that this could have been during the Maldon campaign in 991.[33] Later in this chapter, we shall see that Maldon could have been threatened by a Scandinavian army in 993 as well as 991 and, as we trace the itinerary of the Scandinavian army in England, it will be seen that it visited Essex during 992. It follows that Swein may have been in Essex on several occasions in the early years of the final decade of the tenth century. John of Worcester is silent about his presence at the battle of Maldon and so there is no direct evidence to link him with the battle. As the force that fought at Maldon may have been only part of the Scandinavian army in England at that time, Swein could, of course, have been in the eastern counties and not have participated in the battle.

After the battle of Maldon,[34] the Scandinavian army must have remained in

---

[27] See Scragg, *Maldon*, for an analysis of the sources and the battle, together with a bibliography.

[28] Darlington and McGurk, *John of Worcester*, pp. 438–9, *s.a.* 991.

[29] *II Æthelred*, prologue. For this law in Old English and translation, see Keynes, 'Historical Context', pp. 103–7.

[30] Darlington and McGurk, *John of Worcester, s.a.* 991. *Liber Eliensis*: Kennedy, 'Byrhtnoth's Obits', pp. 65, 68.

[31] *ASC* C D E *s.a.* 991.

[32] S.939.

[33] Lund, 'The Danish Perspective', pp. 132–3. Lund also makes the point that: 'There may well have been raids that went unrecorded', *ibid.* p. 133.

[34] Kennedy, 'Byrhtnoth's Obits', pp. 59–62.

Essex for a time to care for its wounded, bury its dead and harry the country-side. There is no record of it having overrun Maldon itself. It is likely that Swein Forkbeard joined the main body of Scandinavian invaders whilst it was in Essex and that some local thanes received him 'when first he came there with a fleet' and gave him active support. The evidence is in King Æthelred's confirmation of the will of Æthelric of Bocking whose property had been put at risk of forfeiture by a charge of treason which had not been cleared during Æthelric's lifetime. The relevant words are:

> It was many years before Æthelric died that the King was told that he was concerned in the treacherous plan [*he wære on þam unræde*] that Swegn should be received in Essex when first he came there with a fleet[35]

Given Swein's background and ability, he must have been one of the inner council of leaders, although he was probably not the only 'king' in that army.[36] However, the most important leaders of this army appear to have been Jostein and Guthmund. Olaf Tryggvason was probably associated in this leadership soon after his *lið* joined the main army if Jostein accepted him as his nephew.[37]

Activities of the Scandinavian Army

It seems likely that the Scandinavian fleet eventually left Essex and sailed along the Kent coast. The *ASC* records that they caused great terror by their coastal raiding.[38] It also says that Archbishop Sigeric, who appears to have been the representative of royal authority in Kent, advised the king that tribute should be offered in return for peace. The enemy agreed a truce and a payment of 10,000 pounds was paid to them. It is difficult to give such a sum a modern equivalent though it is certain that the writer of the *ASC* annal intended it to be indicative of the great concern that this army was causing.[39]

The Scandinavian army probably over-wintered in England in a position that was inaccessible to a land army and difficult to attack by sea. No doubt some of the army returned to Scandinavia with their booty and their share of the tribute. However, the westerly movement of Scandinavians was continuing and so the

---

[35] S.939. Whitelock, *Anglo-Saxon Wills*, no. XVI (2), 'King Æthelred's Confirmation of Æthelric's Will', pp. 44–7. The likely date of the confirmation and its preamble suggest that Swein was in England some considerable time before his recorded participation in an attack on London in September 993. See Professor Whitelock's introduction to Whitelock *EHD*, no.121, p. 535. See this chapter, pp. 42–3, below, for the date of the attack on London.

[36] Snorri says, in relation to the young St Olaf: 'for it was the custom that those commanders of troops who were of kingly descent, on going out upon a viking cruise, received the title of king immediately, although they had no land or kingdom': Hollander, *Heimskringla*, Saint Olaf's saga, c. 4.

[37] For the relationship between a man named 'Jósteinn' and Olaf, see Jónsson, *Heimskringla*, Olaf Tryggvason saga, K 52.

[38] *ASC* C D E *s.a.* 991.

[39] See the debate between J. Gillingham and M. K. Lawson on the value of payments to Scandinavian armies in *EHR* 104, 1989 and 105, 1990 part 2.

army numbers would have been augmented. The army itself was made up of a mixture of peoples: Scandinavians from Norway, Sweden, Denmark; expatriate Norwegians from Russia; Slavs who had joined forces such as those of Olaf Tryggvason in Russia or Pomerania; Frisians and Celts.[40] There was no obvious place outside England for such an army to retire whilst awaiting the next campaigning season.[41] Sigeric's involvement in negotiating the truce suggests that the army had attacked the Kent coast. If it had not travelled beyond Kent, it could have used the Isle of Sheppey or Sandwich and the Isle of Thanet as a base.

The *ASC* for the annal year 992 indicates that King Æthelred and his councillors were faced with a serious problem that could not be ignored, though we can only surmise its extent. If, for instance, the enemy army controlled Sandwich and the Wantsum Channel they were in a position to disrupt trade to Canterbury and London.[42] The English response to the problem was to summon all the ships that could be put to use to assemble at London,[43] an action with grave economic and social implications for the country since those ships were needed for internal and international transport and trading purposes. Such a summons could only be sustained for a limited time and specific purpose, so the English fleet must have been gathered to deal with an existing and very tangible threat such as an enemy fleet that was already stationed on the English coast. The fact that the English fleet was summoned to London indicates that the enemy army was in Kent: had they been on the Isle of Wight, for instance, the fleet might have been summoned to Sandwich.[44] The fact that there is no mention of a land army being summoned in support of the fleet suggests that it was stationed in a place that was inaccessible by land, such as an island; alternatively, the Scandinavians had built themselves very good defences on their landward side.

What happened next has been confused by accusations levelled at one of the leaders of the English fleet, Ealdorman Ælfric. It appears that he was incompetent and deserved censure but the twelfth-century annalists who wrote about him distorted history in order to attack him. John of Worcester's account (*JW*) levels accusations of treachery against Ealdorman Ælfric in the following passage:

---

[40] The presence of men from various parts of Scandinavia is clear: Jostein was probably from Norway, Swein was from Denmark, runic memorials confirm the presence of Swedes, Olaf had journeyed via Russia and Pomerania. The presence of Frisians and Celts in this force is a deduction. *Knutsdrapa*, verse 7, confirms that Frisian forces came to England: Whitelock, *EHD*, 15, p. 308. The Welshman, Bjorn inn brezki, was a warrior hero in the sagas: Blake, *Saga of the Jomsvikings* (see index), reminding us that the Irish and Welsh Celts were not averse to undertaking raiding expeditions on their own account.

[41] In personal correspondence, Professor Keynes has written: 'I'm still wedded to the notion (as set out in my contributions to the Maldon book and to the *Oxford Illustrated History of the Vikings*) that there was basically one viking force active in England in the period 991–1005, and it doesn't really worry me that from time to time it seems to have taken a nap.'

[42] For the strategic importance of the Isle of Thanet see Hill, *An Atlas of Anglo-Saxon England*, p. 14, map 19.

[43] *ASC* C D E *s.a.* 992.

[44] Compare *ASC* C D E *s.aa.* 1008, 1009.

On the advice and orders of Æthelred, king of the English, and of his nobles, stronger ships were assembled at London from all England, and these the king, filling them with picked soldiers, put under the command of the ealdormen Ælfric (whom we mentioned above) and Thored, and the bishops Ælfstan of Wilton and Æscwig, commanding that if they by any means could, they should take the Danish army in any port where they could blockade it. But the ealdorman Ælfric, secretly sending a messenger to the enemy, urged them to take care they were not surrounded unexpectedly by the king's army. Indeed, the ealdorman himself, an extraordinary example of shameful behaviour, on the night before the day when the English had determined to fight bravely against the Danes, fled secretly to the Danish fleet with all his men, and soon took shameful flight with them. When the royal fleet learned of this, it pursued those fleeing. Without delay one single ship was taken from amongst them, and was plundered when the whole host on board had been slain. The others escaped by flight. By a fortunate chance the Londoners with the East Anglians encountered them and joined battle, slaying many thousands of Danes. In addition, they took the ealdorman Ælfric's ship, with men and arms, when he himself had with difficulty escaped, and they were victorious.[45]

JW follows *ASC* D with additions that help to trigger the imagination. Thus, the ships are filled 'with picked soldiers'. Then *JW* adds some information to identify the English leaders. Thus, Ælfric is the ealdorman 'whom we mentioned above'. However, *JW* appears to be incorrect in identifying Bishop Ælfstan as bishop of Wilton and, when it says that the orders to the English commanders included taking the Danish[46] army 'in any port where they could blockade it', *JW* appears to have misunderstood the problem. The enemy fleet was apparently already in England and in an easily defended position. The problem for the English was to persuade them to move and risk battle. In this context the 'warning' ('Ælfric . . . het warnian þone here') which Ælfric sent to the enemy was in the form of a challenge, a challenge that was accepted since we are informed by the *ASC* that he knew when the battle would take place. So, when *JW* says that Ælfric urged the enemy 'to take care they were not surrounded unexpectedly by the king's army', it was not only an unrealistic action for an English commander but strategically impossible. Then *JW* has the English ealdorman flee to the enemy fleet and escape with them, yet this same ealdorman continued to be one of the king's leading ministers, was given command of an army which was raised against the Danes in 1003 and died fighting for King Edmund in 1016.[47] Finally, *JW* suggests that the Danes were later defeated in a sea-battle and that the ealdorman's ship was recaptured from them; this is a complete misunderstanding of the *ASC* account which tells of a Danish attack on part of the English fleet and the loss of the ealdorman's ship, which was captured by the Danes. Similar distortions appear in the account by William of Malmesbury, although he had access to a copy of the *ASC*. Henry of

---

[45] Darlington and McGurk, *John of Worcester*, pp. 440–3.

[46] In this paragraph I have followed *John of Worcester* in referring to the Scandinavians as 'Danes'. The nationality of the invaders is discussed in Chapter 1, p. 11 and on p. 38, n. 40, above.

[47] Keynes, *Diplomas*, table 6, 'Subscriptions of the Ealdormen'. *ASC* C D E *s.aa.* 1003, 1016.

Huntingdon adds an extra twist to the tale by confusing Ælfric of Hampshire with Ælfric of Mercia who had been banished some years earlier. It should be noted that Version F of the *ASC* encourages the misunderstanding about Ælfric by the context in which it adds that he was 'one of those in whom the king trusted most'.[48] Some modern historians are guided by the twelfth-century chroniclers in their interpretation of the *ASC* and refer to the 'treachery' of one of the English leaders.[49] What follows here is, however, derived directly from *ASC* C D E.

The leaders of the English fleet were ordered to try to 'entrap the enemy army anywhere at sea'.[50] In the context of what has been deduced above, the sense of this order was that the English had to entice the enemy fleet from its safe haven and fight.

The English fleet must have taken up a station as near to the enemy fleet as they could find reasonable land facilities for provisions and water. Having come from London, that station was likely to be between the enemy position and London.[51] The movements of such a large English fleet could not have escaped the attention of the enemy force. Ealdorman Ælfric, one of the English leaders, sent a challenge to the enemy fleet and a day for battle was appointed.[52] This interpretation is supported by the following phrase in the annal, which makes it apparent that Ealdorman Ælfric knew when the battle would take place.

Interpreting the *ASC* version of the story, it seems that Ealdorman Ælfric went on shore the night before the battle and he was probably not alone in doing so. What is surprising is that he was not back with the fleet in time to play his part in directing a sea-battle, as the *ASC* comments, 'to his great disgrace'.[53] The *ASC* indicates that the enemy fleet escaped in the direction of London, because it says that the enemy fleet later encountered the ships from East Anglia and London, which were presumably returning to their home ports.[54] So it seems that the better-disciplined Scandinavians must have set out with their warships and transport vessels (possibly, very early in the morning) and had passed the English station before the fleet could challenge them.[55] The *ASC* says that 'the

---

[48] Giles, *William of Malmesbury's Chronicle of the Kings of England*, p. 167; Forester, *The Chronicle of Henry of Huntingdon*, pp. 178–9; Greenway, *Henry of Huntingdon*, p. 329; *ASC* F *s.a.* 992.

[49] See, for instance, Keynes, 'Historical Context', p. 91.

[50] *ASC* C D E *s.a.* 992. The words are: '7 sceoldon cunnian meahton hi þone here ahwær utan betræppan': Cubbin, *MS D, s.a.* 992, p. 48.

[51] See Figure 5, p. 41.

[52] *ASC* C D E *s.a.* 992. The words are: 'þa sende se ealdorman Ælfric 7 het warnian þone here . . .': Cubbin, *MS D, s.a.* 992, p. 48. The use of the word 'warnian' is confusing. In context it must mean 'challenge' rather than 'warn' in the sense of 'take care', which is the meaning usually given to it. The context is, however, obvious since the immediately following phrase makes it clear that, as a result, a day for battle had been agreed: '7 þa on þære nihte þe hi on þone dæg togædere cuman sceolden'.

[53] 'þa s\c/eoc he on niht fram ðære fyrde him sylfum to myclum bysmore': Cubbin, *MS D, s.a.* 992, p. 48.

[54] See Figure 5.

[55] Most Scandinavians were probably interested in booty before glory and were no doubt pleased to avoid this battle: compare the avoidance of battle in *ASC s.a.* 1009. One may

Figure 5. Scandinavian itinerary: 991–992

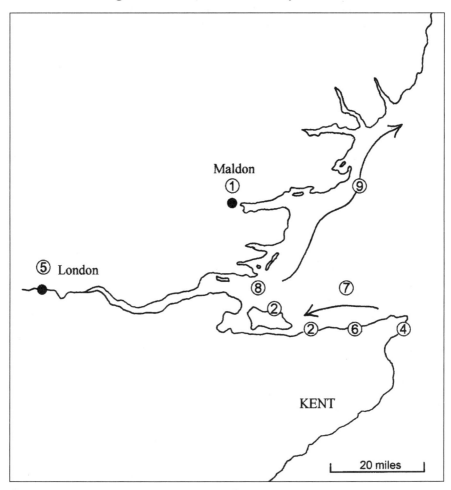

① Battle of Maldon: August 991
② SC coastal raiding: probably Kent
3 *gafol* agreed: 10,000 pounds
④ SC take up winter quarters: probably Kent
⑤ English fleet gathered on Thames at London

⑥ English fleet threatens SC
⑦ SC escape and pass English fleet
⑧ SC encounter the East Anglian and London ships
⑨ SC move up the east coast (towards Bamburgh)

SC = Scandinavians

enemy escaped, except that the crew of one ship was slain'; so one ship through ill luck, mismanagement or, perhaps, bravado was brought to battle by the English ships. Whilst the English ships were thus engaged, the enemy fleet must have been distancing itself and completing its escape.

Although the opportunity to inflict significant damage on the enemy fleet

reflect upon the wisdom of entrusting the leadership of the fleet to four individuals. *ASC* C D E *s.a.* 992 says that the king 'entrusted the expedition to the leadership of Ealdorman Ælfric and Earl Thored and Bishop Ælfstan and Bishop Æscwig'.

had been lost, the Scandinavians had been driven away from their safe moorings and Ealdorman Ælfric could report a partial success. The English presumably discharged their ships to return to their home ports or their next trading destination, because the *ASC* says:

> And then the Danish army encountered the ships from East Anglia and from London, and they made a great slaughter there and captured the ship, all armed and equipped, on which the ealdorman was.[56]

If the English fleet had been in active pursuit of the enemy, their fleet should have included ships from southern ports as well as those from East Anglia and London. Though the East Anglian and London ships were following the same route as the enemy fleet, they, presumably, did not anticipate encountering it. Interestingly, the situation, enemy tactics and result were probably very similar to those described by Snorri in relation to Swein Forkbeard's important victory, some seven or eight years later, at the sea-battle of Svold. There, Swein anticipated that his enemies would sail down the coast in open order, so he hid his fleet in ambush and launched a successful surprise attack.[57] If Snorri's account of the battle is not entirely imaginary, one may suppose that Swein's tactics were influenced by events in England in 992.

To the Scandinavians the opportunity to capture ships must have been irresistible. The ealdorman's ship was a particularly valuable prize and there were possibly others. The object of a sea-battle was to clear and capture ships, not to sink them and the fact upon which the annalist focused was that Ælfric's ship was captured in such a state, 'all armed and equipped', as might suggest that its crew had put up little resistance. As for the rest of the battle, the 'great slaughter' was probably not one-sided and both fleets probably suffered damage before darkness or the weather forced them to part.

There are no reports of enemy activities immediately after the naval battle. The Scandinavian fleet probably re-grouped along the coast of Essex and landed for the purpose of making repairs, dealing with the wounded and obtaining fresh supplies of water and food. The Scandinavians, rich in booty and their share of the 10,000 pounds of tribute, were in a position to make themselves welcome. Documentary evidence that some Essex thegns were prepared to welcome their leaders was noted above.[58] Given a choice of trading or being raided, this is not surprising.

The enemy fleet must have over-wintered in England on the east coast because the *ASC* reports it next at Bamburgh on the north-east coast, then on the Humber and, finally, outside London in September 993. The report of the attack on London is in *ASC* C D E *s.a.* 994. Because of the annal date, there has been a misunderstanding about the date of the attack on London, which is usually ascribed to September 994. The C D and E annals were using an indiction year commencement (*caput anni*) at this time, which means that the annal year 994

---

[56] *ASC* C D E *s.a.* 992. The translation is in Whitelock, *EHD*, p. 213, *s.a.* 992.
[57] Jónsson, *Heimskringla*, Olaf Tryggvason saga, K 100–1.
[58] S.939.

ran from September 993 to September 994. Since the attack on London is the first event in the annal year we are intended to understand that the attack occurred in September 993. The year commencement for annal purposes could vary, according to the source being used or the personal inclination of the scribe and his sponsor. The *caput anni* used in the various versions of the *ASC* changed more than once during this period.[59]

There is a period of some fifteen to eighteen months between the naval battle in 992 and the attack on London. The earliest date for the attack on Bamburgh is late September 992, but it could have taken place in the spring of 993, so whether the enemy took up winter quarters before or after the attack on Bamburgh is uncertain.[60] Because of the prevailing winds, the enemy fleet could journey north to Northumbria more quickly than it could make the return voyage, so late autumn is quite feasible. Scandinavian ships could run very fast before the wind and could sail on a broad reach. However, they could not be close-hauled, so they would depend upon currents and oars to make progress against the wind.[61] *JW*, like the *ASC*, places the attack under the annal year 993 indicating that the attack on Bamburgh took place in spring 993 since its year normally commenced in January, but John of Worcester may simply have been taking a lead from the *ASC* annal year.[62] What is certain is that an assault on Bamburgh was of enormous significance. It was the capital of northern earls who ruled an area that had once been an independent kingdom and who were capable of maintaining their territories against any aggression from their northern neighbour, the king of Scotland.[63] They owed allegiance to the king of England, but in return received the benefits of high office and the use of lands in Yorkshire. The fact that Bamburgh was 'sacked and much booty was captured there' was noted by an English annalist whose interest in the north was spasmodic.

During 993, the enemy army made its return journey to the south. By this time, if not before, Swein Forkbeard had established himself as one of the principal leaders of the army.[64] Sawyer, *Anglo-Saxon Charters*, no. 939, which is dated no later than 999, establishes that the English regarded him as a leader of the invaders *before* he had led his second invasion in 1003/4. One might ques-

---

[59] *ASC* A differed from the other versions of the *ASC* in commencing its annal year in mid-winter (or Christmas) at this time, so its annals align very closely with our own year commencement of 1 January. These matters, together with many other facets of chronology in our sources, are explained in Howard, 'Swein Forkbeard's Invasions of England'.

[60] *ASC* C D E *s.a.* 993. The annal year commenced during September 992; hence the earliest date. Because of the other events described under the annal year 993, the attack on Bamburgh could not have been later than spring 993.

[61] Heaton, *Sailing*, pp. 81, 88.

[62] Darlington and McGurk, *John of Worcester, s.a.* 993. John describes the raiders who attacked Bamburgh as 'the aforementioned Danish army' ('predictus exercitus Danorum').

[63] The old kingdom was Bernicia. For the position of the rulers of Bamburgh between the expanding kingdoms of Scotland and England, see Stafford, *Unification and Conquest*, pp. 121–8. For their successes and failures against Scottish kings, see Stenton, *Anglo-Saxon England*, pp. 417–19.

[64] See *ASC* C D E *s.a.* 994 for Swein's leadership of the attack on London in September 993.

tion why this charter, S.939, did not mention Olaf Tryggvason since he was more significant and also in Essex at the same time as Swein: the probable reason is that, when King Æthelred was remembering the treacherous welcome given to his enemy in Essex in S.939, he deliberately omitted mention of Olaf who was by then his ally and whom he had sponsored at confirmation.[65]

The army spent some time raiding both sides of the Humber in Lindsey and Northumbria and, although English levies were raised to oppose it they apparently avoided fighting a battle.[66] The enemy army must have seemed formidable: the *ASC* estimated that the fleet consisted of over ninety ships, suggesting a force of over 5,000 men. The number of ships as recorded in *ASC* A *s.a.* 993 and in *ASC* C D E *s.a.* 994 must have been estimated to some extent. The ships are unlikely to have been marshalled in one place where they could have been counted easily; also, there is a problem of definition: what constituted a ship for this purpose? To extrapolate a number of men from an estimated number of ships is, necessarily, problematical. Some warships might carry 80 men or more; transport ships were designed to be manned by very few men. However, the Scandinavians must have deployed considerable numbers to protect their booty and their ships whilst providing raiding parties for both banks of the Humber that could intimidate forces gathered locally, which were described as a 'very large English army' in *ASC* C D E *s.a.* 993. Equally, the attack on London, in September 993, described in *ASC* C D E *s.a.* 994, in which they suffered heavy losses and after which they ravaged four counties suggests that the enemy were deploying considerable forces.[67]

Considering the size of the army, the defeat of Byrthnoth at Maldon and the sack of Bamburgh, it is understandable that the English forces avoided direct confrontation. Although the *ASC* condemns their attitude as cowardly, they may have employed a strategy of making it difficult for the enemy to obtain supplies and send out raiding parties, a strategy they may have considered justified when the Scandinavian leadership decided to move further south.[68]

[65] *ASC* C D E *s.a.* 994.
[66] *ASC* C D E *s.a.* 993.
[67] 'Considerable' is, of course, a relative term. If 5,000 people attended a premiership football match today it would be a very disappointing crowd, but at the end of the tenth century 5,000 people was the population of a large city: see Chapter 1, p. 2, and Chapter 2, pp. 21–3 and p. 23 n. 43.
[68] ASC C D E *s.a.* 993 says that a very large army ('mycle fyrde') was gathered to combat the enemy. It names the leaders of the army and says that they fled rather than fight. I suspect that this is an interpretation of the leaders' deliberate decision not to fight a major battle against a superior enemy. Since the Scandinavian army was attacking London by the beginning of September, it did not remain long on the Humber, which suggests that they were not having an easy time there. In the twelfth century, writers such as John of Worcester add the charge of treachery to the failings of the leaders of the English army, saying that they fled 'because they were Danes on the fathers' side'. This charge was more apposite to the late eleventh century when the people of this region actively supported the claims of the kings of Denmark to rule England (their lands were harried by the Normans, as a result). It is not so apposite to the circumstances of the late tenth century. The gloss which the twelfth century writers put upon the history of the late tenth century is described in my paper 'King Edward the Martyr: When, Why and How did he die? The Problem and a Proposed Solution' for the Manchester Centre for Anglo-Saxon Studies, April 2002. It will also be considered in my

Figure 6. Scandinavian itinerary: 992–994

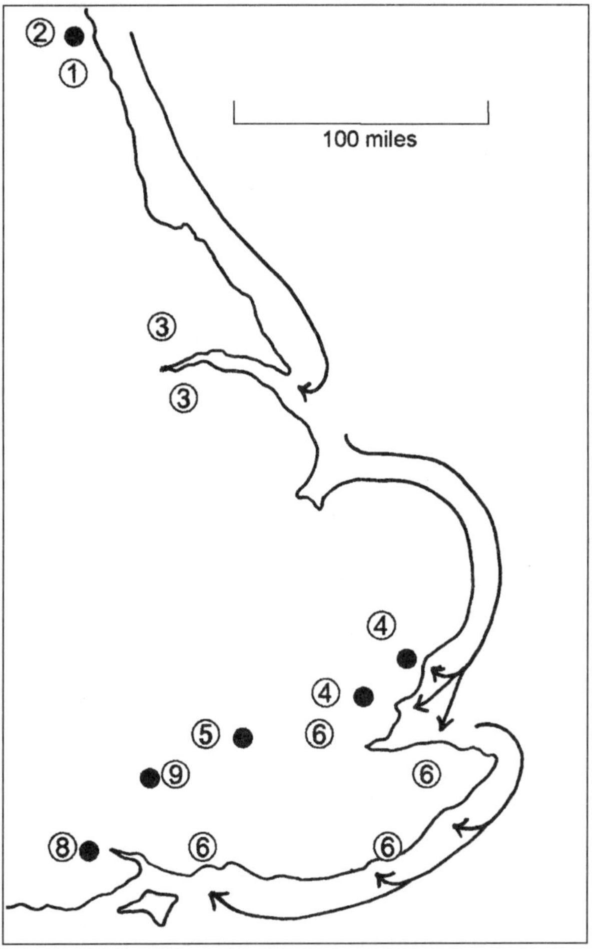

① SC take up winter quarters 992/3: probably in Northumbria
② SC sack Bamburgh
③ SC cause great damage in Northumbria and Lindsey
④ SC attack Ipswich and Maldon
⑤ SC (Olaf and Swein) attack London: September 993
⑥ SC ravage in Essex, Kent, Sussex and Hampshire
7 *gafol* agreed: 16,000 pounds
⑧ SC take up winter quarters 993/4, at Southampton
⑨ Treaty (*II Æthelred*) agreed: probably at Andover

SC = Scandinavians

It was on the following part of the journey that Ipswich and Maldon were threatened once more, an event which one version of the *ASC* associated with the leadership of Olaf Tryggvason.[69] By September 993, the enemy army was on

forthcoming book, *The Reign of Æthelred II (the Unready)*. Compare a similar Fabian strategy that the English national army seems to have adopted after the failure of the English fleet, *ASC* C D E 1009, and the defeat of the army in East Anglia, *ASC* C D E 1010.
[69] *ASC* A *s.a.* 993. See Figure 6, above.

the Thames and it attacked London under the leadership of Olaf Tryggvason and Swein Forkbeard.[70] Because the exemplar for the *ASC* annals was written about three years after Swein had invaded and conquered England in 1013,[71] one might question whether it gave exaggerated significance to the part he played at this time. It is fortunate, therefore, that there is the charter evidence, described above,[72] from before the year 1000, illustrating Swein's significance to King Æthelred and his court. So it seems that Swein and Olaf led the attack on London, whilst older leaders such as Jostein remained in the background.

The siege of London was undertaken with great vigour but the citizens resisted stoutly and the enemy army eventually withdrew having suffered heavy losses. After withdrawing from London it:

> did the greatest damage that ever any army could do, by burning, ravaging and slaying, everywhere along the coast, and in Essex, Kent, Sussex and Hampshire; and finally they seized horses and rode as widely as they wished[73]

Thus, events followed a similar pattern to those of the years 991/92. First there was English resistance and enemy losses; this was followed by raids along the south-eastern and southern coasts. The pattern continued with Æthelred and his councillors agreeing to give the enemy provisions and pay them tribute if they would cease from harrying the country. Once again, Archbishop Sigeric was heavily involved in advocating the payment of tribute.[74] A payment of 16,000 pounds was agreed according to *ASC* C D E. Again the enemy force took up winter quarters, this time at Southampton.[75] However, they no doubt made use of the Isle of Wight, which they were increasingly to regard as a 'safe haven'.[76] In any event, the enemy army held a strategic position from which it could disrupt English trade.

King Æthelred's Treaty with the Army: *II Æthelred*

During the winter of 993/94, Æthelred's government appears to have devised a strategy that differed from that tried in 992. Instead of using the respite gained by paying tribute to raise a fleet, it was proposed that the enemy fleet should remain in England, receiving pay and provisions, and defend the country. *ASC* C D E *s.a.* 994 says that the king sent Bishop Ælfheah and Ealdorman Æthelweard to negotiate with Olaf:

[70] *ASC* C D E *s.a.* 994. See Figure 6.
[71] Chapter 1, pp. 3–5, above.
[72] S.939.
[73] *ASC* C D E *s.a.* 994. The translation is in Whitelock, *EHD*, p. 214, *s.a.* 994.
[74] *II Æthelred*, clause 1. Archbishop Sigeric probably died in October 994 and some writers have had difficulty accepting Sigeric's involvement because they believed that the attack on London and subsequent events occurred a year later than appears to have been the case. Because of my revised dating, Sigeric's involvement is no longer a problem.
[75] *ASC* C D E *s.a.* 994. See Figure 6.
[76] In *ASC* C D E *s.a.* 1006 there is a reference to the Isle of Wight as their sanctuary or safe haven: *friðstole*.

And they then brought Olaf to the king at Andover with much ceremony, and King Ethelred stood sponsor to him at confirmation, and bestowed gifts on him royally. And then Olaf promised – as also he performed – that he would never come back to England in hostility.[77]

There exist copies of the treaty which Æthelred made with the Scandinavian army at this time. It is numbered among the laws as *II Æthelred* and names the leaders of the army as Olaf, Jostein and Guthmund, Steita's son. Olaf is Olaf Tryggvason, Jostein is probably his uncle, Guthmund is not mentioned in other extant sources. The treaty established a permanent peace between the English and the Scandinavian army and that the Scandinavian army would protect England from invasion, and attack its foreign enemies. The treaty also provided laws for the conduct of the English and members of the army towards each other both in England and when they met on territory outside Æthelred's jurisdiction. There is a final clause, clearly an annotation to the original treaty, which says that:

> twenty-two thousand pounds in gold and silver were paid from England to the army for this peace [*fride*].[78]

The treaty, *II Æthelred*, was presumably the result of Bishop Ælfheah's and Ealdorman Æthelweard's efforts but, were it not for the existence of the treaty, the conclusion could be drawn from the *ASC* annal that Olaf simply promised to leave England. This would beg questions about where the Scandinavian army came from in 997, which *JW* referred to as the 'army which had remained in England'.[79] It is interesting to note that the C D and E versions of the *ASC* avoid reference to the deployment of mercenaries until late in Æthelred's reign, when his arrangement with Thorkell the Tall could not be ignored. It should be noted that Archbishop Wulfstan strongly disapproved of this policy if the homiletic passage in *ASC* D *s.a.* 959 may be taken as evidence. Also, it was not part of the chronicler's remit from his sponsor to add anything positive about Æthelred's military policy, since the objective was to provide a contrast with the very positive military exploits of Edmund Ironside. It is possible that the treaty, *II Æthelred*, became an exemplar for similar agreements with Scandinavian leaders such as Pallig in 1000 and Thorkell the Tall in 1012, hence its preservation.

The *ASC* account of the attack on London, perhaps with the benefit of hindsight, gives equal prominence to Olaf and Swein. However, *ASC* A *s.a.* 993 names Olaf as the army leader, making no mention of Swein. *ASC* C D E only refers to Olaf's presence at Andover. Similarly, *II Æthelred* identifies Olaf but not Swein, raising the question whether Swein was still with the Scandinavian

---

[77] Whitelock's translation. The *ASC* does not describe the treaty terms.
[78] See the discussion of *heregeld* in Chapter 2, p. 19, above.
[79] Darlington and McGurk, *John of Worcester, s.a.* 997. See n. 41, above, for Keynes' opinion that 'there was basically one viking force active in England in the period 991–1005'.

army when the treaty was agreed.[80] It is probable that he was, as the events in Scandinavia and Saxony, described below, which may have encouraged him to return to Denmark, occurred after the agreement of the treaty in England. Failure to mention his name in *II Æthelred* may simply reflect his status at that time in an army led by the Norwegians, Olaf and Jostein.

England enjoyed a period of peace following the agreement of the treaty. It may have been because the Scandinavian army was committed to protecting England from further invasion, that new raiders, journeying west from Scandinavia and eager for booty, turned their attention to Saxony. In 994 they made a great raid into the mouth of the river Elbe, defeated a Saxon army, attacked the city of Stade and mutilated their hostages before fleeing from Saxony. The chronicler, Thietmar of Merseburg, was himself nearly taken hostage and one of his uncles was killed leading the Saxon army.[81] Adam of Bremen agreed with the account given by Thietmar and added that 'Duke Benno and Margrave Siegfried came up with an army and took vengeance for that disaster. And those very pirates who, we said, had landed at Stade were destroyed by them.'[82] Adam said that the enemy army consisted of Swedes and Danes. He also said that another army of Scandinavians raided into the mouth of the River Weser and that they were finally defeated and suffered considerable losses. Thietmar's account suggests that the raiders who were on the Elbe withdrew from Saxony, probably suffering losses on the way but were not 'destroyed' as stated by Adam.

These events must have had an impact upon Jutland and appear to have destabilised Denmark politically. It may have been changes occasioned by these events that persuaded Swein Forkbeard to return to Denmark in the following year to restore his rule.

In England the treaty between Æthelred and the Scandinavian fleet probably remained in force during the two campaigning seasons, 994 and 995, and the annals portray Olaf and Æthelred as good friends,[83] so when, in 995, Olaf set off on the expedition which was to make him king of Norway, he may have been given assistance by King Æthelred in addition to his share of the 22,000 pounds *heregeld*.[84]

Both Olaf Tryggvason and Swein Forkbeard seem to have turned their attention to the Irish Sea during 994, which would have accorded with the terms of *II Æthelred*.

Heimskringla says that Olaf was active in the Irish Sea at about this time, campaigning in places where there could have been Scandinavian and Celtic strongholds such as the Hebrides, the Isle of Man, Ireland and Strathclyde

---

[80] See Sawyer, 'Ethelred II, Olaf Tryggvason and the Conversion of Norway'.
[81] Pertz, *Annales Hildesheimenses, s.a.* 994; Pertz, *Annales Corbienses, s.a.* 994; Pertz, *Annales Quedlinburgenses, s.a.* 994; Trillmich, *Thietmari Merseburgensis*, Bk IV, c. 23 (16) – 25 (16).
[82] Tschan, *Adam of Bremen*, Bk II, c. xxxii (30).
[83] *ASC* C D E *s.a.* 994.
[84] See Sephton, *The Saga of Olaf Tryggwason*, cc. 269, 285, for the friendship between Æthelred and Olaf. For further discussion of the agreement made between King Æthelred and Olaf Tryggvason, see: Andersson, 'The Viking Policy of Ethelred the Unready', and Sawyer, 'Ethelred II, Olaf Tryggvason and the Conversion of Norway'.

('Cumberland'). *Heimskringla* includes Olaf's Irish Sea campaigns in sequence with his other warlike activities as if they occurred before he made peace with the English because Snorri, following his skaldic source, assumed that Olaf travelled round the British Isles in an anti-clockwise direction, which is what a seaman might anticipate.[85] Unlike Snorri, we have the evidence of the *ASC* that the army turned south from Bamburgh to the Humber, London and Southampton, a clockwise direction that was more difficult to sail. It is apparent from the *ASC* that he was fully occupied on the eastern and southern coasts until after the winter of 993–4.[86] This would indicate that his activities elsewhere must have been after the agreement of *II Æthelred*.

A reference in the Welsh annals to Swein Haraldsson ravaging the Isle of Man indicates that Swein Forkbeard was active in the Irish Sea and probably fulfilling the treaty terms.[87] The Welsh annals are sparse and the dates appear to have been added later. Under the year 994 they say 'And then the Isle of Man was devastated by Swein son of Harald.' It is apparent from internal evidence that the most likely year for the devastation of the Isle of Man by Swein was 995. The identity of Swein is confirmed a few lines later under the annal year 1012 which says:

> And then Swein, son of Harald, came to England, and expelled Edelred, son of Edgar, from his kingdom, and reigned in his territory, in which he died in that year.[88]

This annal belongs to the year 1013 and the reference to Swein's death in the same year is perhaps due to the original annalist using a March *caput anni* or to the practice of keeping sequential information together when closely related in time.[89]

The Return of Swein and his *Lið* to Denmark

Allowing time for Olaf Tryggvason to fulfil his treaty obligations makes autumn 995 the most likely time for his return to Scandinavia. It is likely that Swein Forkbeard returned at about the same time. Why they returned to Scandinavia is a matter for discussion at this point.

[85] Jónsson, *Heimskringla*, Olaf Tryggvason saga, K 30 – K 32. *ASC* C D E *s.a.* 993.

[86] *ASC* A *s.a.* 993; *ASC* C D E *s.aa.* 993–4.

[87] Whilst noting the evidence that Swein campaigned in the Irish Sea, attacking the Isle of Man, Keynes suggests that he (presumably with his *lið*) might have broken away from the main Scandinavian army by this time: Keynes, 'Historical Context', p. 92.

[88] Williams ab Ithel, *Brut Y Tywysogion*, pp. 32–5. The edition is based on the Red Book of Hergest, Jesus College, Oxford and it has been collated with an older and some later manuscripts. The oldest manuscripts refer to Swein as 'Yswein uab Herald'; later versions have the variant 'Ywein vab Harald'. Interestingly, there are references to an earlier 'son of Harald', named Godfrey ('Gotbric', later variants: 'Godfrid', 'Gotfrit') in the annals dated 970, 979, 981 and 986.

[89] Swein died in February 1014. In the *ASC* for this period there are examples of annal 'years' with more than four seasons and some with less, for similar reasons.

Heimskringla says that Olaf had been taken from Norway to the eastern Baltic as a baby. Swein may have been driven out by an alliance of enemies headed by the families of Erik of Sweden and Hákon of Norway who had a common interest in keeping the heirs of Harald Bluetooth away from Scandinavia.[90] In England, the treaty arrangement was open-ended, providing a guaranteed base with supplies and ample scope for raiding in the Irish Sea against the enemies of King Æthelred. According to *Heimskringla*, Olaf married a wealthy widow, related to the king of Dublin, who had property in England and Ireland.[91] The arrangements in England were such that most of the mercenary fleet remained when Olaf and Swein departed and Olaf sailed to Norway with only five ships.[92] So there were reasons why Olaf and Swein might have considered remaining in England at this time.

Olaf and Swein probably left the British Isles because of a mixture of ambition and opportunity. In Olaf's case, there were good contacts between Norway and the British Isles. *Heimskringla* says that Earl Hákon, the ruler of Norway, knew of Olaf's activities and was alarmed at his increasing power, popularity and rumours of his claim to the throne of Harald Fairhair through his father, Tryggvi Olafsson. Hákon was increasingly unpopular for reasons that are well documented in *Heimskringla*,[93] and many people in Norway wanted a change in government and a restoration of the kings. As a result there was an uprising against the earl, who was killed, and his family fled, seeking sanctuary with their allies in Sweden. Although the Swedish royal family offered them sanctuary, they apparently gave no practical support towards re-establishing Hákon's sons' rule in Norway, perhaps because they had considerable problems of their own.[94] It was against this background that Olaf returned to Norway and was 'restored' with popular acclaim to the throne of his ancestors.[95]

Although it is possible to question the accuracy of the detailed record in *Heimskringla* concerning Olaf and how he became king of Norway, it is preferable to the lack of information about Swein Forkbeard at this time. The *Encomium* says nothing about this expedition to the British Isles and, therefore, nothing about his return. Historians such as Professor Sawyer questioned the account which may be derived from the German chronicles and annals.[96] However, a case has been proposed, above, that Swein had lost control of Denmark and that, after the death of Erik of Sweden, probably in 994,[97] Swein

---

[90] See Chapter 1, p. 9, and Chapter 3, p. 34, above, for Erik of Sweden, and this chapter, below, for evidence of the relationship between Hákon's family and the Swedes.

[91] See Jónsson, *Heimskringla*, Olaf Tryggvason saga, K 32, K 46–7.

[92] *Ibid.* K 47.

[93] *Ibid.* K 48.

[94] Including the disruptive effects of the *lið*s that had attacked Saxony: see above.

[95] Jónsson, *Heimskringla*, Olaf Tryggvason saga, K 49, K 51. Whether Olaf was a successful opportunist who learned the story of the disappearance of Tryggvi's baby son from Norwegians such as Jostein, or whether he was genuinely the child of Astrid and Tryggvi is a matter for debate.

[96] See Sawyer, 'Swein Forkbeard and the Historians'.

[97] After the Scandinavian invasion of Saxony in 994, according to the chronology of Adam's account. Lappenberg, *Mag. Adami*, cc. 29, 37.

returned to Denmark and re-conquered his kingdom. If Adam of Bremen is to be believed there may have been setbacks during Swein's campaign but he was eventually successful following his marriage to the widow of Erik of Sweden.[98]

In 1991, Lund argued that Swein might have parted company with the main army before the treaty, *II Æthelred*, was concluded but he accepted that he was back in Denmark in 995 'when he began to mint coins with his own name on them'.[99] Keynes suggested that the omission of Swein's name from the treaty, *II Æthelred*, need not indicate that he had left the army but may be because 'he did not seem as important to the contemporary draftsman of the treaty as he seemed in retrospect to the chronicler'[100] Keynes went on to write:

> A certain 'Swein, son of Harald' is said by the Welsh annals to have ravaged the Isle of Man in 995, and is conceivably to be identified as the Danish ruler, son of Harald Bluetooth; but if so, he was soon afterwards back in Denmark, doing whatever may have been necessary to re-establish his position as king.[101]

Whether it was because the Swedish hold on Denmark had been shaken or for other reasons, it may be concluded that Swein had probably returned to Denmark by the end of 995.

The Scandinavian Army in England

After the departure of Olaf and Swein most of the Scandinavian army remained in England.[102] Neither the leaders of the army nor the leaders of individual *liðs* are identified in the *ASC* with the possible exception of Pallig who is mentioned in an annal for the year 1001.[103] The army may have continued to comply with the treaty, but the *ASC* makes no mention of the treaty terms that transformed it into a mercenary army and, although the treaty arrangements were presumably in force during the campaigning seasons of 994, 995 and 996, no mention is made in the *ASC* of the army's activities. Indeed, were it not for *II Æthelred*, it might be inferred, from *ASC* C D E, that the agreement with Olaf led to his immediate departure together with his army:

> And then Olaf promised – as also he performed – that he would never come back to England in hostility.[104]

---

[98] Queen Sigrid: see Chapter 1, p. 9, above.

[99] Lund, 'The Danish Perspective', pp. 138–9.

[100] Keynes, 'Historical Context', p. 92.

[101] *Ibid.* p. 92. M. K. Lawson, *Cnut*, p. 23, supports this, quoting the Welsh annals for Swein's presence in the Irish Sea in 995.

[102] Darlington and McGurk, *John of Worcester*, *s.a.* 997; Keynes, 'Historical Context', pp. 88 and 93.

[103] Pallig is named by *ASC* A *s.a.* 1001 in terms that suggest that he had been a leader of part of the army in 1000 and possibly before.

[104] *ASC* C D E *s.a.* 994.

The annals for 997, 998 and 999 in *ASC* C D E provide evidence of problems with this army, informing us of savage attacks on many places in the south and implying that the response by local forces and by King Æthelred's government was inadequate.

Having made no reference to the terms of *II Æthelred*, *ASC* C D E does not give any reasons for the army's conduct during the period 997 to 999. We can only surmise at local difficulties and at a failure to provide supplies, land, land-rents and, perhaps, *heregeld* at a level that the army felt was warranted. It may have been that the army was destabilised by the addition of *liðs* and new leaders joining it subsequent to the treaty agreement. Whatever the reason, *ASC* C D E describes an army that appears to have been, increasingly, out of control. In Chapter 1, pp. 3–5, above, it was proposed that *ÆE*, the exemplar for the *ASC* C D E annals, was created for political purposes and was a biased source: we have evidence of bias in the annal *s.a.* 1001, which is compared with a detailed independent source in Chapter 4, pp. 57–9, below. No such separate source exists for the annal years 997, 998 and 999, but, for reasons discussed below, we may suspect the *ASC* C D E exemplar of bias and exaggeration.

In 997, there is charter evidence that Æthelred convened several great councils.[105] Meetings probably took place at Cookham, Calne and Wantage. The meeting at Wantage may have been to promulgate a law-code, in which case there was probably another meeting at Woodstock in that year for a similar reason.[106] The activities of the Scandinavian army did not interfere with this full government programme, which would seem to indicate that the events recorded in the *ASC* were regarded as temporary, local difficulties.

In 998, *ASC* C D E says that the army stayed in the Isle of Wight and obtained provisions from Hampshire, yet *ASC* A, which evidences a particular interest in this area,[107] made no reference to the army's incursions.

In 999, *ASC* C D E informs us that King Æthelred called out naval and land forces to deal with the Scandinavian army but that direct confrontation was avoided. The annal concludes:

> And then at the end neither the mobilisation of the fleet nor the mobilisation of the army achieved anything, except hardship for the people, and a waste of money, and an emboldening of their enemies.

Yet the same annalist records at the beginning of his next annal that King Æthelred was able to send a fleet into the Irish Sea and himself lead his army to ravage in the north-west, probably into Strathclyde. Without explanation, the annalist records that the 'enemy fleet' departed to Normandy.

Æthelred's campaign in the north-west is significant. His attack on 'Cumberland', which in those days included Strathclyde, was evidently successful since he is said to have ravaged nearly all of it. His fleet ravaged the Isle of Man. This

[105] Keynes, *Diplomas*, appendix 2, pp. 269–73; and appendix 1, p. 255, *s.a.* 997. Whitelock *EHD*, no. 43, 'King Ethelred's Code Issued at Wantage (*III Ethelred*, 978–1008)', pp. 402–3. Also, S.890, S.891, S.939.
[106] Wormald, 'Æthelred the Lawmaker', pp. 61–2. Keynes, *Diplomas*, appendix 2, p. 273.
[107] *ASC* A *s.aa.* 993 (for 991 and 993) and 1001.

campaign was reminiscent of those conducted by King Æthelred's predecessors, particularly King Æthelstan.[108] It was a strong political message both to the king's subjects in the north and to the rulers of neighbouring territories. As well as this evidence of a strong government safeguarding its frontiers, there is also evidence of a responsible government promoting internal reform, as exemplified by improvement of the coinage and promulgation of law codes,[109] and so we would be justified in questioning the judgement of the writer of the exemplar for *ASC* C D E in respect of the years 997 to 999 as exemplified by his remarks quoted above.

[108] *ASC* A B C D *s.aa.* 934, 937.
[109] For coinage and laws, see Chapter 2, pp. 14–22, above, and Wormald, 'Æthelred the Lawmaker', pp. 47–80.

4

Swein Forkbeard's Second Invasion

The Scandinavian Army Leaves England

The annal for 1000 in *ASC* C D E records that 'the king went into Cumberland[1] and ravaged very nearly all of it' and his fleet ravaged the Isle of Man. It adds that the enemy fleet had gone to Normandy. This is a strange sequence of events, since there is no explanation for the Scandinavian army ceasing its raiding activities and going to Normandy. John of Worcester amends the order of events so that the enemy fleet went to Normandy first.[2] This seems logical since King Æthelred could hardly have led an army to ravage 'Cumberland' if he had not been assured that southern England was safe.

To try to understand why the Scandinavian army left England, it is necessary to consider the circumstances in which the members of that army were placed. The core of the army consisted of men who had remained behind in the pay of Æthelred's government when Olaf Tryggvason departed in 995. They had been settled on land in the south-west, probably in Devonshire,[3] and continued to be available as a military force to attack the king's enemies. Originally, some of them would have taken part in the campaign of 991; others would have rein-forced the fleet as it journeyed south in 993. Thus, in 999, many of the members of this army would have been away from Scandinavia for six or even eight years. They had been settled in England since 994 and they had no other obvious home base to which they might return. They had journeyed west with the *lið*s. Rune-stone evidence shows that some of them returned to Scandinavia at various times[4] and, although in 994/5 the westward impetus was diverted from England,[5] in the following years the army would have been reinforced with *lið*s, fresh from Scandinavia and eager for booty. These reinforcements probably destabilised the army in England and continued to do so on an increasing scale during the period 997 to 1001. This army had rebelled and had attacked the

---

[1] 'At this date Cumberland means the kingdom of Strathclyde, not merely the modern county': note *s.a.* 1000 in Whitelock *et al.*, *The Anglo-Saxon Chronicle*.
[2] Darlington and McGurk, *John of Worcester, s.a.* 1000.
[3] *ASC* C D E *s.a.* 997 infers that they were based in Devon; *s.a.* 998 says that they came back east into Dorset, implying that they were based west of the river Frome. *ASC* A *s.a.* 1001 has settled Scandinavians joining a raiding army in Devon.
[4] Lund, 'The Danish Perspective', pp. 119–133, explains the rune-stone evidence in the section entitled 'The Scandinavian *Lith* and its Members'.
[5] Chapter 3, p. 48, above.

English, according to the *ASC*.[6] It must have had grievances, whether real or imagined, that caused it to break its treaty obligations and it was to Æthelred's advantage to restore the army to its former allegiance. Given the outcome of events it may be deduced that, in addition to mobilising an army and a fleet in 999, Æthelred entered into negotiations with the army. There is evidence that part at least of this army was re-settled subsequently in the south-west and that Æthelred lavished gifts of gold, silver and estates upon its leaders.[7] Part of this army probably formed the nucleus of the forces which invaded 'Cumberland' under the command of King Æthelred in 1000 and which also ravaged the Isle of Man.

If Æthelred renegotiated his agreement with the army leaders in 999 it does not explain why a large part of the army should go to Normandy. There is uncertainty about Æthelred's relations with the Norman court at this time. In 990/1, a papal legate, Bishop Leo of Trèves, had brokered a peace agreement between Æthelred's government and the government of Richard, duke of Normandy.[8] Although Richard had since died and was succeeded by his son, Richard II, the treaty terms may still have been in force since, in 1002, King Æthelred married Richard II's sister.

The causes of the enmity between the two rulers in 990/1 were not stated in the Pope's letter confirming the peace agreement. There were several causes that might have contributed to it, including disputes over shipping in the Channel concerning fishing rights, trading, smuggling and piratical attacks by ships of one nation upon those of another. The geographical location of Normandy and Wessex points to these possibilities and it is perhaps significant in this context that Pope John's letter refers to Æthelred as 'king of the West Saxons'. The final sentence in the letter indicates that both courts had been harbouring exiles from the other's country. Difficulties with raiding forces might have further exacerbated matters. In the annal for 980, for instance, *ASC* C records that raiders made citizens of Southampton captive; this almost certainly means that many of them were sold into slavery and they may have been taken to the market at Rouen, in Normandy, for that purpose.

> a recent survey of Rouen's commercial development has shown that the city's trading prosperity was mediocre right up until the tenth-century boom, which derived from its role as a mart at which Viking booty was liquidated.[9]

---

[6]   *ASC* C D E *s.aa.* 997–1001 and Chapter 3, pp. 51–2, above.

[7]   See references to Pallig joining the enemy army in Devon with the ships he could muster: *ASC* A *s.a.* 1001. Significantly, the evidence appears in version A only and does not feature in *ASC* C D E.

[8]   Whitelock *EHD*, p. 823: 'Letter of Pope John XV to all the faithful, concerning the reconciliation of Ethelred, king of England, and Richard, duke of Normandy (991)'. The letter is quoted in Giles, *William of Malmesbury's Chronicle of the Kings of England*, pp. 171–2. Since doubts are expressed about some of the content of this chronicle for this period later in this chapter, it is fortunate that a copy of the letter is also in an early eleventh-century manuscript: BL, Cotton Tiberius A xv. (For discussion of William's alleged amendment of an earlier papal letter, see Thomson, *William of Malmesbury*, pp. 172–3.)

[9]   Bates, *Normandy before 1066*, p. 98.

However, it should be observed that there is no specific reference to such activities in the letter. If there were a variety of causes for the dispute between the two countries, the agreement brokered by the papal legate in March 991 and confirmed in the papal letter may not have prevented disputes re-emerging since their respective rulers were powerless to police all the activities of their subjects.[10] Also, in 998 the Scandinavian army was stationed on the Isle of Wight and some of the booty which it took from the coastal areas of Hampshire and Sussex could have found its way to Normandy.

With this activity as a possible cause of a resurgence of the enmity between the two countries, it is not possible to deduce whether or not the old treaty agreement between them was still in force. It is even possible that Æthelred and his advisers may have directed the Scandinavians to campaign in Normandy since there is a reference to an invasion by King Æthelred's forces in the chronicle of William of Jumièges, who wrote that King Æthelred sent an army against his brother-in-law, Duke Richard, but that it was met and defeated by forces under the command of Nigel, Vicomte of the Cotentin. The account is highly exaggerated and William's chronology is suspect (for instance, Æthelred did not marry Richard's sister until 1002) but as an indication of an invasion for which Æthelred was blamed it could reflect the events of the year 1000.[11] Roger of Wendover says that the Viking fleet invaded Normandy in 1000.[12] *ASC* C D E's bland statement that the enemy fleet went to Richard's land does not help to resolve this issue:

7 se unfryðflota wæs þæs sumeres gewend to Rikerdes rice.[13]

Other than the reference in the work of William of Jumièges, the visit of the army to Normandy did not make a sufficiently significant impact for it to be recorded in the Norman chronicles.

We can only say for certain that *ASC* C D E fails to explain why an army that was ravaging England in 999, despite the reported ineffectiveness of an English army and fleet, left the country to go to Normandy. The *ASC* says that Æthelred ravaged 'Cumberland' with an army but fails to give a reason, nor does it explain why the ineffective English leadership should suddenly prove so decisive and why it felt that it could leave the south coast and the southern shires apparently unprotected.

That the north-west coast of Britain and the Isle of Man were centres of Scandinavian activity and that they were a potential threat to English trade and English ports was probably sufficient reason for Æthelred to attack them,[14] but, without direct confirmation from the chronicler, this must also remain supposition. In the 980s the *ASC* indicates that England suffered from raids on the

10 For an account of what a rich merchant or nobleman might fear if he were driven ashore at the wrong place on the Channel coast, taken from the writings of William of Poitiers, see Brown, *Norman Conquest*, pp. 22–3.
11 Brown, *Norman Conquest*, pp. 4–5; p. 4 n. 1 discusses the date of these events.
12 Roger of Wendover, *s.a.* 1000: Giles, *Roger of Wendover's Flowers of History*.
13 Cubbin, *MS D, s.a.* 1000.
14 Keynes, 'Historical Context', p. 93.

northern coasts of Cornwall, Devonshire and Somerset; even an attack on Cheshire.[15] One of the apparent results of the treaty, *II Æthelred*, was that Olaf Tryggvason and Swein Forkbeard campaigned in Irish Sea locations. The mercenary army which Olaf left behind was probably settled in the west of England and is recorded as campaigning in the Severn Estuary in 997. So far as they were able, Æthelred and his government seem to have directed much warlike effort in the direction of the Irish Sea and the Severn Estuary. Celts, 'Welsh' and Scandinavians operated in this area and there was a political struggle for mastery of the important trade routes. Arguably, England had much to gain both from defending its existing interests and from further asserting itself. It should not be forgotten that Æthelred was heir to a tradition of success and territorial acquisition; dominance of the Irish Sea trade routes and the north-west coast of Britain, up to and including Strathclyde, would have been a realistic political ambition. Æthelred's father, King Edgar, had his rule over all England recognised in a coronation that had taken place only a quarter of a century previously, and Æthelred needed to assert his authority in the north. Because we know the disastrous outcome of the reign, many years later, there is a temptation to expect Æthelred and his ministers to have taken a defensive approach to affairs of state throughout his reign. This must be an untenable concept given all the known circumstances.

The Invasion in 1001 and its Aftermath

In 1001 the Scandinavian army returned from Normandy.[16] *ASC* C D E, all derived from the same *ÆE* exemplar, records the events that followed. Unusually, we have a detailed independent source for comparison: the *ASC* A annal *s.a.* 1001. *ASC* C D E records that the Scandinavian army:

(a) came to the mouth of the Exe and journeyed inland, attacking Exeter unsuccessfully;

(b) ravaged through the land 'as they were accustomed' ('⁊ dydon eall swa hi bewuna wæron');

(c) destroyed an 'immense army' ('ormæte fyrde'), drawn from Devon and Somerset, which was brought against them at Pinhoe;

(d) overran the land;

(e) retired to the Isle of Wight with much booty.

After this *ASC* C D E records that:

(f) no naval force nor land force dared go against the enemy army.[17]

---

[15] *ASC* C *s.aa.* 980, 981, 988.

[16] *ASC* A does not say where the army came from. *ASC* C D E implies that it was the army that had gone to Normandy in the previous year.

[17] The Old English quotations are from BL, Cotton Tiberius B iv.

ASC A provides a more detailed account of the activities of 'a naval force' ('sciphere') that ravaged and burnt almost everywhere. This can be compared with the above account, using the paragraph letters for cross-reference. A naval force:

> journeyed inland to Dean ('æþelinga dene', which was probably in Sussex, near the Hampshire border);

> fought a battle against an army from Hampshire and lost more men than the English but inflicted severe losses on them, killing many important leaders and retaining control of the battlefield;

> went westwards into Devon where it was reinforced by Pallig[18] who, breaking the pledges of loyalty he had given King Æthelred, joined it with the ships he could collect;

> burnt Teignton and forced the local population to buy peace;

(a)   came to the mouth of the Exe and journeyed inland 'in one journey until they reached Pinhoe' ('on ænne sið oð hy coman to peonho'), thus, indicating that there was no attack on Exeter;

(b)   (the reference to 'one journey', 'ænne sið', raises doubts about how far they 'ravaged through the land as they were accustomed');

(c)   defeated the king's reeves who commanded 'what army they could gather' ('mid ðære fyrde ðe hy gegaderian mihtan'); the army was put to flight and many were killed; (the passage contradicts *ASC* C D E's record that the English gathered an 'immense army');

(d)   burnt the residence at Pinhoe and at Clyst and many more (confirming that it 'overran the land');

(e)   went back east to the Isle of Wight from where it continued to raid;

and soon afterwards accepted peace terms.[19]

There is a remarkable contrast between these two accounts of the same campaign. *ASC* C D E describes only part of the campaign[20] and indicates that the invading army ravaged the countryside as it pleased and easily defeated an immense English army. It concludes by stating that no English force dared oppose it. This account also includes a failed siege of Exeter. *ASC* A describes how the invaders were opposed valiantly, probably on the Sussex, Hampshire border, with great loss of life on each side. The invading army then went westwards, gaining reinforcements in Devonshire, because a Scandinavian in the pay of the king betrayed his pledges to King Æthelred. The Scandinavian army was

---

18 William of Malmesbury claims that Pallig was Swein Forkbeard's brother-in-law. This is discussed below.
19 Old English quotations are from Cambridge, Corpus Christi College, MS 173: Flower and Smith, *The Parker Chronicle and Laws, A Facsimile*, 29b and 30a.
20 Evidence that *ÆE* also omitted part of an account of events in 1003 and 1011 is considered later in this chapter and in Chapter 5, pp. 91–4.

then opposed by an inferior English army that suffered many casualties. After further raids the two accounts in the *ASC* agree that the enemy army went to the Isle of Wight but, whereas the C D E version states that no English force dared oppose it, the A version closes its account by saying that peace terms were agreed. The A version, in effect, also contradicts the C D E account of an attack on Exeter.

The A version of the annals was being written at Winchester and we probably owe this account to the fact that it was of local significance and that important men died when the army from Hampshire fought the invaders. *ASC* A says that 81 men in all died on the English side and this is described as 'a great loss of life'. This figure provides an insight into the numbers being deployed. Assuming that 81 men represented between 10% and 20% of the English army, the total would have been between 800 and 400 men.[21] The Scandinavian army lost more men than the English but was able to hold the battlefield. This suggests that their numbers were larger. Also, they were campaigning inland so they should have left a sizeable force to protect their ships. This suggests that the total Scandinavian army consisted of between 1,500 and 1,000 men. Allowing that many more men would have been wounded than were killed, the consequences of this battle for the invaders must have been serious. Pallig's reinforcement of this army was timely to say the least. These estimated numbers, for the size of the forces involved, serve to provide a realistic impression of the logistical and strategic issues.[22]

The contrast between the two accounts of events in 1001 is part of the evidence indicating the biased and misleading nature of *ASC* C D E, and, therefore of *ÆE*. Professor Keynes has noted that:

A reading of the CDE-chronicler's account of events in the one year (1001) for which we have an independent and reasonably detailed annal (in manuscript A) shows just how unfortunate it is that we are normally dependent on his word alone;[23]

The Winchester additions to *ASC* A cease with the annal for 1001. The manuscript was later transferred to Canterbury.[24]

---

[21] The explanation for the assumption that between 10% and 20% of the English army was killed is based on the knowledge that 81 were killed and is arrived at as follows. If 100% of the English army had been killed, then the total army would have been 81, but the chronicler would have certainly informed us of a massacre of 100% of the English army. If 5% of the English army had been killed, then the total army would have numbered (81 x 100/5=) 1,620; this is unlikely because the passage says that men of name were killed and the losses were very heavy; so, losses would have been at least 10% (with 81 killed, 10% equates to an army of 810). Because there were so many important leaders in the battle (six of them were killed), it is unreasonable to expect the army to number less than 400 because of the number of personal retainers the leaders would have brought with them in addition to the levy from the Hampshire hundreds. (81 dead would be approximately 20% of an army of 400.)

[22] To show the figures in another context, Exeter had over 2,000 inhabitants about a century later: Darby, *Domesday England*, p. 308.

[23] Keynes, 'Historical Context', p. 85.

[24] Swanton, *Anglo-Saxon Chronicle*, p. xxii and n. 48.

The different versions of the *ASC* agree that the invasion of England in 1001 caused substantial damage and loss of life and that the English were eventually forced to ask the army for a truce, presumably at the end of the campaigning season when the English *fyrd* was disbanded.[25]

The annal for 1002 in *ASC* C D E records that peace was made with the enemy army and that a tribute of 24,000 pounds was paid to them.[26] The fact that *ASC* A records that peace terms were agreed in 1001 need not be read as a disagreement between the two versions; it may simply reflect the fact that, at this time, the C D E annal year ended during September whilst version A ended its year in December.[27] If time is allowed for gathering a vast sum of money, 24,000 pounds, the fact that *ASC* A does not record the payment in 1001 need not conflict with the C D E version of events. As there is no annal for the year 1002 in *ASC* A, we must rely on *ASC* C D E alone at this point.

Attempts have been made to relate changes in the coinage to the pattern of tribute payments and there is some correlation.[28] Close correlation should not be expected, however, having regard to the impact on the exercise of the full range of expenditure occasioned by the Scandinavian invasions.[29]

ASC C D E says that the payment of 24,000 pounds was made on condition that the enemy army should cease its evil doings. In 991, a truce left the army to be dealt with, and an English fleet was prepared for action in the following year.[30] In the winter of 993/4, after a payment of 16,000 pounds, the enemy army went on to discuss terms for a treaty by which, as a mercenary force, it was to defend England and fight its enemies. Since the *ASC* does not record the departure of the army following the payment of tribute in 1002 and does not mention English preparations to fight it, the likelihood is that the army agreed to remain as a mercenary force under the direction of the king and subject to the treaty terms made some eight years earlier in the spring of 994.

In spring 1002 the sister of Duke Richard of Normandy came to England to be married to Æthelred. *ASC* F says her name was Emma or, to the English, Ælfgifu.[31] Emma's marriage to Æthelred presumably marked the settlement of any outstanding disputes between the two rulers. When the enemy army had been ravaging in England, it may have seemed that there was a potential danger, common to them both, which should supersede any ongoing causes of enmity. The subsequent alliance between the two rulers is deduced not only from the marriage but also because a Norman was put in charge of Exeter and because of

---

25 For the Scandinavian itinerary, see Hill, *Atlas*, map 116.

26 Version E of the Anglo-Saxon Chronicle refers to 23,000 pounds but this appears to be a scribal error, since F, which follows an earlier version of E, records 24,000 pounds.

27 For indiction *caput anni* at this time, see Howard, 'Swein Forkbeard's Invasions of England', figure 10, p. 89.

28 Lawson, ' "Those Stories Look True" ', pp. 385–406.

29 See Chapter 2, pp. 17–19, and Figure 4, p. 20, above, for discussion of the expenditure.

30 Chapter 3, pp. 37–8, above.

31 The name 'Ælfgifu' is inserted in the manuscript over the name 'Ymma': Dumville, *MS F*, f. 61v.

the favourable treatment accorded Æthelred and his family, by Duke Richard, during a period of exile in 1013–14.[32]

Although the king and his counsellors had paid tribute of 24,000 pounds and may have renewed the treaty agreement with the Scandinavian army, *ASC* C D E indicates that they had little confidence in the loyalty of that army and its leadership. In the period 997 to 999 they had broken the treaty agreement, *II Æthelred*. In 1001 they had conducted a vigorous campaign against the English and, according to *ASC* A, the king had reason to feel especially betrayed by leaders such as Pallig who may have been under his personal command during the north-western campaign in the year 1000 and who had received substantial rewards.[33] There seems to have been an expectation that the mercenaries might turn against their paymaster yet again and *ASC* C D E says that King Æthelred received warnings of plots against his life coupled with a plan to overthrow the government.[34] Whether Æthelred had planned the action for some time or whether he was reacting to an imminent threat is not clear, but on St Brice's Day, 13 November 1002, an attempt was made to slay all the 'Danish men' who were in England, on the orders of the king.[35] This could not have been a massacre directed against the Danes of the Danelaw, but at 'Danes', probably mercenaries, who had been given peace land in 'English' territory.[36] There is dramatic evidence of how the massacre was carried out in a charter renewing the privileges of a monastery in Oxford that had been burnt when 'Danes', vainly, sought sanctuary there. This charter suggests that, in their enthusiasm, the English extended the massacre to include Scandinavian traders and settlers who were not directly involved with the mercenary forces further south. The following passage is taken from King Æthelred's charter:

> it will be well known that, since a decree was sent out by me with the counsel of my leading men and magnates, to the effect that all the Danes who had sprung up in this island, sprouting like cockle amongst the wheat, were to be destroyed by a most just extermination, and this decree was to be put into effect even as far as death, those Danes who dwelt in the afore-mentioned town [Oxford], striving to escape death, entered this sanctuary of Christ, having broken by force the doors and bolts, and resolved to make a refuge and defence for themselves therein against the people of the town and the suburbs; but when all the people in pursuit strove, forced by necessity, to drive them out, and could not, they set fire to the planks and burnt, as it seems, this

---

[32] *ASC* C D E *s.aa.* 1002, 1003, 1013.

[33] *ASC* A *s.a.* 1001: 'eac se cyng him wel gegifod hæfde on hamon 7 on golde 7 seolfre': Flower and Smith, *The Parker Chronicle and Laws (Corpus Christi College, Cambridge, MS 173): A Facsimile*, f. 30a. Pallig's participation in Æthelred's northern campaign is based on the assumption that the king's substantial gifts were in recognition of Pallig's services.

[34] *ASC* C D E *s.a.* 1002.

[35] *ASC* C D E *s.a.* 1002. The indiction year commenced in September. The specific date of the massacre is deduced in the context of events in the adjacent annals and because it *follows* events recorded as spring 1002. The sources for *ÆE* were moving away from an indiction *caput anni* at this point: Howard, 'Swein Forkbeard's Invasions of England', figure 10, p. 89.

[36] Keynes, *Diplomas*, pp. 203–5.

church with its ornaments and its books. Afterwards, with God's aid, it was renewed by me and my subjects, . . .[37]

King Swein's Revenge

However justified the action may have seemed, the massacre on St Brice's Day was a long remembered event for which Æthelred has taken much blame. William of Jumièges, writing some seventy years later, regarded the massacre as the cause of Swein Forkbeard's enmity towards Æthelred and his subsequent invasions as acts of revenge.[38] This explanation for Swein's invasions is also in William of Malmesbury's *Gesta Regum*:

> Sweyn . . . principally designing too avenge his sister Gunhilda. This woman, who possessed considerable beauty, had come over to England with her husband Palling [*sic*], a powerful nobleman, and by embracing Christianity, had made herself a pledge of the Danish peace. In his ill-fated fury, Edric [*sic*] had commanded her, though proclaiming that the shedding her blood would bring great evil on the whole kingdom, to be beheaded with the other Danes. She bore her death with fortitude; and she neither turned pale at the moment, nor, when dead, and her blood exhausted, did she lose her beauty; her husband was murdered before her face, and her son, a youth of amiable disposition, was transfixed with four spears. Sweyn then proceeding through East Anglia against the Northumbrians, received their submission without resistance . . .[39]

This chronicle, as noted by its editor, confuses the events of 1003 and 1013 in this passage,[40] and it is accompanied by many errors as compared with the *ASC* account. However, some historians have concluded that the account is based upon fact. Thus, Professor Whitelock quotes William of Malmesbury regarding Pallig, saying that he was King Swein's brother-in-law and that he and his wife and their child were victims of the massacre.[41] Despite this, the passage and the surrounding paragraphs are such as to throw doubt upon William as a viable source, so we cannot be sure of Pallig's relationship with Swein, although, in that Pallig is one of the few Scandinavians mentioned by name in the *ASC*, we

---

[37] 'Renewal by King Ethelred for the monastery of St. Frideswide, Oxford, of a privilege for their lands at Winchendon, Buckinghamshire, and Whitehill, Cowley, and Cutslow, Oxfordshire, after their church and deeds had been burnt down during the massacre of the Danes (7 December 1004)': Whitelock, *EHD*, no. 127, pp. 545–7, and S.909. Note that the charter is dated 7 December 1003, not as recorded by Whitelock. The date of the charter is '1004, 2nd indiction', a year that goes from September 1003 until September 1004; the regnal year quoted in the charter supports a December 1003 dating. For 'indiction year', see Cheney, *Handbook of Dates*, pp. 2–3. (The massacre must have been popular in the south of England, and in this charter, only a year after the massacre, Æthelred is seen associating himself with some of the excesses which occurred.)

[38] Brown, *Norman Conquest*, p. 5.

[39] Giles (trans.), *William of Malmesbury's Chronicle of the Kings of England*, p. 185.

[40] *Ibid.* p. 185.

[41] Whitelock *et al.*, *The Anglo-Saxon Chronicle, s.a.* 1001.

can be assured of his importance. Whether revenge was Swein's prime motive for attacking England is also uncertain, but it would be strange if there were no connection between these events and Swein's invasion in 1003.[42] Although William of Malmesbury's highly detailed account may be regarded as suspect, it may be based upon a credible tradition. The massacre was an important event and it may be presumed that many Scandinavians were killed, 'many' in this instance being a figure in excess of a hundred, possibly several hundreds. Given the relatively small populations and the social structure, many Scandinavians of the warrior class would have lost relatives and/or friends in the massacre and would consider themselves obliged to seek revenge. Given also that the Scandinavians who were subjected to the massacre had probably settled in England, it may be presumed that women and children suffered in the massacre. The motive for revenge, which William of Malmesbury ascribed specifically to Swein Forkbeard, may have existed in reality for many Scandinavians. Whether or not Swein had suffered a direct loss, there would have been considerable moral and political pressure upon him to lead an army to avenge the dead.

The defeat and death of Olaf Tryggvason of Norway at the sea-battle of Svold and Swein's alliances with his son-in-law, Erik of Lade, and his stepson, Olof Skotkonung of Sweden, had secured Swein a dominant position in Scandinavia.[43] His marriage to Sigrid, the dowager queen of Sweden and mother of Olof, helped him to create a political hegemony in Denmark and the rest of Scandinavia, which, in turn, allowed him to contemplate overseas adventures. The events of the previous two decades meant that there were many Scandinavians who had a taste for foreign adventure and it was sound policy to lead them overseas rather than allow them to disrupt peace and trade in the Baltic. There were many reasons, therefore, why Swein should seize upon a reason to direct an invasion force against England.

The *ASC* C D E annals for the year 1003 are particularly puzzling. They record that the enemy army stormed Exeter, destroyed its fortifications and seized much booty; a great English army, drawn from Wiltshire and Hampshire and led by Ealdorman Ælfric was gathered but then dispersed, apparently without fighting; Swein led the enemy army first to Wilton, which was ravaged and burnt, and then to Salisbury, and from there back to the sea and his ships.[44]

The *ASC* annals are difficult to interpret. We do not know how the army that stormed Exeter was constituted. At the end of the previous year King Æthelred had ordered all the Danish men who were in England to be slain. There is charter evidence that a massacre was carried out. There is chronicle evidence that leaders of the mercenary force, such as Pallig, may have been included in the massacre. If the massacre had been ineffective in Devon and the mercenary force retaliated by taking up arms against Æthelred, it is surprising that the *ASC*

---

[42] Saga evidence that Swein boasted some years before the massacre that he would conquer England may be discounted as imaginative accretion: Blake, *The Saga of the Jomsvikings*, p. 28, and Jónsson, *Heimskringla*, Olaf Tryggvason saga, K 35.

[43] See Chapter 1, pp. 9–11, above, for events in Scandinavia.

[44] See Figure 7, p. 65, below, for this itinerary.

makes no comment about it. If the massacre was effective and included members of the mercenary force and their families, it could be inferred that a new army was led to England by Swein Forkbeard; yet, again, it is surprising that the *ASC* does not say so. A third possibility is that Swein led an invasion force that reinforced an existing army in England.

Swein's name appears part way through the annal in a context that suggests he had been mentioned earlier, perhaps indicating that part of this or an earlier annal had been omitted. A comparison with *ASC* A for the year 1001 suggests that *ASC* C D E is being selective in recording the activities of the enemy army in that year; there must be a suspicion that there is similar selectivity in the annal for 1003.

The enemy army overran the fortifications at Exeter, contrasting with the supposed successful defence of Exeter in 1001. The *ASC* blames the failure at Exeter on the incompetence, or worse, of a French *ceorl* named Hugh who had been appointed reeve by the new queen. This leads us to consider the influence of Normans at Æthelred's court at this time but charter evidence suggests no great changes in this regard, although John of Worcester says that Hugh had been put in charge of Devon.[45]

The *ASC* omits to inform us what the enemy army did after taking much booty at Exeter. It next appears in Wiltshire and an English army, drawn from Wiltshire and Hampshire, was gathered to oppose it. Yet again, we are left with unanswered questions for this great English army was apparently dispersed. Are we to suppose that there were negotiations and the enemy broke a truce as they did in the following year? The *ASC* explains the dispersal of the English army as being a consequence of the feigned illness of one man, Ealdorman Ælfric, and quotes a saying that 'when the leader gives way the whole army will be much hindered'. The consequence of the army's dispersal was that Swein was able to seize an opportunity to march on Wilton and destroy its fortifications.[46] This is the first mention of Swein's presence with the army and there is no supporting evidence that Swein Forkbeard was in England at this time.

There is little other, nearly contemporary evidence to support or enhance the information in the *ASC* for the annal for 1003. Turning to the chronicle of John of Worcester, it seems that he has tried to show matters in a more logical manner; alternatively one may conjecture that he had access to another source. Professor Whitelock suggested that his more explicit account of events 'seems more than mere surmise from the Chronicle'.[47] John starts his annal for the year with an immediate reference to Swein, King of Denmark and says that he attacked Exeter. The fortification at Exeter fell because of the negligence or treachery of the Norman Count, Hugh, who had been put in charge of Devon by Queen Emma. The walls of the fortification were destroyed and Swein and his army took enormous booty back to the ships. Afterwards the enemy army was

---

[45] 'quem Regina Emma Domnaniae prefecit' (whom Queen Emma had put in command of Devon): Darlington and McGurk, *John of Worcester, s.a.* 1003.
[46] Hill and Rumble, *The Defence of Wessex*, pp. 224–5.
[47] Whitelock, *EHD*, p. 217 n. 5, *s.a.* 1003.

Figure 7. Scandinavian itinerary: 1003–1005

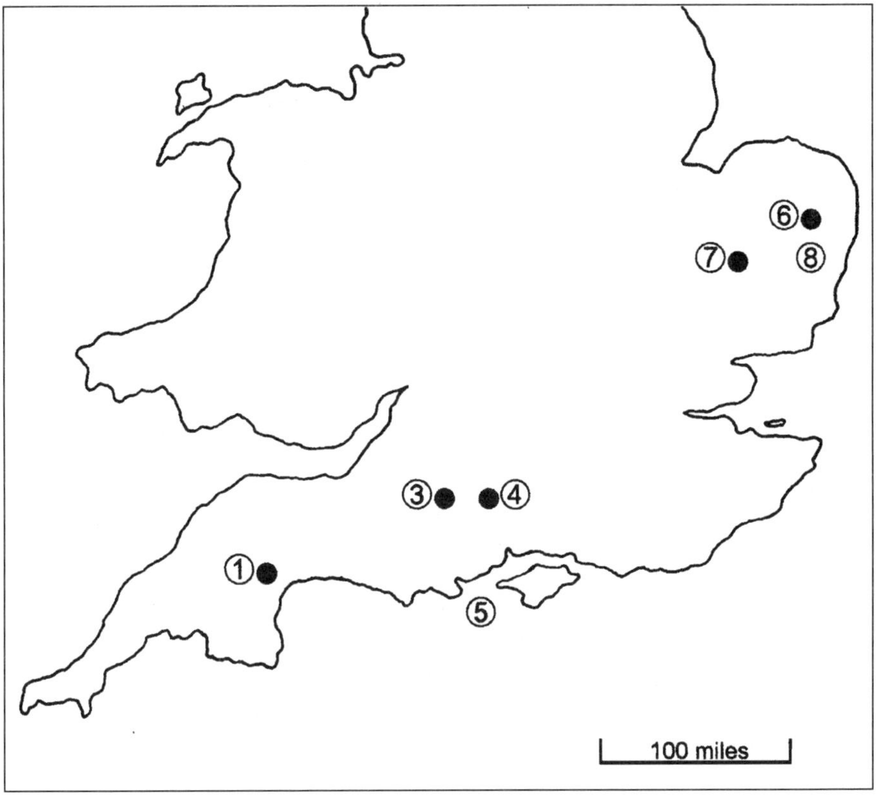

1003
① SC stormed Exeter and seized much booty
2 SC went inland into Wiltshire: English army gathered and dispersed
③ SC ravaged and burnt Wilton
④ Swein went to Salisbury
⑤ Swein returned to the sea

1004
⑥ Swein came with his fleet and ravaged and burnt Norwich

⑦ SC broke a truce and ravaged and burnt Thetford
⑧ SC fought against Ulfcetel and the East Anglians: many slain on each side

1005
9 SC fleet returned to Denmark

SC = Scandinavians

ravaging in Wiltshire when a strong English army, drawn from Wiltshire and Hampshire, came against them. John then tells the story of Ealdorman Ælfric's feigned illness and quotes the saying from the *ASC* which, he says, is an ancient proverb. Swein was then able to proceed against Wilton, followed by the devastation of Salisbury. After this Swein and the enemy army returned to the ships. Thus, many of our questions fall away as we read John's account. They are replaced with a question as to whether he had another source or whether he used his imagination to create a more logical account than that in *ASC* C D E.

Finally, the annal for 1003 says that Swein and his forces went back to the sea after attacking Salisbury. It is not clear whether we are meant to infer that

Swein's army left England and returned the next year, although a departure of the whole army may seem unlikely.[48]

Swein's Attack on East Anglia

In contrast to the annal for 1003, that for 1004 in *ASC* C D E is straightforward and unequivocal. John of Worcester follows the *ASC* for this year without additional matter or interpretation. *ASC* D may be translated:

> In this year, Swein came with his fleet to Norwich and completely ravaged and burned the fortification ('burh'). Ulfcytel decided, with the *witan* of East Anglia, that it was better to buy peace ('fryþæs') from the force before it did great damage through the land, for it had come upon them unawares and he had not time to gather his army. Then under cover of the truce ('gryþe') that should have been kept between them, the force stole inland from its ships and made its way to Thetford. When Ulfcytel realised this, he ordered that the ships should be hewn apart but those who were intended to do this failed him. Then he gathered his army secretly and as quickly as he could. And the force came then to Thetford some three weeks after it had ravaged Norwich and it was there one night and ravaged and burned the fortification ('buruh'). Then in the morning when they wanted to return to their ships, Ulfcytel came with his troop to fight and they fought fiercely together and there was great loss of life on either side. There were the noblest men of East Anglia slain. But if their full might had been there, they (Swein's army) would never have got back to the ships. For they themselves said that they had never met harder hand to hand fighting in England than Ulfcytel had brought against them.[49]

There can be little doubt that the Swein referred to by the *ASC* is Swein Forkbeard. His presence in England demonstrates that the political situation in Scandinavia was such that he felt he could leave Denmark and lead a foreign campaign over a period of many weeks. Depending upon our interpretation of the *ASC* and of John of Worcester's account of the previous year, he was also able to lead a similar campaign in 1003, or, at least, join that campaign at a later stage. There is nothing in the Scandinavian records and traditions to suggest that Swein could not have led campaigns in those years. Although it must be counted unusual for a Scandinavian monarch to feel sufficiently secure to remain away from his country for so long, Denmark was the most politically and economically advanced country in Scandinavia with a tradition of loyalty to one royal family. Swein presumably considered that his rule was firmly established by 1003, that he had trustworthy ministers, that Denmark was politically stable internally and that his alliances and relationships with the rulers of Sweden, Norway, Pomerania and, presumably, Saxony were securely based. These

---

[48] Keynes, 'Historical Context', p. 98. For Keynes' continuing view that there was basically one 'viking force' in England throughout the period 991–1005, see above, Chapter 3, n. 41.
[49] My translation. Compare also Whitelock, *EHD*, p. 217, *s.a.* 1004. See Figure 7, p. 65, for the itinerary.

considerations seem justified following the overthrow of Olaf Tryggvason and the political settlement that followed the sea-battle at Svold.[50]

At some date following his return to Denmark in about 995, Swein must have recovered his sons who may have been sheltered in Pomerania whilst he was in England. It seems very likely that his son, Cnut, accompanied him on these English campaigns in 1003 and 1004.[51] Swein presumably left his son, Harald, in Denmark but whether that was his eldest son, the son of Gunnhild, or a younger son, the son of Sigrid, is uncertain, although the account in the *Encomium* of Swein's political arrangements for Denmark in 1013 may be derived from these earlier events.[52] Norse/Icelandic sources, particularly *Heimskringla*, distinguish between Swein's wives, 'Gunnhild' and 'Sigrid'. However Professor Lund has expressed the view that:

> Although it is quite likely that Sven Forkbeard had another wife before he married the widow of Erik of Sweden, this fact does not permit us to distinguish between Erik's widow and Sigrid Storråde. Sigrid, as Lauritz Weibull demonstrated in 1911, is no historical figure but a product of 12th and 13th century Norse and Icelandic fiction; she is what these late authors made of the Polish princess.[53]

This is a reminder of the continuing debate about how far we may trust and use the Norse/Icelandic manuscript sources for the history of Scandinavia and the impact of Scandinavians on neighbouring countries.

Although Swein was leading an army constituted of *lið*s, it should be observed that his position at this time was quite different from that during his previous expedition to England. Then, he had been the leader of a *lið* but not the leader of the army in England. On this occasion he was the undoubted leader, according to the *ASC*, and had probably been responsible for leading a number of *lið*s to England, gathered from different parts of Scandinavia.

The opening sentence of the annal and the geographical location of Norwich suggest that Swein may have returned to Denmark at the end of his campaign in 1003 and that this was the start of a new campaign. Alternatively, and equally likely, the enemy force may have taken up winter quarters in England in a secure place, such as the Isle of Wight, moving east along the Channel coast and up the east coast of England for the start of a new campaign in 1004. If the enemy army remained in England, this did not, of course, preclude Swein from returning to Denmark for several months. In either case, Swein was leading *lið*s which may have previously been based in England as well as *lið*s formed in Scandinavia.

A new and important character is introduced to the *ASC* account of the campaigns in this year. Ulfcytel is accorded respect as a warrior by the *ASC* and

[50] Chapter 1, pp. 9–11, above.
[51] Chapter 6, pp. 101–2, below.
[52] Campbell, *Encomium*, Bk I, cc. 3, 4.
[53] From correspondence to me, in December 1998, concerning Harald Sweinsson and whether he succeeded to the Danish throne in 1014.

by Scandinavian skaldic sources.[54] His name indicates that he was of Danish extraction and his position at court suggests that his family may have been settled in the Danelaw for some time. The will of the ætheling Æthelstan speaks of 'the silver-hilted sword which belonged to Ulfketel', which may refer to a gift from Ulfcytel of East Anglia.[55] He was numbered amongst the king's thegns, *ministri*,[56] but there is no evidence that he was made an ealdorman even though John of Worcester accords him the title *dux East-Anglorum*.[57] He wielded considerable influence in East Anglia, and featured as the leader of subsequent campaigns.

It is interesting to note that Ulfcytel's initial action, on realising that he would have to fight, was to order an attack on the enemy's ships. This was their most vulnerable point but the fact that Ulfcytel's men failed to destroy Swein Forkbeard's ships suggests that he must have fortified the beach-head and left a substantial guard over his ships when he ventured inland. It seems surprising that we do not read more about attacks on enemy ships and that they apparently suffered no major losses whilst ravaging inland. By contrast, the English fortifications were now increasingly vulnerable and in this campaign two important ones, Thetford and Norwich, were destroyed.

The *ASC* records that many Scandinavians fell in the battle with Ulfcytel's forces.[58] There is no record of the enemy army receiving reinforcements, as it did in 1001 when Pallig went over to them. It is perhaps a reflection on their losses that this army left England in 1005 without there being any record of further campaigns nor any indication of an agreement with the English government for the payment of a tribute. The *ASC* records that the fleet returned to Denmark, but that it was soon to return.[59]

There was no respite from disaster in England, however, during 1005. *ASC* C D E records a great famine, 'such that no man could recall one so fierce'. John of Worcester follows *ASC* C D E in recording the great famine and the departure of the enemy army. He adds that it was on account of ('quapropter') the famine that King Swein returned to Denmark.[60] The famine may well have been a contributory factor in Swein's decision to leave or it may have been the deciding factor and once more we are left to ponder whether John is using his imagination or whether he is recording information from an alternative record of events; either interpretation of his words is possible.

The return of Swein and his army to Scandinavia in 1005 marked the end of his personal involvement in this second invasion, although the annal for 1005 implies that the invasion of 1006 may be regarded as a continuation when it says that 'little time elapsed before it [the enemy army] came back'.

The campaign Swein led personally against England in the years 1003 to

---

54 Hollander, *Heimskringla*, Saint Olaf's saga, c. 14 (quoting Sigvat the scald), c. 25 (quoting Thord Kolbeinsson).
55 Whitelock, *Anglo-Saxon Wills*, no. XX, pp. 57–63. S.1503.
56 Keynes, *Diplomas*, pp. 208–9 and n. 199.
57 Darlington and McGurk, *John of Worcester*, s.a. 1004.
58 *ASC* C D E s.a. 1004.
59 *ASC* C D E s.a. 1005.
60 Darlington and McGurk, *John of Worcester*, s.a. 1005.

Figure 8. Ealdorman Ælfhelm's family connections

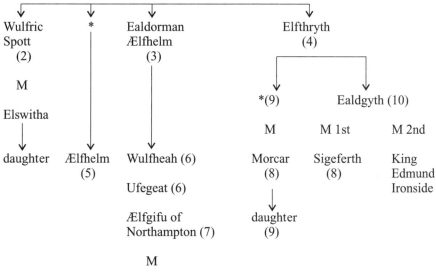

Wulfrun (a Mercian lady) (1)

(1) See *ASC* D, *s.a.* 943 and Whitelock, *Wills*, p. 152.
(2) Important landowner in the Danelaw. Probably the brother of Ealdorman Ælfhelm. See Whitelock, *Wills*, p. 153 and Sawyer *Charters of Burton Abbey*.
(3) Ealdorman of southern Northumbria; witnessed charters from 990 to 1005; killed in 1006; according to *JW*, father of Wulfheah and Ufegeat; father of Ælfgifu who married King Cnut. See Whitelock, *Wills*, pp. 152–3.
(4) Only daughter of Wulfrun; she died before 994. See Whitelock, *Wills*, p. 152.
(5) Whitelock, *Wills*, p. 156, line 13: *Ælfthelme minan mæge*: a relative of Wulfric Spott but not the ealdorman. See Whitelock *Wills*, p. 155 for a tradition that King Swein invaded England in 1013 on the invitation of Ælfthelm and Morcar.
(6) Wulfheah and Ufegeat were blinded: *ASC* C D E *s.a.* 1006. See note (3), above.
(7) Mother of Swein Cnutsson and Harald Cnutsson (Harefoot), Swein Forkbeard's grandsons, who were kings of Norway and England respectively.
(8) *JW* says Morcar and Sigeferth were brothers, the sons of Earngrim: for this and the relationship between them and Wulfric Spott, see Whitelock, *Wills*, pp. 153–5.
(9) For the relationship between Morcar's daughter and wife with Wulfric Spott see Whitelock, *Wills*, p. 155.
(10) Ealdgyth was married to Sigeferth, according to *JW s.a.* 1015. She married Edmund Ironside after her first husband was killed in 1015. In my opinion, she was probably not the mother of King Edmund Ironside's sons [because Edmund died in November 1016].

M = 'Married to'   *JW* = *John of Worcester*

1005 was far from being a triumph. Although the Scandinavian army probably took much booty back with it, there is no record of a tribute payment from the English government nor even of Swein forcing negotiations upon it. Also, there had been a hard-fought battle and many Scandinavians had been slain or wounded. The outcome of this campaign can hardly have enhanced Swein's reputation at home or abroad when it was compared with the outcome of campaigns in England in, say, 1002 or 994. The situation at the beginning of 1005 may also be contrasted with Scandinavian triumphs in England during the following year when the annals do not suggest that Swein was in personal command of the campaign.

Æthelred II in 1005

By contrast with Swein, the position of Æthelred II and his government in 1005 might be described as buoyant. In England, art and literature were flourishing, the economy was prospering, the Church was at its most influential and was receiving great endowments.[61] The Scandinavian army had caused considerable problems but in 1002 Æthelred had freed himself from dependence upon mercenaries in dramatic fashion when he ordered the massacre on St. Brice's Day. In 1004, an invasion led by the King of Denmark had been brought to the brink of disaster by English resistance in East Anglia and he had returned to Denmark in 1005. However, a change in political direction became apparent in the year 1006 and, from that year, Æthelred and his government experienced a period of disaster rarely equalled in English history and the country was devastated by invasions and civil war until Æthelred's death in 1016. As Professor Stafford expressed it, '1006 marked a turning point in political and military thinking'.[62]

It is possible to look back and find indications of a change in direction before 1006.[63] In 1002, Æthelred's military policy changed drastically when he ceased to rely on mercenaries and, more significantly, when he chose to fight treachery with treachery by ordering the massacre on St Brice's Day. Also in 1002, there was a change in foreign policy. The previous rivalry with Normandy over the control of the Channel, which had sometimes led to local conflict, was replaced by an alliance. This alliance was sealed by the marriage of Æthelred to Emma, the sister of the Duke of Normandy, with a marriage agreement which appears to have placed at least one port on the Channel coast under the control of Emma's Norman representative. These were significant changes in policy and suggest a change in the advisers who counselled the king. Such a change is evidenced by the events recorded for 1006 in *ASC* C D E:

> In this year, Archbishop Ælfric died and Bishop Ælfheah succeeded him to the archiepiscopal see. In the same year, Wulfgeat was deprived of all his property, and Wulfheah and Ufegeat were blinded and Ealdorman Ælfhelm killed.[64]

---

[61] Chapter 2, pp. 14–16, above.
[62] Stafford, *Unification and Conquest*, pp. 64–5.
[63] See Stafford, 'Reign', pp. 31–5, for discussion of the signs of change.
[64] *ASC* C D E *s.a.* 1006, Whitelock's translation. See Figure 8, p. 69, for Ealdorman Ælfhelm's family connections.

According to *ASC* F *s.a.* 995, Ælfric had been a great reforming archbishop. Wulfgeat and Wulfheah, together with Ordulf and Æthelmær who had apparently retired in 1005, had been amongst the leading *ministri* for many years.[65]

John of Worcester describes Wulfgeat as a man whom Æthelred had loved almost more than anyone: 'quem pene omnibus plus dilexerat'. He ascribes the murder of Ealdorman Ælfhelm to Eadric Streona and he says that Ælfhelm's sons Wulfheah and Ufegeat were blinded at the king's command.[66] As always, for this period, John's account must be read with some caution.

Professor Keynes summarised the changes in government at this time in the following manner:

> The coincidence in time between the apparent retirement of Ordulf and Æthelmær in 1005 and the alarming sequence of events in 1006 which left Wulfgeat disgraced, Ealdorman Ælfhelm murdered and Wulfheah and Ufegeat blinded, is certainly remarkable – and one might be forgiven for suspecting that it is not entirely fortuitous. Indeed, it seems to reflect something approaching a palace revolution amongst the principal lay associates of King Æthelred, and, if we may trust Florence of Worcester, one that had perhaps been engineered by Eadric Streona.[67]

Thus, the change in political direction was fully apparent by the year 1006. The following chapters will trace the disasters which were to try King Æthelred and his close advisors.

---

[65] Keynes, *Diplomas*, p. 210.

[66] Darlington and McGurk, *John of Worcester, s.a.* 1006.

[67] Keynes, *Diplomas*, pp. 211–12. Ealdorman Ælfhelm and his sons, Wulfheah and Ufegeat, were important northern leaders. It is significant that Swein Forkbeard allied himself with this family, during his invasion in 1013, by marrying his son, Cnut, to Ealdorman Ælfhelm's daughter, Ælfgifu of Northampton: see Figure 8, p. 69.

5

The Invasion in 1006

The Great Invasion

As noted in Chapter 4, p. 68, above, the invasion in 1006 may in some respects be regarded as a continuation of the invasion of 1003–1005, which had been directed by Swein Forkbeard. Writing in the twelfth century, Henry of Huntingdon said that Swein led the invasion:

> In the fifth year [1005], the Danes sailed for their own country; but meanwhile there was no lack of calamity to the English, for they were visited with a desolating famine, beyond any known in the memory of man.
>
> In the sixth year [1006], the audacious Sweyn reappeared off Sandwich with a powerful fleet. He was accompanied by his three usual attendants, fire, slaughter, and pillage: and all England trembled before him, like the rustling of a bed of reeds shaken by the west wind.[1]

This account is probably inaccurate, however. Henry of Huntingdon seems to have presumed that if the army returned, as stated in the *ASC*, then its leader, Swein Forkbeard, would have returned with it, but there is no suggestion of this in the *ASC* and the evidence, examined in this chapter, indicates that the Scandinavian army in 1006 and later was led by others.

ASC C D E *s.a.* 1005 indicates that it was Swein's fleet that 'came back' in 1006. If so, it was greatly reinforced, for the *ASC* says that a great fleet came to Sandwich.[2] The immense size of this army may be deduced from the fact that the whole nation (*þeodscipe*) from Wessex and Mercia was called out but apparently avoided fighting a significant battle against it.[3]

It is likely that this immense army had been gathered on the directions of King Swein and that it was led by men who were loyal to him. This accords with the political situation in Scandinavia at the time. Comment has been made in the previous chapter about Swein's alliances in Scandinavia and on the southern Baltic coast and about the fact that he had sufficient confidence in the political stability of Scandinavia in general, and Denmark in particular, to lead the

---

[1] Forester, *Henry of Huntingdon*, c. vi, p. 186. For the Latin text and a more recent translation, see Greenway, *Henry, Archdeacon of Huntingdon* Historia Anglorum *The History of the English People*, p. 343.

[2] Cubbin, *MS D, s.a.* 1006: '⁊ ða ofer þone midne sumor com se micla flota to Sandwic'. *ASC* version E describes it as 'the Danish fleet'. See Hill, *Atlas*, map 119.

[3] *ASC* C D E *s.a.* 1006.

campaign of 1003 to 1004 in person. In effect, as king of Denmark and through his alliance with the rulers of Norway, Erik of Lade and his brother, Swein controlled all the land and sea routes through which Scandinavian *liðs* must pass in order to reach England. Because of its size, the fleet that invaded England in 1006, which had to be marshaled, supplied and await favourable weather before it set sail, must have spent some time in Danish ports and coastal waters. Thus, there is a further implication that this 'great fleet' was raised by King Swein and that it was led by his trusted lieutenants.

The army must have included ships and men from many parts of Scandinavia – Denmark, Norway and Sweden. The leader of this army may have been named Tostig and may have been related to King Swein. His name and relationship with Swein Forkbeard may be deduced from two separate pieces of information. A quotation from Neils Lund explains the evidence for his name:

> A famous inscription in Uppland was carved in commemoration of Ulf of Borresta. He was a very active viking in his youth and shared in three gelds paid by the English: first Toste paid, then Thorketil paid, and then Cnut paid.
>
> (U343–4)[4]

Although Professor Lund identifies Thorketil and Cnut, he says that 'Toste, whose mention in this context suggests that to contemporaries he was a chieftain of comparable importance, is unknown from other sources.' Cnut's geld was paid in 1018, Thorkell's geld was paid six years earlier in 1012 and the geld paid previous to that was the 36,000 pounds paid in 1007. It seems likely, therefore, that 'Toste' was the leader of the invading army in 1006/1007.[5] For possible evidence of his relationship with King Swein we must move on two generations to the children of Earl Godwine of Wessex. The earl owed his advancement to King Cnut and, for many years, he was the King's most trusted adviser. His marriage to Gytha, the daughter of the Scandinavian Jarl Thorgils, was probably arranged by Cnut. His three eldest sons were given the Scandinavian names Swein, Harold and Tostig; there was also a daughter, Gunhild. His younger children were Gyrth, Leofwine, Wulfnoth and a daughter, Edith.[6] We do not know who was the godfather of Godwine's elder children, but, given their close working relationship and the circumstances of his marriage, it could easily have been Cnut. Certainly, Godwine would have wished to please and flatter his king at this time. It seems more than a coincidence that Godwine's eldest son bore the name of Cnut's father, his second son bore the name of his grandfather and his daughter, Gunhild, bore the name of Cnut's mother. It is possible, therefore, that Tostig was related to Cnut and to his father King Swein.[7] This identification of a

---

[4] Lund, 'The Danish Perspective', pp. 117–18; plate 6.1, p. 118, shows the relevant inscription on this stone (U 344) very clearly.

[5] For 'Tostig' see Keynes, 'Historical Context', n. 39, p. 109. Incidentally, there was a geld in 1002 but this is less likely to be the one referred to in the inscription. 1006 to 1018 indicates membership of a *lið*, or *liðs*, for more than twelve years; a relatively long time. The army, which was paid geld in 1002, had been active for several years before that.

[6] For Godwine's family tree, see the appendix to Swanton, *Anglo-Saxon Chronicle*.

[7] Though perhaps not a blood relative. Queen Sigrid's father was Skogla-Tosti, according to

name for the leader of the invading army in 1006 and his relationship with the king of Denmark should be regarded as tenuous[8] but it serves as a further indication that the army in 1006 was led by men loyal to King Swein.

The English reaction to the invasion may be accounted a change in policy. Instead of local armies drawn up from the shires most endangered by the invasion, the king called out 'the whole nation from Wessex and Mercia' to undertake military service against the enemy,[9] an English example of what, in later times, Danes might have termed *leding*. However, there is no evidence that this great English army tried to force the invaders into battle. For their part, and bearing in mind what the forces of East Anglia alone had achieved in 1004, the enemy army was probably keen to avoid a decisive engagement.[10] One may deduce, therefore, that the English army adopted Fabian tactics, following the enemy around, cutting off and destroying small raiding parties and generally making it very difficult for them to loot and forage.[11] The enemy army did manage to forage sufficiently to maintain itself in good order and the English army, many of the soldiers being far from their home shires, foraged in a like manner so that *ASC*, C D E *s.a.* 1006 records that:

> the English levy caused the people of the country every sort of harm, so that they profited neither from the native army nor the foreign army.[12]

The *ASC* then says that, when winter came, the English army was dispersed and went home and the enemy force retired to the Isle of Wight and provisioned itself from the neighbouring countryside. John of Worcester indicates that they were able to take an enormous amount of booty with them ('cum enormi praeda') to the Isle of Wight. This seems unlikely. Whether the English were pursuing Fabian tactics, or whether the Scandinavians were adopting evasive tactics, or both, the nature of such a campaign should have reduced looting opportunities to a minimum. Since the Church probably had to pay its proportion of the costs of the English levy and since the population generally suffered from the movements of two armies around the country, the chronicler had more than one reason for being aggrieved at the Fabian tactics of the native force.

Jónsson, *Heimskringla*, Olaf Tryggvason saga, K 43, K 91, so it is possible that this Tostig was a blood relative of the Swedish queen and, in accordance with Scandinavian practice, he may have been Cnut's 'foster-father'.

[8]   Lund says that an identification of 'Toste' with 'a Skoglar-Tosti mentioned in the saga of St Olaf' is 'very dubious': Lund, 'The Danish Perspective', p. 117. For chronological reasons, I agree with this assessment, but the possibility of 'Toste' being a *relative* of 'Skoglar-Tosti' cannot be excluded.

[9]   *ASC* C D E *s.a.* 1006.

[10] A view supported by John of Worcester: Darlington and McGurk, *John of Worcester, s.a.* 1006.

[11] There is no reason to doubt our sources, which say that the English army did not engage the enemy army in battle. The English army remained in the field and there are complaints in our sources about it foraging. The enemy army mounted a winter campaign to take advantage when the English army dispersed. The tactics I have ascribed to the English army best fit these known circumstances.

[12] Whitelock's translation in *EHD s.a.* 1006.

The *ASC*'s reference to the enemy army provisioning itself from the neighbouring countryside indicates that no winter truce had been agreed. It was perhaps anticipated that the enemy force would do nothing over the winter period. The English army had disbanded and King Æthelred and his court went into Shropshire to spend the Christmas season. Perhaps it was a particularly mild winter, and/or, perhaps the enemy had been frustrated by the English tactics, which had prevented them taking much booty. Whatever, the reason, the enemy force mounted a winter campaign through Hampshire and Berkshire,[13] 'fetching themselves food and treasures from more than 50 miles from the sea'.[14] The English gathered an army, which challenged the enemy force on its return journey, but it was soon put to flight and the enemy was able to travel, in triumph, within sight of Winchester, as they went back to their base on the coast. The result of this disaster was that the king and his *witan* decided that they should make a truce with the enemy and they agreed to provision the force and pay tribute to it. This was duly done and the tribute was paid in 1007.[15]

ASC C D E uses some interesting phrases in describing the events of 1006/7. It should be remembered that the chronicler was writing with the benefit of hindsight and it is notable, therefore, that he describes Æthelred going to Shropshire for Christmas '7 nam þær his feorme', taking his food rents as lord and master of the land. When the Scandinavians left the Isle of Wight to progress through Hampshire and Berkshire, the chronicler says 'eodon him to heora gearwan feorme' ('they went for their ready food rents'). Perhaps we are intended to read into this balanced phraseology an anticipation of the conquest that was to follow.

Whatever the chronicler may be anticipating in his annals, the situation at this time was not hopeless from the English point of view. They had negotiated a truce and they were prepared to take warlike action to drive away the enemy during the next campaigning season. However, in many ways, the events of 991 to 994 were about to be replicated: the English had failed to drive the Scandinavians away; a truce was agreed and tribute paid; an English fleet was prepared to drive the Scandinavians away but failed; the English negotiated with the Scandinavians and persuaded a large number of them to take service as a mercenary army to defend England. It was this final action, in 1012, that apparently precipitated Swein's third invasion and conquest of England. The following pages trace the events leading to that invasion.

---

[13] John of Worcester says that they felt able to undertake a campaign 'quia rex tunc temporis in Scrobbesbyriensi prouincia morabatur' ('as the king was at that time staying in Shropshire'): Darlington and McGurk, *John of Worcester*, s.a. 1006.

[14] *ASC* C D E s.a. 1006. See Hill, *Atlas*, map 119, for this itinerary.

[15] In providing a record of this invasion and its outcome, *ASC* CDE has included events which relate to the beginning of the year 1007 under the annal heading for 1006.

The English Fleet

According to the *ASC*, a *gafol* of 36,000 pounds was paid to the enemy army in 1007. This followed *gafol* payments of 10,000 pounds in 991, 16,000 pounds in 994 and 24,000 pounds in 1002.[16] The *ASC* implies that the immense army, which it refers to as *unfriðhere*,[17] continued to be based on the Isle of Wight, which it had come to regard as its sanctuary.[18]

The *ASC* does not refer to the Scandinavian army again until the annal for 1009 when it says that the immense raiding army, *unfriðhere*, came to Sand wich.[19] It does not say where this army came from in 1009 but, because a late addition to *ASC* C describes it as the army 'which we called Thorkel's army',[20] it is sometimes inferred that it was a different army from that of 1007, which was not led by Thorkell. Following this interpretation, Professor Keynes wrote:

> A 'great fleet', possibly led by a certain Tostig, arrived at Sandwich in July 1006, causing disruption wherever it went, and using the Isle of Wight as a base for its further operations in Wessex during the winter of 1006/7. The English sued for peace, and the handsome sum of 36,000 pounds was paid to the army in 1007; whereupon it seems to have returned whence it came. As if that was not enough, an 'immense raiding army', led by Thorkell the Tall, arrived at Sandwich in early August 1009, and proceeded to overrun the greater part of southern England.[21]

An alternative interpretation can be justified. John of Worcester says that Thorkell arrived in England in 1009, at the head of a *lið*, and was joined by a larger army, led by Heming and Eglaf, before proceeding to Sandwich.[22] John gives Thorkell the title *comes* and describes Heming and Eglaf as *duces*; the implication of the titles is that Heming and Eglaf were superior to Thorkell in status at this time. The reference to 'Thorkel's army' in *ASC* C, which was a late addition to its exemplar \C,[23] does not necessarily mean that Thorkell commanded the army in 1009; it is referring to the fact that he eventually

---

[16] *ASC* C D E *s.aa.* 991, 994, 1002, 1007. Payments to Scandinavian armies are discussed in Chapter 2, pp. 17–19, above. See also Figure 4, p. 20.

[17] Cubbin, *MS D, s.a.* 1007.

[18] *Ibid. s.a.* 1006: 'his frydstole'.

[19] Cubbin, *MS D, s.a.* 1009: 'ða com sona æfter Lafmæssan se ungemetlica unfriðhere to Sandwic'. *Lafmæssan* (Lammas) is on 1 August.

[20] Whitelock, *EHD, s.a.* 1009.

[21] Keynes, 'The Vikings in England', p. 75. Compare Keynes, 'Historical Context', p. 95, and Stafford, *Unification and Conquest*, p. 65.

[22] Howard, 'Swein Forkbeard's Invasions of England', pp. 112–13, discusses the authenticity of John's information; also, Darlington and McGurk, *John of Worcester*, *s.a.* 1009.

[23] It is demonstrably a late addition to \C, because it does not feature in either *ASC* D or E, and so was almost certainly not in *ÆE*, the exemplar from which \C received the annal for 1009.

became the leader of the army, after which he became a very significant figure in English history.[24] He had become the leader of the combined army by 1012, probably on his return to England having participated in piratical activities with Olaf helgi at some time in the period 1010/11 off the coast of Jutland.[25]

Because of this distinction between two armies, there is a real possibility that the main Scandinavian army did not leave England but remained there, safe on its base in the Isle of Wight. The argument for the army remaining is much the same as that provided in Chapter 3, pp. 37–8, above, for a similar situation that appertained in 992. It may be argued that the actions of Æthelred and his government, as reported in *ASC* C D E for the years 1007 to 1009 and analysed below, make most sense if the army remained in England.

If the immense army remained in England, we should consider what happened to it after receiving tribute in 1007, when it was presumably still based on the Isle of Wight. No doubt some ships would have dispersed after receiving *gafol*, but there was no obvious place for the main part of the fleet to go. It had been based on the Isle of Wight for several months. The Scandinavians were rich with booty and had an enormous amount of money besides. If they spent their money as freely as sailors have been wont to over the centuries when in port, the local economy would have been thriving. In such circumstances, the isle and the mainland opposite would be exciting places to be. The Scandinavians already had an arrangement with the English government for the provision of supplies from the whole of England.[26] They were now in a position to supplement such provisions by paying for any additional supplies or luxuries they might require. One would expect them to be in no hurry to move. Since there is no record of the fleet dispersing, going to Scandinavia, or visiting the Continent, a presumption is raised that it remained on the Isle of Wight. What it did in this period is not recorded, but some idea of the threat that it posed may be gathered from the English reaction and the immense preparations that were considered necessary to deal with the problem.

There appears to have been a reorganisation of the administration of the country at this time. The most significant change in this context was the appointment of an ealdorman of Mercia – a post that had remained vacant since ealdorman Ælfric had been banished in 985.[27] The man appointed was Eadric Streona, who was to play a very significant part in the conduct of affairs during the remainder of Æthelred's reign. His appointment suggests a move towards a more traditional organisation of internal defences in which forces drawn from larger territories, such as Mercia, would be better able to deal with the inroads of an invading army. This change reflects the increased size of the enemy armies and a change in the nature of the threat they posed.

In addition to this internal reorganisation, the *ASC* says that the king ordered ships to be built, the implication being that they were intended to deal with the

---

[24] As evidenced in the *ASC*, *The Chronicle of John of Worcester* and the *Encomium* during the period 1012 to 1023.

[25] See this chapter, pp. 93–4, below.

[26] *ASC* C D E *s.a.* 1006.

[27] *ASC* C D E *s.aa.* 985 and 1007.

Scandinavian threat at sea. This may indicate the continued presence of a Scandinavian army on the Isle of Wight where land forces were unable to dislodge it. Such a situation could explain why Æthelred and his counsellors were prepared to undertake the creation of a great fleet over a period of more than a year, knowing that ultimately, unless the enemy army agreed to withdraw, they would need to use force. The length of time taken to prepare their fleet suggests that the English were not expecting to resist an enemy fleet whose arrival was imminent.

The size of the English fleet impressed the writer of the annals and he appears to have used a contemporary 'taxation' schedule in describing it. Unfortunately, the passage has been transmitted inaccurately so that versions C D E and F each have individual versions which vary slightly from the others. From a detailed analysis of the words in each version of the *ASC* it is possible to reconstruct what the original document probably stated.[28] It was a very large fleet and, as interpreted in the reconstruction, and in *ASC* F *s.a.* 1008, it contained some very large warships.

Such a fleet was quite different from the provision of a coast-guard to deter potential invaders such as is described by Professor Lund in relation to the situation appertaining in Denmark in the late twelfth century,[29] although the law, *V Æthelred*, which is quoted below in this section, envisages the annual provision of ships to the king at about this time, suggesting the possibility of a similar coast guard.

Naval forces had been used previously by the English. In 992, a national naval force had been organised by commandeering available ships for a specific purpose. It was possible to call out a local ship force, just as it was possible to call out a local land force, when there was an urgent need. Thus, in 999, a naval force and a land force were called out against a Scandinavian army attacking Kent.[30] Alternatively, the king might employ a mercenary fleet for the protection of England as he did under the terms of his treaty with Olaf Tryggvason and as he may have done with Pallig and others in 1000. This suggests that building ships to create the greatest fleet yet gathered by an English king[31] was driven by a specific need. Allowing for the cost of such a fleet and the disruption to the economy when it was manned, the need would have been one that the nation as a whole recognised. It was planned and built over a period of a year, so its objective would have been to deal with a threat so great and tangible that it could warrant such lengthy preparations. The existence of an immense enemy army on the Isle of Wight would have been such a threat.

The reconstruction of the annal in *ASC* C D E F says that, in 1008, King Æthelred and his councillors ordered the creation of an English war fleet with ships built specially for the purpose on the basis of:

---

28 Howard, 'Swein Forkbeard's Invasions of England', pp. 65–73. This reconstruction also serves as part of the proof that version D of the ASC is most closely aligned to the original exemplar, *ÆE*. A synopsis of the reconstruction is provided in Appendix 2, below.
29 Lund, *Lið, Leding og Landeværn*, pp. 298–301.
30 *ASC* C D E *s.a.* 999.
31 *ASC* C D E *s.a.* 1009.

(a) selected units of three hundred hides should provide a ship plus, possibly, a helmet and corselet for every ten hides, and

(b) selected units of ten hundred hides should provide a large battleship plus a helmet and corselet for every eight hides.[32]

This decree must have generated much activity in England; the economic stimulus of these events is discussed in Chapter 2, pp. 16–22, above.

The decision to raise a great English fleet may have been taken at the Council of Enham in Hampshire, which may be dated to Pentecost 1008. The legislation promulgated by the king was preserved in various manuscript versions associated with Archbishop Wulfstan of York.[33] The law code, known as *V Æthelred*, says that:

> . . . people are to be zealous about . . . the supplying of ships, as zealously as possible, so that each may be equipped immediately after Easter every year.[34]

It seems that, when King Æthelred promulgated the law code, it was already accepted that the fleet would not be ready until Easter 1009. An interesting feature of the law code is that it anticipates the continuing need for a fleet each year, perhaps as a coast guard operation after the immediate threat, requiring an immense fleet, had been addressed.

If we may accept John of Worcester's chronology,[35] a significant number of ships and crews gathered during autumn 1008 and Æthelred and many of his counsellors were with them at Sandwich. The *ASC s.a.* 1009 explains what happened:

> Then it happened, during this same time or a little earlier, that Brihtric, Ealdorman Eadric's brother, accused Wulfnoth *cild*, the south-Saxon, to the king. And he (Wulfnoth) then withdrew and then enticed (men) to him so that he had twenty ships. And he then ravaged everywhere along the south coast and wrought every (kind of) harm.[36] Then it was made known to the fleet that they could easily blockade them, if they should so wish. The (aforementioned) Brihtric took with him eighty ships and thought that he ought to make good his boast ['micles wordes'] that he would capture Wulfnoth alive or dead. However, when they were on their way, there came against them a wind such as no one could remember before, and then the ships were completely broken and shattered and thrown up onto the land. And immediately the (aforesaid) Wulfnoth came and burned the ships.[37]

Because John of Worcester relates the story of the storm under the annal year 1008, it is possible he concluded that it was a late autumn storm. However, it is possible that Wulfnoth spent several weeks on his piratical mission before action

[32] Howard, 'Swein Forkbeard's Invasions of England', figures 8 and 9, pp. 72–3. See also Appendix 2, below.
[33] Wormald, 'Æthelred the Lawmaker', pp. 48–58.
[34] *V Æthelred*, clause 27: Whitelock, *EHD*, pp. 405–9.
[35] Darlington and McGurk, *John of Worcester, s.a.* 1008.
[36] *ASC* C D E F *s.a.* 1009, my translation. *ASC* C omits 'the south-Saxon'.
[37] *ASC* C D E *s.a.* 1009, my translation. See Figure 9, p. 80.

Figure 9. The English fleet: 1008–1009

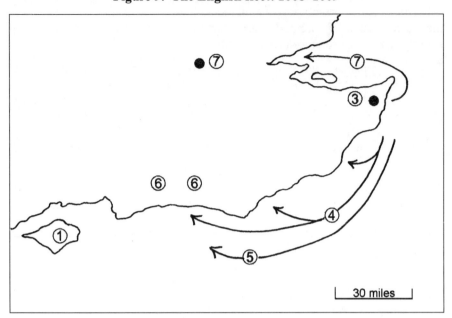

①   *SC* receiving *metsunge* and *gafol* on the Isle of Wight. *ASC* C D E *s.aa.* 1006, 1007. *JW s.a.* 1007.
2   King Æthelred ordered the creation of an English fleet. *ASC* C D E *s.a.* 1008. *JW* s.a. 1008.
③   Fleet assembled at Sandwich. *ASC* C D E *s.a.* 1009. *JW s.a.* 1008.
④   Wulfnoth *cild* fled with 20 ships and ravaged south coast. *ASC* C D E *s.a.* 1009. *JW s.a.* 1008.
⑤   Brihtric, with 80 ships, followed Wulfnoth. *ASC* C D E *s.a.* 1009. *JW* s.a. 1008.
⑥   Brihtric's ships driven ashore by a storm and destroyed. *ASC* C D E *s.a.* 1009. *JW s.a.* 1008.
⑦   King Æthelred sent remainder of the fleet to London. *ASC* C D E *s.a.* 1009. *JW* s.a. 1008.

SC = Scandinavians
JW = John of Worcester

was taken and, because there is the law code evidence that the main body of the fleet was expected to be ready about Easter, it is more probable that these events, including the great storm, took place in the spring of 1009. In the circumstances of the early eleventh century a determined and well-supported man, such as Wulfnoth, could maintain himself for a considerable time against the authority of the government.[38]

When Brihtric set out against Wulfnoth, his eighty ships must have represented a considerable proportion of the fleet. That Wulfnoth escaped the storm suggests that he was still in port when it arose and that Brihtric's objective of a blockade was feasible. For Brihtric there must have seemed a reasonable expectation of finding Wulfnoth's fleet and capturing most if not all of the twenty ships. It is difficult to believe that the capture of those twenty ships was the only objective. If there had been a major enemy fleet in the east, Brihtric should not

---

[38] For charter evidence of how a man named Wulfbald and members of his family defied royal authority in the final decade of the tenth century, see Whitelock, *EHD*, pp. 531–4; S.877; Robertson, *Anglo-Saxon Charters*, no. LXIII.

have been allowed to sail west. The fact that we are told that he was sailing in a westerly direction, from Sandwich along the south coast, is further evidence that the enemy fleet was based on the Isle of Wight. If so, Brihtric's plan would presumably have been to blockade and capture Wulfnoth's ships, make repairs, and await further ships and supplies from Sandwich before continuing down the coast in a westerly direction. John of Worcester says that they had an uneventful voyage and were caught unawares by the great storm.[39] Not only was the storm unexpected but it was of unprecedented ferocity, according to *ASC* C D E. The resulting destruction of the fleet adds substance to the description of the storm. It seems that the fleet was blown on shore and shattered; one may assume a substantial loss of life in these circumstances.[40] The Chronicle says that Wulfnoth then came and burned what was left of the vessels. It does not say that he looted the vessels, but, no doubt he did and no doubt also the coastal inhabitants did likewise, as was normal custom. Archbishop Wulfstan appears to have had a clause added to the Enham legislation concerning the punishment of anybody who damaged or destroyed 'a warship of the people'.[41] It is tempting to believe that the amendment was a reaction to these events.

It is difficult to imagine the enormity of this disaster to the English nation. As a gradual realisation of its full extent became apparent there must have been an atmosphere of deep despair in Sandwich. *ASC* C D E continues the story:

> Thus when this was made known in full to the other ships where the king was, how the others had fared, it was as if all was in confusion. And the king took himself home and the ealdormen and the chief councillors ['heahwitan']; and they abandoned the ships thus lightly. And the people then, who were on the ships, sailed the ships afterwards to London.[42]

John of Worcester adds that the fleet went to London on the orders of the king.

The disaster was complete. There were a substantial number of ships still at Sandwich but the vanguard had been destroyed, presumably with a considerable loss of life. The chronicler says that the king abandoned the fleet and went home. Strictly, the king would have had no one home to go to; he withdrew from Sandwich to one of the royal residences such as Cookham and, presumably, most of his ealdormen and counsellors went with him. The king and his court were itinerant and there was no further reason for them being in Sandwich. The chronicler possibly gives the impression that the fleet was abandoned to its own devices but this is very unlikely to have been the case and John is almost certainly correct in saying that the fleet sailed to London on the orders of the king. The fleet was presumably deemed no longer capable of undertaking the task for which it had been gathered. Many ships had been built specifically for the fleet but many more must have been commandeered from other enterprises. There would have been a need for those ships for coastal and river transport

---

[39] Darlington and McGurk, *John of Worcester, s.a.* 1008.
[40] There appears to be no evidence of Brihtric's existence after these events. See Keynes, *Diplomas*, p. 216.
[41] *VI Æthelred*, clause 34. Whitelock, *EHD*, p. 408 n. 2.
[42] My translation from Cubbin, *MS D*. See Figure 9, page 80.

purposes as well as foreign trade. Since there is no further record of this fleet being used during 1009, the implication is that it was dispersed. Given the time-scale involved, the return to London and the dispersal of the fleet were probably completed by early summer. In *ASC* C D E, the chronicler allows himself a comment about this disaster:

> And (they) allowed all the toil of the ships to take place thus lightly; and there was no victory and that in which all England had trusted was no better (than this).[43]

Versions C E have 'nation' instead of 'ships' in D. Version E has a word '['ege']' in place of 'victory' which Thorpe indicates as a possible error and which Swanton translates as 'deterrent'. John of Worcester simply says 'and thus all the great labour of the people perished'. In the circumstances all the comments are very restrained.

The Scandinavian Army Attacks the South-East

The next event in the *ASC* is the arrival of an immense enemy army in August 1009:

> When this ship muster was thus ended, then, immediately after Lammas [1 August], the immense enemy army came to Sandwich, and immediately made its way to Canterbury and would quickly have captured the fortified town if they [the citizens] had not more quickly begged them for peace; and all the East Kentish people made peace with the army and gave it 3,000 pounds. Then, immediately after, the army turned around until it came to the Isle of Wight, and there, both in Sussex and Hampshire and also in Berkshire, ravaged and burned, as their custom is.[44]

The only break in the *ASC* account, between the English fleet going to London and the arrival of this army, is a two-line reflection on the failure of the English fleet. It might be thought that the enemy army arrived at Sandwich immediately after the English fleet sailed away, but John of Worcester indicates a lapse of time by placing the two events in different years.[45] He says that Thorkell's fleet came to England and the other immense fleet, led by Heming and Eglaf, joined it at the Isle of Thanet; then both fleets went to Sandwich. He distinguishes the relative importance of the leaders, describing Thorkell as *comes* and the other leaders as *duces*, indicating that Thorkell was not, at that time, leader of the

---

[43] My translation from Cubbin, *MS D*.
[44] My translation: *ASC* C D E *s.a.* 1009. The words 'which we call Thorkell's army', describing the 'immense enemy army', were probably added to \C and so are in version C of the *ASC*. This and other translations in this section may be compared with Whitelock, *EHD*; Garmonsway, *Anglo-Saxon Chronicle*; Swanton, *Anglo-Saxon Chronicle*.
[45] Darlington and McGurk, *John of Worcester, s.aa.* 1008, 1009.

immense army.[46] It is likely that Heming was Thorkell's brother and Eglaf was a Dane who subsequently featured as a witness to some of King Cnut's charters.[47]

John says that Thorkell 'came to England' with his fleet, a comment which is not extended to the 'other innumerable fleet of Danes'. John last mentioned the enemy army as being on the Isle of Wight and describes an agreement with the English by which 'from that time provisions were given to them by the whole of England and tribute amounting to 36,000 pounds was paid'.[48]

If, as seems likely, Thorkell and his fleet came to England from Scandinavia, it is probable that King Swein Forkbeard was aware of it and approved its gathering and its departure from lands he ruled directly or over which he had great influence, via his relatives through marriage. The same reasoning would apply to the other immense army if it had come from Scandinavia. However, for the reasons considered above, the main Scandinavian army may have been in England already. Although it has been deduced earlier in this chapter that this army was led by men loyal to King Swein in 1006, its leadership may have changed subsequently since John of Worcester makes no mention of Tostig, the probable leader when the *gafol* was paid in 1007,[49] and so it is not possible to ascertain what influence, if any, Swein had in 1009, although the evidence that the army joined forces with Thorkell's fleet might suggest that there was a continuing relationship.

Thorkell's father was Strut-Harald, a Danish earl,[50] so his family may have been subjects of the kings of Denmark.[51] The sagas indicate that the family of Strut-Harald was powerful and influential. Given his background, Professor Lund's description of Thorkell as 'probably the leader of a gang of thugs based somewhere in the Baltic'[52] may seem harsh, though the people who suffered at the hands of this, or any other, Scandinavian warlord might have agreed. Both Keynes and Campbell have published detailed accounts of Thorkell and of his career[53] and there is further discussion in Chapters 6 and 7, below. We can only

---

[46] 'Danicus comes Turkillus sua cum classe ad Angliam uenit. Exinde mense Augusto alia classis Danorum innumerabilis, cui preerant duces Hemmingus et Eglafus, ad Tenetland insulam applicuit, et predicte classi sine dilatione se iunxit. Deinde ambe Sandicum portum subeunt . . .': Darlington and McGurk, *John of Worcester, s.a.* 1009.

[47] Keynes, 'Cnut's Earls', pp. 54–7, 58–60, 62–4. Campbell, *Encomium,* pp. 73, 82–4, 87. Blake, *The Saga of the Jomsvikings,* pp. 27–8. Darlington and McGurk, *John of Worcester,* pp. 462–3 n. 5.

[48] Darlington and McGurk, *John of Worcester, s.a.* 1007.

[49] See this chapter, pp. 73–4, above. Thorkell was apparently leader of the Scandinavian army in England by 1012: *ASC* C D E *s.aa.* 1012, 1013. Darlington and McGurk, *John of Worcester, s.aa.* 1012, 1013.

[50] Campbell calls Thorkell 'Þorkell Strut-Haraldsson inn havi, son of Strut-Haraldr, Earl of Zealand': Campbell, *Encomium,* p. 73. See also Blake, *The Saga of the Jomsvikings,* p. 18. Thorkell's by-name, 'inn havi' means 'the Tall'. In the sagas, Thorkell's brother, Earl Sigvaldi, was said to be the leader of the Jomsvikings and they say that he (and probably Thorkell) played an important part in bringing about the battle of Svold.

[51] This relationship with the kings of Denmark is to be found in Blake, *The Saga of the Jomsvikings,* and Jónsson, *Heimskringla,* the Olaf Tryggvason saga.

[52] Lund, 'The Danish Perspective', p. 116.

[53] Keynes, 'Cnut's Earls', pp. 54–7. Campbell, *Encomium,* pp. 73–82.

surmise about internal politics in Denmark at this time. For instance, Swein may have allowed Thorkell to reinforce his brother in England because he felt confident of his own power-base in Denmark and of his ability to control this influential family. Equally, he may have allowed Thorkell to join Heming because the Strut-Harald family was too influential to cross openly. The fact that Thorkell was allied to King Æthelred against Swein in 1013 demonstrates the dangers inherent in the situation in 1009. Sawyer, referring to the events of 1012 and 1013, wrote:

> Thorkell was no friend of Swein Forkbeard and the king had reason to fear that, strengthened by his success and with English support, he might pose an even more serious threat to Swein's power than Olaf Tryggvason had done. Swein's decision to conquer England in the next year [1013] seems to have been partly intended to prevent such a challenge; he may even have suspected that Thorkell hoped to conquer England himself.[54]

Whatever may have been the later political considerations, Swein appears to have allowed Thorkell to go to England in 1009 and also allowed him to return to England in c. 1011, since evidence in the *Encomium* and in the verses of Sigvat the Skald indicates that Thorkell left England and returned again, in c. 1011, to avenge the death of his brother, Heming.[55]

Whether or not the immense fleet owed any sort of allegiance to Swein Forkbeard, it was a considerable threat to England. It concentrated much attention on Kent and Essex in the south-east and it also attacked the Channel coast and up the Thames valley. It left Kent, having received 3,000 pounds, and moved its base to the Isle of Wight to campaign in Sussex, Hampshire and Berkshire during autumn 1009. The *ASC* records the action which the king took against the enemy army:

> Then the king ordered the whole nation [national army] to be called out, so that they should be withstood on every side. But, for all that, they travelled however they wished [i.e. by sea and/or land]. Then on a certain journey [venture], the king got in front of them with all the national army, when they wanted (to return) to (their) ships; and all the army [folk/nation] was ready to capture them [or, possibly, 'fight a battle with them']. But then it was hindered because of Ealdorman Eadric, as it always was.[56]

In the translation of the final sentence, the national army was 'hindered', but the translation might be: 'it [the enemy army] was allowed to continue'.[57]

John of Worcester provides additional information:

> Then (their) fortune changing, whilst they were away as usual raiding far from the sea and were returning laden with booty, the king occupied the road by which they were returning to their ships, with many thousand armed men, and

54 Sawyer, 'Cnut's Scandinavian Empire', p. 17.
55 See this chapter, pp. 92–5, below.
56 My translation, *ASC* C D E *s.a.* 1009.
57 Cubbin, *MS D, s.a.* 1009: 'ac hit wæs þa þuruh Eadric ealdorman gelæt swa hit gyt æfre wæs'.

he was ready, as was his whole army, to conquer or die. But the treacherous Duke Eadric Streona, the king's son-in-law, for he had married his daughter Edith, strove in every way, by speeches (which were) both treacherous and cunning, that they should not engage in battle, but should permit their enemies to go on their way. He urged and persuaded so that, like a traitor to the country, he rescued the Danes from the hands of the English and allowed them to get away. They, in fact, turning away from them, returned to their ships with great rejoicing.[58]

We do not know whether John's information is imaginative addition, or from the 'Lost Life of King Edmund',[59] or from some other source. However, Ealdorman Eadric must have had persuasive reasons, for not engaging the enemy in battle, for his counsel to have prevailed. The failure of the 'national army' to engage the enemy in battle may be indicative of the size of the Scandinavian force and is certainly a pointer to the physical state of the English forces and their morale after the destruction of a large part of their fleet and the probable loss of a great number of men. In such circumstances, Eadric was unlikely to have had treacherous motives in avoiding battle; he may, reasonably, have calculated that the risks were too high and that a Fabian strategy, similar to that pursued in 1006, was most suited to the situation.

John adds the information that Eadric was, by this time, the king's son-in-law. Eadric was consolidating his position rapidly and, if correct, the marriage is further evidence of the great personal influence he had gained over the king.

The autumn campaign came to an end and the *ASC* says:

Then, after St Martin's Day [11 November], they journeyed back again to Kent. And they took up winter quarters on the Thames and lived off Essex and off the adjoining shires on both sides of the Thames. And frequently they fought against the fortified city of London. But, praise be to God, it still remains unharmed; and they always suffered harm there.[60]

John agrees with the *ASC* on this passage. The Scandinavians remained in their winter quarters until after Christmas. According to this *ASC* account, the enemy army was taking an increased interest in the south-east. However, the *ASC* chronicler may have had a special interest in London and the south-east so that events further west attracted less of his attention.[61] The Isle of Wight probably continued as a base. For instance, in 1013, when most of England, including London, had submitted to King Swein, Æthelred, who was then under Thorkell's protection, spent Christmas on the Isle of Wight, the implication being that the island was controlled by Scandinavian forces loyal to Thorkell.

At this stage, the enemy fleet which had returned to Kent was probably stationed at or near Greenwich, because *ASC* C D E says that the Scandinavians were on the Thames and that they lived off Essex and the adjoining shires on

---

[58] Darlington and McGurk, *John of Worcester, s.a.* 1009, my translation.
[59] Chapter 1, pp. 5–6, above.
[60] My translation, *ASC* C D E *s.a.* 1009.
[61] For a discussion of this aspect see Keynes, 'Declining Reputation', pp. 232–3.

both sides of the Thames. They were east of London which effectively prevented them sailing further up the river and the reference to frequent attacks on London is a reminder of its strategic importance. Until they captured London, the Scandinavians could not take their ships up the Thames valley to plunder the countryside and carry away booty. They failed to capture the city and so, later, they took an overland route through the Chilterns to get into the rich Thames valley. From the English viewpoint, the Scandinavian presence meant that sea travel and trade to and from London was blockaded. This created an economic, strategic and political problem of great proportions.

Early in the new year the enemy army undertook a winter campaign:

> Then, after mid-winter, they took an inland venture out through the Chilterns and so on to Oxford and burned the fortified town. And then it [*sic*] went on both sides of the Thames towards the ships. Then they were warned that there was an army gathered at London against them, so they crossed over at Staines. And thus they behaved all winter; and that spring [Lent] they were in Kent and (they) repaired their ships.[62]

Although these events belong to the modern calendar year 1010, the winter campaign and the ship repairs are recorded under the annal year 1009. However, John of Worcester records the events in the year 1010, saying the host of 'Danes' disembarked in January and went through the pass (*saltum*) known as Chiltern to Oxford.[63] He expands the story, explaining that part of the army which was on the north bank of the Thames crossed at Staines and so was able to retreat through Surrey to the ships, the implication being that the Scandinavians avoided the army which was waiting for them at London. Since their river access to the sea was being blockaded, the Londoners would probably have been keen to inflict damage on them. However, the enemy, returning laden with booty, seems to have been equally keen to avoid battle and they took a route, according to John, which enabled them to return to their base on the Thames, avoiding the English forces which were near London.

According to the *ASC*, the Scandinavian army continued in this manner throughout the winter. This was presumably because the English had not negotiated a truce and paid *gafol* and provided *metsunge*. Certainly, there is no mention in the *ASC* of negotiations or a truce at this time.

The Missing Annals

After Easter 1010, the Scandinavians embarked on another raid:

> In this year the aforementioned army ['here'] came, after Easter [9 April], to East Anglia and landed at Ipswich. And (they) went straightway ['anreces'] where they sought ['geacsedon'] Ulfcytel with his army ['fyrde']. This was on Ascension Day [18 May] and then the men of East Anglia immediately fled.

[62] My translation, *ASC* C D E *s.a.* 1009.
[63] Darlington and McGurk, *John of Worcester, s.a.* 1010: 'per saltum qui dicitur Ciltern' for the *ASC*'s 'þuruh Ciltern'.

Figure 10. Scandinavian itinerary: 1009–spring 1010

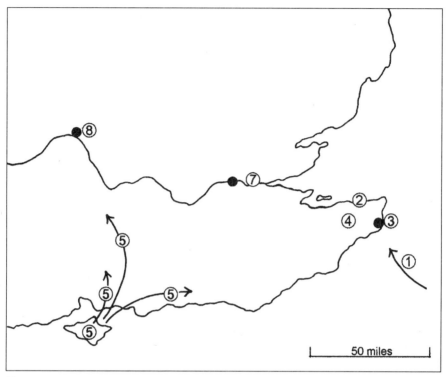

① Thorkell's fleet came to England
② The other fleet, led by Heming and Eglaf, joined it on the Isle of Thanet
③ Both fleets went to Sandwich
④ SC received 3,000 pounds from the people of Kent
⑤ SC went to the Isle of Wight and ravaged in Sussex, Hampshire and Berkshire
6   King Æthelred called out the national army but a battle was avoided
⑦ SC took up winter quarters on the Thames and attacked London unsuccessfully
⑧ After mid-winter, the SC went through the Chilterns and burned Oxford

SC = Scandinavians

Then the men of Cambridgeshire stood steadfastly against (the enemy). There were slain Æthelstan the king's relative ['aþum'], Oswig and his son, Wulf son of Leofwine, Eadwig brother of Æfice and many other good thegns and innumerable other folk. Thurcytel Mare's Head first started the flight.[64]

As usual the Old English provides a distinction, difficult to achieve in translation, between the invading army [*here*] and the English army [*fyrde*]. The translation of the second sentence is influenced by *ASC* F, which makes it clear that the Scandinavians sought out Ulfcytel and his army deliberately. If correct, this was a change in their policy. Generally, whilst prepared to fight, they

[64] *ASC* C D E *s.a.* 1010. C E have 'Wulfric' for D's 'Wulf'. All the translations of the *ASC* in this section are mine, unless otherwise stated. This and other translations in this section may be compared with Whitelock, *EHD*; Garmonsway, *Anglo-Saxon Chronicle*; Swanton, *Anglo-Saxon Chronicle*.

avoided battle where possible, as they did in 1009 and earlier in 1010. John of Worcester supports the view that the Scandinavians deliberately sought a battle saying that they approached Ringmere[65] where they knew Ulfcytel and his army to be. Perhaps, knowing Ulfcytel would oppose them, they chose to fight him sooner rather than later, possibly before all his troops were ready. The *ASC* date, 18 May, is contradicted by John who says that the battle took place on 'tertio nonas Maii', 5 May. Professor Whitelock noted that 5 May 'is shown to be correct by the entry of Oswig's death on that date in the Ely calendar'.[66] John describes Æthelstan, who was slain, as the king's son-in-law, though it is not clear which of Æthelred's daughters he had married.

The enemy army had won a great victory. The *ASC* continues:

> The Danes had control of the place of slaughter and, there, took to horseback and afterwards had control of East Anglia and burned the country (for) three months. And first they set out into the wild fens and they killed and burned men and cattle throughout the fens; and they burned Thetford and Cambridge.[67]

This passage accounts for the enemy army's activities from the battle in May until about mid-August 1010.

> Afterwards, they made their way southwards again into (the) Thames (valley); and the men on horseback rode back to the ships. And afterwards, they made their way swiftly westwards again into Oxfordshire; and from thence into Buckinghamshire; and so along the (river) Ouse until they came to Bedford; and so forward until Tempsford; and always burned as they went. Then (they) made their way again to the ships with their booty.[68]

The *ASC* does not say where the ships were when the enemy horsemen rejoined them; they were previously mentioned at Ipswich. John of Worcester does, saying:

> These things done, the men on foot being transported by ships, the mounted men travelling on horse-back, they returned to the river Thames.[69]

It seems that the enemy ships returned to their base on the Thames; this base may have been at Greenwich. John, or his source, may have been correct in saying that the Scandinavian foot soldiers returned to their ships and then into the Thames valley, but that is not what the *ASC* says. My interpretation of the *ASC*, in Figure 11, p. 89, has the main Scandinavian army approaching the Thames valley to the west of London whilst the mounted men diverted to return

---

[65] Ringmere features more than once in the sources as a place of battle. The reason for this and its strategic importance were explained by Russell Poole in 1987: Poole, 'Skaldic Verse', pp. 278–80.

[66] Whitelock, *EHD*, p. 220 n. 10.

[67] *ASC* C D E *s.a.* 1010. The words 'and, there, took to horseback and afterwards had control of East Anglia' are omitted from *ASC* C.

[68] *Ibid.*

[69] My translation of the Latin text in Darlington and McGurk, *John of Worcester, s.a.* 1010.

Figure 11. Scandinavian itinerary: 1010

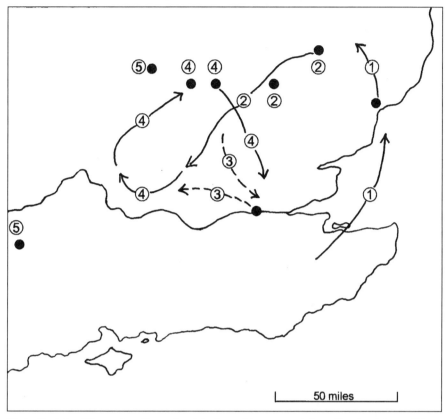

① April to May: SC went from Kent to Ipswich; then to Ringmere to defeat Ulfcytel and the English levies from East Anglia and Cambridge

② May to September: SC ravaged the country; burned Thetford; burned Cambridge; then turned southwards into the Thames valley

③ The mounted SC rode to the ships and then quickly back to west

④ SC raided Oxfordshire and Buckinghamshire, then Bedford, then went as far as Tempsford, before returning to their ships

⑤ SC burned (North)hampton, and ravaged in Wessex around Cannings Marsh

SC = Scandinavians

to the ships and then rejoined the main body of the army. More than one inter-pretation of this army's itinerary is possible.[70]

The *ASC* continues:

> When they were going to their ships, then the (English) army should have come out again (in case) they wanted (to go) inland. Then the (English) army went home; and when they were in the east then the (English) army was kept in the west; and when they were in the south, then our army was in the north. Then, all the *witan* was summoned to the king so that they could advise how this land should be defended. But although they quickly gave advice, it stood

[70] See Hill, *Atlas*, map 121.

no more than a month. Eventually, there was no leader who would gather an army, but each fled as best he could, and in the end no shire would support another.[71]

An English army ['fyrd'] had been called out and, to judge from the chronicler's complaints, it pursued a Fabian policy and avoided battle. From the chronicler's description, it seems to have been completely ineffective, although he also complains that it went home and allowed the enemy army the opportunity to conduct a late autumn campaign, a complaint which seems a little strange if the army was indeed so completely ineffective. The chronicler then describes a complete breakdown in morale and even, it seems, in the king's authority since no plan was followed consistently and leaders were refusing to put armies in the field. However, it should be observed that it was unusual to call out the *fyrd* so late in the year. The *ASC* says how the Scandinavians took advantage of the situation:

Then before St Andrew's Day [30 November], the (enemy) army went to Hampton and immediately burnt the *port* ['market-town' or 'harbour'] and went about there much as they pleased. And thence (they) went over the Thames into Wessex and so to Cannings Marsh and burnt it all. When they had gone as far as they wished (they) then came to their ships in mid-winter.[72]

When *ASC* C D E says the enemy army attacked 'Hampton', it is not entirely clear whether Southampton or Northampton is meant. The reference to the enemy army crossing 'the Thames into Wessex' after the attack indicates Northampton, an interpretation that is supported by John of Worcester. John adds that afterwards the 'Danes' ('Dani') burnt much of Wiltshire in their usual manner and returned to their ships about Christmas time. He does not explain why they should have gone so far across country to attack Northampton, from a base he had said was on the Thames, presumably east of London in a location such as Greenwich, in the late autumn when there must have been easier targets closer to their camp. The location of Northampton and Cannings Marsh shows that it was a strange itinerary for one separate raid.[73] There are other interpretations of this itinerary that start in East Anglia, but supporting maps tend to ignore the geographical location of the ships, to which the enemy army returned before its Northampton/Canning campaign. These ships were either still at Ipswich or, following John of Worcester, had already returned to the Thames.[74]

Beginning with the attack on Sandwich in August 1009, *ASC* C D E explains the major events of the Scandinavian invasion season by season. The record of events becomes vague with the commencement of the annal year 1011. On a casual reading this is not apparent because *ASC* C D E has much to say. It starts:

---

[71] *ASC* C D E *s.a.* 1010.

[72] *Ibid.* In the final sentence *ASC* D has 'rypon' (lower case 'r') which I have translated as 'ships', following Thorpe who thought it a mistake for *scypon*: Thorpe, *The Anglo-Saxon Chronicle, s.a.* 1010. *ASC* C and E have 'scipon'.

[73] Figure 11, p. 89, above.

[74] See Hill, *Atlas*, map 121, and N. J. Higham, *The Death of Anglo-Saxon England*, p. 53.

Here in this year, the king and his *witan* sent to the (enemy) army and begged for peace, and promised them tribute and provisions on condition that they should cease their ravaging. They had then overrun: (i) East Anglia (ii) Essex (iii) Middlesex (iv) Oxfordshire (v) Cambridgeshire (vi) Hertfordshire (vii) Buckinghamshire (viii) Bedfordshire (ix) half Huntingdonshire (x) much of Northamptonshire; and south of the Thames all Kent, Sussex, Hastings, Surrey, Berkshire, Hampshire and much of Wiltshire.[75]

Northamptonshire does not feature in the list according to versions E and F; otherwise they agree with C D. The word 'Hamtunscire' features twice in the list and is translated as 'Northamptonshire' when it first appears and as 'Hampshire' on the second occasion since the latter shire is said to be 'south of the Thames'. The omission by the E and F versions of the first 'Hamtunscire' (Northampton-shire) may be accidental or it may reflect some confusion in the mind of a copyist who thought the same name should not appear twice in the listing of shires. An interesting feature of the listing of the shires is that those north of the Thames are numbered, those to the south are not. The raid in the late autumn involved the last shire in each of the northern and southern lists: Northampton-shire and Wiltshire. This raid, which has just been discussed, is a strange itin-erary and it is tempting to consider the possibility that *ASC* C D E was written to conform with lists that an annalist had in front of him and that he did not have itineraries for the raids which were as clear as might appear from his annal.

However the annal was derived, there can be no doubting the extent of the devastation since the most prosperous areas of Wessex and Mercia had suffered at the hands of the Scandinavian army within a relatively short period. The *ASC* annalist comments on the situation:

All those misfortunes befell us through bad policy [ill-advice, 'unrædas'] in that they were neither offered tribute nor fought against in time. But when they had done most to harm (us), then peace and truce were made with them. And nevertheless, for all this truce and tribute, they travelled in all directions in (armed) bands and ravaged our poor people and plundered them and killed them.[76]

If, as the *ASC* says, the English asked for peace ['fryðes'], apparently during the winter of 1010/1011, and promised the enemy army tribute and provisions ['gafol ⁊ metsunge'], it seems strange that there is no mention of a payment of *gafol* until the Easter of the following year. This does not conform to what had become the normal pattern. Despite the annalist's complaints, he does not record any major incident concerning the enemy army until the sack of Canter-bury in September 1011. The possibility that important information about invading armies is missing has already been considered in relation to the annals for 1001, 1003 and 1009. It is possible that the *ASC* may have omitted infor-mation, including the payment of *gafol*, from the annals for 1011. John of

---

[75] *ASC* C D E *s.a.* 1011.
[76] *ASC* C D E *s.a.* 1011.

Worcester's account indicates that this is so. After listing the shires that had been devastated, he says:

> Æthelred, king of the English, and the leading men of his kingdom sent his envoys to them to sue for peace, and to promise them maintenance and tribute to give up their marauding. When they had heard them, they accepted the offers, not without guile and deceit, as the outcome of the matter showed, for, although ample provisions were prepared for them and the tribute paid in accordance with their wishes, yet they did not desist, but scoured the country everywhere in bands, and plundered townships, despoiling some wretches of their possessions, even killing others. Finally, between the nativity of St Mary and the feast of St Michael, they surrounded and besieged Canterbury.[77]

John's account effectively deals with the period between a payment of *gafol* and the attack on Canterbury in September 1011 by describing the treacherous behaviour of the enemy army. This may be accurate but it begs a question because it does not conform to the established pattern and there is other relevant evidence to consider. The pattern established earlier in the *ASC* is for *gafol* to be paid for a winter truce and thereafter the English might go to war with the invaders or else persuade the enemy to become a mercenary force in the employment of the king.

From other sources we may deduce the possibility that Thorkell left England during this period and that his brother was killed after he had gone.[78] That Thorkell departed from England suggests that a payment had been made and, since the main body of the Scandinavian army stayed in England, that negotiations were taking place for it to become a mercenary force. Heming's death suggests some act of treachery, but the fact that Thorkell made an alliance with King Æthelred in 1012 or 1013 indicates that he did not hold the king personally responsible for his brother's death. What happened during this period must be conjecture, but we have enough information to suspect that there were some significant events concerning the Scandinavian army which have not been recorded in the extant versions of the *ASC* and that there may have been some justification for the attack on Canterbury.

There are two pieces of information that indicate Thorkell's departure from England at this time. The first piece of information is in the *Encomium*, which says that King Swein's soldiers persuaded him to lead them in an invasion of England (in 1013):

> Thorkell, said they, your military commander, Lord King, having been granted licence by you, has gone to avenge his brother, who was killed there [in England][79]

---

[77] Translation from Darlington and McGurk, *John of Worcester, s.a.* 1011.
[78] This is explained later in this section. See also Campbell, *Encomium*, Bk I, c. 2.
[79] ' "Turchil", inquiunt, "princeps miliciae tuae, domine rex, licentia a te accepta abiit, ut fratrem suum inibi interfectum ulcisceretur" ': Campbell, *Encomium*, Bk I, c. 2, Campbell's translation.

According to John of Worcester, Heming and Thorkell were in England together in 1009, so it must be considered likely that Thorkell went back to Scandinavia at some stage so that he could return to avenge his brother with King Swein's permission. Campbell, editor of the *Encomium*, identifies Heming as Thorkell's brother[80] but does not recognise the possibility that Thorkell left England for some months during the years 1010 to 1011, writing:

> It is, of course, well known that Thorkell Hávi conducted a vigorous campaign in England just before Sveinn's final invasion, and that he concluded peace with Æthelred in 1012, and entered his service with forty-five ships. It is also confirmed by an early Icelandic tradition that he avenged a brother in England some time before the death of Sveinn, although, since the brother in question seems not to have arrived in England till just after Thorkell, the Encomiast is not correct in stating that vengeance was the original object of Thorkell's invasion. It is highly improbable that Thorkell was ever in Sveinn's service, or took any forces with him to England which could be considered part of Sveinn's army, but, on the other hand, it is more than likely that his progress was regarded by Sveinn with disquiet, for the latter had himself long cherished designs upon England.[81]

There is a second piece of evidence that Thorkell left England for a time, in the verses of Sigvat the Skald. Sigvat was a follower of St Olaf and he wrote a praise poem about that king's early campaigns and battles. Because he numbers each battle, we can be reasonably sure of the chronological sequence of events. There is a verse about St Olaf (Olaf helgi) joining Thorkell for a campaign.[82] It seems to me that with such highly technical, stylised verses, a skald would depend for his impact upon his audience having some foreknowledge of the related events, and, in *Heimskringla*, Snorri, a skald himself, provides a background explanation for this verse:[83]

> Then King Oláf sailed to Denmark. There he met Thorkel the Tall, the brother of Earl Sigvaldi, and Thorkel joined him, because he was at that time all ready to set out on a warlike expedition. So they sailed south along the coast of Jutland, and at a place called Suthrvík they won a battle over many viking ships. Such vikings that always were at sea and commanded a large force, had themselves called kings though they had no lands to rule over. King Oláf gave battle to them, and it was a hard one, but he won the victory and much booty.[84]

80 Campbell, *Encomium*, pp. 73, 87.
81 Campbell, *Encomium*, p. lii.
82 Hollander, *Heimskringla*, p. 251.
83 I am indebted to Dr Whaley for her observations on this matter. She agrees that skaldic verses 'have a supporting, authenticating role', but adds that there is some debate about whether verses such as these would have been accompanied by a prose explanation and whether any accompanying explanation would have covered both technical complexity and lack of specificity in the content. Dr Whaley tells me that the idea of 'accompanying prose' is 'known in the trade as *Begleitprosa*'.
84 Hollander, *Heimskringla*, p. 250, Hollander's translation; he says that Suthrvík was 'on the west coast of Jutland'.

Because of the chronological sequence of the battles in the verses, and because two verses later St Olaf is helping Æthelred re-conquer England (1014), it seems likely that this expedition occurred in c. 1011 rather than before Thorkell's invasion of England in 1009. Campbell agreed that Snorri was probably correct in stating that St Olaf's fourth battle was in Denmark and considered the possibility of 'Suðrvík' being Søndervig in Jutland. However, he has St Olaf join Thorkell before the 1009 invasion of England and consequently relates the following verses to events in England during the period 1009 to 1012, in contradiction to the words in *Heimskringla*.[85] A reason why Campbell rejected Snorri's interpretation is that Snorri's chronology of events did not align with his expectations. This is a complex subject, but it seems likely that Campbell's interpretation is influenced by his understanding that St Olaf had a fifteen-year reign in Norway. However, it can be shown that the chronology that gives St Olaf a fifteen-year reign is suspect because the same chronology extends Cnut's reign by about five years and shortens King Swein's life by about four years, among other anomalies. A detailed analysis of all the chronological references in *Heimskringla* from the birth of Olaf Tryggvason to the death of St Olaf reveals the real possibility that St Olaf's reign lasted between ten and eleven years. So far as I am aware the chronology, on which Campbell's interpretation is based, has not previously been questioned. In 1987, Russell Poole followed the same chronology and the same interpretation of events as Campbell.[86] A synopsis of my investigation of the chronological evidence in *Heimskringla* is attached as an appendix to this book.

For the present, we have an *ASC* account that does not provide information about events between the king asking the Scandinavian army for a truce early in 1011and the sack of Canterbury in September 1011; we have the John of Worcester information that *gafol* and *metsunge* were given to the enemy army in 1011 and that the Scandinavians accepted the truce but then behaved in a treacherous manner; and we have considered the possibility that *gafol* was paid, some Scandinavians, including Thorkell, left England and the rest remained, making an accord with the king. For some reason that accord broke down, the Scandinavian leader, Heming, was killed, Canterbury was sacked and Thorkell returned to England to avenge his brother.

It should be noted that the quotations from Campbell in this section and from Sawyer in the previous section suggest that Thorkell was not subordinate to King Swein but might be regarded as his rival. The development of a rivalry in the period 1012 to 1013 remains to be considered. For their relationship prior to that, there is circumstantial evidence and the words in the *Encomium*. It is relevant to observe that both Lund and Sawyer have commented on the security of Swein's position in Denmark at this time and for some years before.[87] My own interpretation is that Thorkell and his brother Heming, the sons of Strut-Harald, were Danes. Another leader of the Scandinavian army was probably also a Dane, if Eglaf is the same man who later witnessed King Cnut's charters. Swein was

---

85 Campbell, *Encomium*, pp. 81–2.
86 Poole, 'Skaldic Verse', pp. 265–98.
87 See the quotations in Chapter 3, pp. 33–4, above.

king of Denmark and, at the very least, had an influence over Sweden and Norway. The *liðs* which invaded England with Thorkell in 1009, and if my interpretation of the *Encomium* and Sigvat the Skald is correct, in c. 1011, were gathered in Scandinavia. It should be considered at least possible, if not probable, that Thorkell had submitted to King Swein and gathered forces with his permission, even encouragement, in 1009 and also in c. 1011. There is very little evidence to help us judge the strength of the relationship between King Swein and the Scandinavian army in England during the period 1006 to 1012, since the comments in the *Encomium* on this subject are probably biased. However, it would be wrong to discount the possibility that Swein continued to assert a strong, if indirect, influence over developments in England during this time.

Renewal of the Treaty with the Scandinavian Army

The major event of the year 1011 was the attack on Canterbury. It is described in *ASC* D:

> Then in this year between the Nativity of St Mary and St Michael's Day [8 September and 29 September] they surrounded Canterbury; and they got into (it) through treachery, because Ælfmær betrayed it (a man) whose life the archbishop, Ælfheah, had previously saved. And then they captured the archbishop, Ælfheah, Ælfweard the king's reeve, Abbess Leofrun and Bishop Godwine; and Abbot Ælfmær they allowed (to go) away. And inside there they captured all the ordained men and (other) men and women – it was not possible for any man to describe how many people that was. And after they were in that stronghold for as long as they wished and when they had searched the stronghold thoroughly, they then went to their ships and led the archbishop with them.
>
> > There was prisoner who before was primate of England and of Christendom. There might one see hardship where often before one saw happiness; in that wretched stronghold where first came Christianity and joy for God and for the world.
>
> And they had the archbishop with them until the time when they martyred him.[88]

Version C spells Ælfmær without an 'l'; this is presumed to be a copying error, as is the lack of an 'f' in version D. Versions E and F list an Abbot Leofwine in place of Abbess Leofrun, possibly in error.

John of Worcester adds a description of the events following the capture of Canterbury. From the wording of *ASC* C D E it might be supposed that Abbot Ælfmær was responsible for betraying the city, but John says that this was not the case and distinguishes between an Archdeacon Ælfmær who betrayed Canterbury and Abbot Ælfmær of St Augustine's monastery who was released, but John offers no explanation for his release. John also provides more infor-

---

[88] *ASC* D *s.a.* 1011. The inset passage may be intended as a verse but is not written as such in the manuscript: examined courtesy of the British Library.

mation about the people captured along with Archbishop Ælfheah, saying the king's reeve was named Ælfred (not Ælfweard), Leofrun was abbess of St Mildrith's,[89] and Godwine bishop of Rochester.

There is no record of the reaction of the king and his *witan* to the sacking of Canterbury. Nor is there any further record of events in the *ASC* until Easter 1012. We are informed then, by *ASC* C D, that:

> Here in this year, Ealdorman Eadric and all the most senior counsellors of England, ecclesiastic and lay, came to London before Easter. That (year), Easter was on 13 April. And they were there until all the tribute payment was completed after Easter: that was 48,000 pounds.[90]

ASC F does not mention Eadric. *ASC* E F says that the tribute payment was 8,000 pounds, using the Roman numeral viii., but John of Worcester agrees with *ASC* C D that the tribute was 48,000 pounds (XLVIII). Since F is derived from E, it seems possible that the discrepancy reflects a clerical error either in \E or in E when it was copied from \E. The *ASC* describes Eadric's arrival in London as if he were the king in person. He was the leading ealdorman and represented the king, who may have been ill. The king was relatively old by the standards of the time; the *ASC* tells us that he was ill, at Cosham, in 1015 and that he died in April 1016. Eadric and the *witan* came to London to supervise the payment of a *gafol*. There is no mention of an undertaking to pay *gafol* and *metsunge* after the first sentence of the annal for the previous year, 1011, so there is an implication that this is the *gafol* promised a year previously. The possibility that this was not so has been considered above. If the *ASC* omitted important information about the activities of the enemy army, it is likely that it has omitted an agreement for the payment of *gafol* and *metsunge*, which would have been made in the winter of 1011/1012. A payment of *gafol* at Easter 1012 would then accord with the time-scale of earlier payments of *gafol*. All other events were overshadowed by the martyrdom of Archbishop Ælfheah:

> Then on the Saturday, the (enemy) army was greatly incensed against the bishop because he would not promise them any money, but forbade that anything should be given or allowed in return for him [i.e. for his release]. They were also very drunk because southern wine was brought there. Then they took the bishop, led him to their meeting place, on the eve of Sunday in the Easter Octave, which was 19 April, and there pelted him with bones and with ox-heads, and one of them struck him then with the back of an axe, on his head, and with that blow he fell down and his holy blood fell on the ground and his holy soul was sent to God's kingdom. And, in the morning, his body was taken to London and there bishops Eadnoth and Ælfhun and the citizens accepted it with all honour and buried him in St Paul's Minster and there God now reveals the powers of the holy martyr.[91]

---

89 On the Isle of Thanet.
90 *ASC* C D *s.a.* 1012.
91 *ASC* D *s.a.* 1012.

There are some minor differences between C, D and E. C has the words 'shamefully killed (him)' before he was pelted with bones, presumably a late addition that emphasises an intention of killing the archbishop, thus making him a martyr.[92] Versions E F differ from C D in stating that bishops Eadnoth and Ælfhun, with the citizens, came to fetch the archbishop's body to London. John of Worcester agrees with the C D version on this matter; he expands on the story to describe the archbishop's brave refusal to bend to the Danes' demands for a 3,000 pounds ransom and so the archbishop was brought to trial, condemned and found martyrdom at their hands.

The account in *ASC* C D E *s.aa.* 1012 and 1013 suggests that Thorkell was with the Scandinavian army at this time and was probably the leader of that army. Thietmar's chronicle says Thorkell was with the army when it sacked Canterbury and captured the archbishop and that he did all he could to prevent the death of Ælfheah.[93]

The *ASC* continues:

> Then the tribute was paid and peace was sworn by oath. Then the (enemy) army dispersed as far as it had been gathered. Then forty-five ships from the (enemy) army made submission to the king, and they promised him that they would defend this country, and he was to feed and clothe them.[94]

The sequence of events in the *ASC* has Eadric and the *witan* meeting in London for the payment of the largest *gafol* yet made to the Scandinavians. There is no mention of any attempt on their part to negotiate the archbishop's release, nor is there mention of their reaction to the archbishop's death. The tribute payment was more than just 'paid': the word 'gelæst' suggests that an undertaking and a ceremony were 'performed' or 'carried-out'.

The wording of the *ASC* is ambiguous in saying that the fleet dispersed but then forty-five ships came over to the king. It is not clear whether there were two separate events or whether the fleet dispersed except for forty-five ships. John of Worcester says that forty-five ships remained ('remansere') when the fleet dispersed. It is presumed that Thorkell was the leader of the forty-five ships that came over to the king at this time, although he is not mentioned by name until the annal for 1013, when he was in London with King Æthelred. The assumption that he was the supreme commander of the enemy army in 1012 is partly based on the late addition to *ASC* C *s.a.* 1009, which refers to the army as 'Thorkell's army', and partly inferred from the important role he played in defending the king during Swein's third invasion. Stenton, following Thietmar, considered that Thorkell's men appeared to have defied him in killing Archbishop Ælfheah and wrote:

---

[92] I have followed Whitelock in translating 'pelted him with bones and with ox-heads': Whitelock, *EHD*, p. 222. 'Oftorfedon' (from *oftorfian*) may be translated 'stoned to death' or 'pelted to death', so the additional emphasis may have seemed justifiable to a later annotator of *ASC* \C.

[93] Trillmich, *Thietmari Merseburgensis*, Bk VII, cc. 42–3.

[94] *ASC* C D E *s.a.* 1012.

A viking commander whose men had once got out of hand was never secure among them afterwards, and the ugly incident at Greenwich helps to explain the remarkable fact that before the end of the year, when the greater part of the army left England, Thorkell came over to King Æthelred with forty-five ships.[95]

Campbell, Keynes and Higham agree that Thorkell was the leader of the great army in 1012 and went over to King Æthelred with forty-five ships.[96] Keynes says that Thorkell:

is conceivably to be identified as the 'Thurcytel *miles*' who attested a charter of King Æthelred in 1012.[97]

The agreement with the Scandinavians described in the *ASC* and the behaviour of Thorkell and his fleet in 1013, when England suffered Swein Forkbeard's third invasion, suggests that the terms of King Æthelred's agreement with Thorkell were very similar to those agreed with Olaf Tryggvason nearly twenty years earlier, which were preserved in *II Æthelred*. Olaf Tryggvason had eventually become king of Norway, possibly with the help of English money and supplies. Thorkell's action in taking service with King Æthelred in 1012 was not only a withdrawal of any allegiance that he may have owed to King Swein, but could be regarded as a potential threat to the king's authority in Denmark. The writer of the *Encomium* says, in Book I, c. 2, that it was a betrayal of King Swein's interests and this may be an informed view because, although the encomiast probably did not know either King Swein or Thorkell the Tall, his patroness and informant was Queen Emma who must have got to know Thorkell very well when he was at King Æthelred's court, and when he was King Cnut's leading ealdorman in England. The *Encomium* states that it was this betrayal of King Swein's interests which led directly to Swein's third invasion in 1013.

---

[95] Stenton, *Anglo-Saxon England*, p. 384.
[96] Campbell, *Encomium*, p. 74; Keynes, 'Historical Context', p. 95; Higham, *The Death of Anglo-Saxon England*, p. 56.
[97] Keynes, 'Cnut's Earls', p. 55, quoting S.926 and Campbell, *Encomium*, p. 75 n. 3.

6

Swein Forkbeard's Third Invasion

Swein Forkbeard's Diplomatic Offensive

The victory achieved by King Swein Forkbeard and his allies at Svold, over Olaf Tryggvason of Norway, allowed Swein to feel sufficiently confident of his control over Denmark to undertake an overseas campaign in England during the period 1003 to 1005.[1] However, there is some contradictory evidence in our sources about Swein Forkbeard and the political situation in Scandinavia, evidence that was examined by Sawyer in 1991, when he answered some of the criticisms of sources favourable to Swein, particularly the *Encomium Emmae Reginae*.[2] The *Encomium* was evidently written on the instructions of Queen Emma: she was in a unique position to supply the encomiast with information, which she had received directly from participants in events. Sawyer's assessment of the encomiast, on the subject of Swein Forkbeard, was that 'we should take him [the encomiast] seriously; his judgement was sounder than Thietmar's, and he was better informed than Adam'.[3]

Keynes has written recently:

> It would be easy to dismiss the *Encomium* as a thoroughly unreliable and ten-
> dentious piece of work, which it is, though to do so would be to deny oneself a
> useful account of the Scandinavian conquest of England in 1013–16, a con-
> temporary impression of Cnut's rule, and an inside view of English politics in
> the immediate aftermath of Cnut's death. We may be sure, however, that it was
> not the Encomiast's intention to provide posterity with anything of the sort.[4]

Keynes' assessment of the *Encomium* neatly summarises a dilemma: where our principal source of information is the *Encomium*, may we trust it as a historical record of events, or is its credibility too seriously flawed?

In the *Encomium*, Book I, chapter 1, the encomiast assures us that King Swein lived in peace in his kingdom, secure in its defences and in the absolute loyalty of his forces ('milites'). This information may be aligned with evidence, mentioned earlier in this study, that from about 996 Swein was secure in his authority over Denmark and that his influence probably extended into the rest of

---

[1] Chapter 1, pp. 9–10, and Chapter 4, p. 63, above.
[2] Sawyer, 'Swein Forkbeard and the Historians', pp. 27–40.
[3] Sawyer, 'Swein Forkbeard and the Historians', p. 39.
[4] Campbell, *Encomium*, 1998 reissue, p. [lxvi].

Scandinavia.[5] Historians such as Lund have noted that Swein's ability to lead foreign campaigns evidenced that he must have felt confident of his authority in Denmark even during a prolonged absence.[6]

In Book I, chapter 2, the encomiast explains Swein's political perspective of events in England, a perspective that was shared by his followers. Thorkell had been allowed by Swein to lead Danish forces to England to avenge the death of his brother. He had betrayed King Swein by taking service with King Æthelred and persuading the crews of forty (not forty-five, as in the *ASC* version) ships to join him. Swein's supporters were keen that he should lead an invasion of England to return Thorkell and the Danes to their proper allegiance and to punish the English. The encomiast was writing some thirty years after the events and with knowledge of societies which may have been politically more sophisticated than Denmark was at that time, but that does not necessarily negate his explanation of the Scandinavian background to the invasion of England. The political perspective in Denmark in 1012 as proposed by the encomiast is possible and, arguably, even likely.[7]

In Book I, chapter 3, the encomiast describes how Swein summoned his army and commanded the arming of a fleet against the English. He then describes how Swein organised political authority in Denmark during his absence. Professor Lund has considered whether the encomiast is describing the gathering of a national *leding*, and concluded that Swein was not in a position to command a *leding* for a foreign campaign.[8] It seems that Swein was summoning his chief followers, that they were gathering *lið*s around them and that the combination of those *lið*s created a great army, which Swein led to England.

The encomiast says that King Swein took his elder son, Cnut, with him and left behind his younger son, Harald, some trusted counsellors and a military force to keep his kingdom of Denmark secure. That Cnut was older than Harald is stated more than once and without equivocation.[9] Cnut was born either c. 990 or c. 999.[10] Knytlinga saga says that Cnut did not accompany his father on this expedition and that he was too young to go to England until three years after his father's death.[11] The author of this saga was not aware of the account in the *ASC*

---

5   Chapter 1, pp. 9–11, above.
6   See the passage from Lund quoted in Chapter 3, pp. 33–4, above; the passage from Sawyer, in the same section, is also relevant.
7   Chapter 5, pp. 92–5, above, discusses Thorkell's relationship with King Swein during the years before 1012, and Chapter 4, p. 63, discusses the likelihood that Scandinavian *lið*s were seeking outlets for raiding activities and that it was in Swein's political interests to encourage them to direct their energies away from Scandinavia towards England.
8   Chapter 3, pp. 31–2, above; also N. Lund, 'Jellingekongerne', in *Lið, Leding og Landeværn*, pp. 110–25 and 294–5. Lund says that there is evidence that the king could only summon the *leding* for defensive purposes. He also argues that the centralisation of Danish government was not sufficiently advanced in Swein's time and that even at a much later date, 1085, St Cnut's abortive plan to conquer England reveals no indication of *leding*.
9   Campbell, *Encomium*, Bk I, c. 3; Bk II, c. 2. An older brother, named Harald, may have predeceased Swein: Chapter 1, pp. 10–11, above.
10   Chapter 4, p. 67, above: if he was the son of the Slav, Gunnhild, he was born c. 990; if he was the son of Queen Sigrid he was born c. 999.
11   Pálsson and Edwards, *Knytlinga Saga*, c. 8, pp. 27–8.

s.a. 1013 and his misunderstanding may have arisen from following the chronology and time-scale of events for this period that he found in *Heimskringla* and its source material.[12]

There is saga evidence that boys were considered old enough to participate in raiding expeditions when they were twelve years old,[13] so, whether he was born in c. 990 or in c. 999, Cnut was old enough to have accompanied his father on the invasion of England in 1013. Consideration of Cnut's age is relevant to an appreciation of the part he played in events. The suggestion, derived from Adam of Bremen,[14] that he was the son of Queen Sigrid, and therefore born about 999, should be compared with evidence in *Heimskringla* that he was born in about 990.[15] Any debate on this question is likely to be inconclusive and Lawson, who has written extensively about Cnut, says he was born '990–999'. In support of the view that Cnut may have been born as early as 990, Lawson takes stanza 9 of Knútsdrápa, with its reference to Norwich, as possible evidence of Cnut's presence with Swein Forkbeard during his invasion of England in 1003 to 1005, when Norwich was attacked.[16] In this he is following Campbell's opinion in *Skaldic Verse*, an opinion that was discussed by Poole, who found that it was not entirely persuasive when Knútsdrápa was compared with other skaldic verses.[17]

If, as I consider likely, Cnut was born c. 990, he would have been about thirteen years old at the start of Swein's second invasion of England in 1003.[18] If so, the opening verses of Knútsdrápa may refer to this:

> Destroyer of the chariot of the sea, you were of no great age when you pushed off your ships. Never, younger than you, did prince set out to take his part in war. Chief, you made ready your armoured ships, and were daring beyond measure. In your rage, Cnut, you mustered the red shields at sea.[19]

Arguably, it makes most sense to suppose that this first stanza in the *drápa* refers to the period 1003/4 rather than that of 1013/14 when Cnut's active participation in warfare was restricted. Also, it gives a better balance to the poem: stanzas 1 to 3 referring to the 'raid' in 1003/4; stanzas 4 and 5 to the invasion of 1013/14; stanzas 6 to 10 to the invasion of 1015/16; and stanza 11 to Cnut's

---

12 See Appendix 1, below.
13 For an example, see Hollander, *Heimskringla*, Saint Óláf's saga, c. 4, p. 246.
14 Tschan, *Adam of Bremen*, p. 81, Bk II, c. xxxix (37) and note 126; also, p. 78, schol. 24 (25).
15 Jónsson, *Heimskringla*, Olaf Tryggvason saga, K 34.
16 Lawson, *Cnut*, p. 174.
17 Poole, 'Skaldic Verse', pp. 277–8.
18 I. Howard, 'The Anglo-Saxon Chronicle *s.a.* 1013 and Some Problems of Chronology', a paper read at the Leeds International Medieval Congress on 13 July 1998.
19 Whitelock, *EHD*, p. 308. Following Lawson and Campbell and the possibility that stanza 9 relates to the invasion of 1003 to 1005, it would follow that this first stanza would relate to the same campaign and that Cnut must have been born c. 990. However, whilst agreeing with the earlier date for Cnut's birth and that stanza 1 relates to the invasion of 1003 to 1005, I find Poole's arguments the more persuasive as regards stanza 9 probably relating to the invasion of 1015/16.

Scandinavian campaign.[20] In his article on 'Skaldic Verse and Anglo-Saxon History', Poole analyses stanzas 5 to 9 of Knutsdrapa and considers the possibility of stanza 5 relating to either the invasion of 1013/14 or to Cnut's later invasion in 1015/16. He prefers the latter because the northern campaign of Cnut in 1016 was more heroic and successful, but considers the possibility of it referring to the 1013/14 campaign in Lindsey, after King Swein's death, and that 'Knútr might have mounted more of a rearguard action than the *Chronicle* here gives him credit for'.[21]

If Cnut was born in c. 990, he would have been about twenty-three years old in 1013. The encomiast's account of King Swein consulting his son about invading England and his son's reply are probably better suited to a young man than to a boy of about fourteen:

> He, questioned by his father, fearing to be accused, if he opposed the proposal, of wily sloth, not only approved of attacking the country but urged and exhorted that no delay should hold back the undertaking.[22]

The question of Cnut's age will be considered further in relation to his participation in his father's conquest of England, later in this chapter.

Arguably, Swein's perception of England would have changed fundamentally over the years so that, by 1013, England was more than a venue for raiding expeditions. In the opening years of the eleventh century, Scandinavian forces appear to have been creating bases on the Isle of Wight and the Wessex coast and also in the rich Thames valley to the east of London, probably at Greenwich. The eastern parts of England were prospering and trade with northern Germany and with Scandinavia was expanding.[23] Scandinavian armies had exacted increasing amounts of tribute from the English government[24] and in many ways Scandinavian economic, political and military power was increasing. Denmark was well placed to benefit from the changes and by the end of the first decade of the eleventh century Swein Forkbeard could have been contemplating a future relationship with England that included, possibly, a complete dominance over that country. Whether that dominance should be through a native king or whether it should be more direct could also have been a question exercising his mind. English history had seen Northumbrian hegemony, followed by Mercian hegemony, followed by West Saxon hegemony. Given that people of Danish extraction dominated what was increasingly the most prosperous part of the country, it may have occurred to Swein that a Danish hegemony, directed from Denmark itself, was not impossible. Thorkell's action in taking service with King

---

[20] The stanza numbers follow Whitelock, *EHD*. Ottar the Black's Knútsdrápa is embodied, along with verses by other skalds, in chapters 8, 10, 12 of Knytlinga saga, except for the final stanza, which is in *Heimskringla*. The author of Knytlinga saga relates all the verses to events after King Swein's death, probably because of the confusion about Cnut's age, mentioned above. Pálsson and Edwards, *Knytlinga Saga*, 27–35, show the verses in context.

[21] Poole, 'Skaldic Verse', pp. 271–7. Cnut's actions after King Swein's death are considered in Chapter 7, below.

[22] Campbell's translation: Campbell, *Encomium*, Bk I, c. 3.

[23] Chapter 2, pp. 14–22, above.

[24] *Ibid.* and Figure 4, p. 20.

Æthelred may well have brought matters to a head. His treaty arrangement with Æthelred cannot have been welcomed by King Swein. The forty-five ships' crews that remained in England were effectively under Thorkell's control and in the pay of the English. There was little or no room in this arrangement for an acknowledgement of the Danish king's authority. Not only was the treaty arrangement a threat to King Swein's possible ambitions in England, it posed a potential threat in Scandinavia itself. Olaf Tryggvason had conquered Norway with English support in the form of Christian missionaries and money in c. 995.[25] He had then proceeded to threaten to dominate Scandinavia until he was defeated by a formidable alliance at the battle of Svold. Swein himself may have used the wealth accumulated from tributes and looting in England as the basis for a successful return to recover the throne of Denmark in c. 995. The possibility of Thorkell attempting to emulate these examples may have troubled Swein. Thorkell had become a rival not a subject by the end of 1012.

The *Encomium* explains that Swein and his military forces in Denmark were concerned about events in England and felt there was a need for direct intervention to return Thorkell to his true allegiance.[26] Other reasons have been advanced for Swein's invasion in 1013. Adam of Bremen says that Swein wanted to avenge the death of a brother who had been killed in England many years previously and also that he wished to be avenged upon King Æthelred for refusing him refuge in England when he was exiled from Denmark, but Adam's chronicle lacks conviction at this point.[27] Adam says that Swein's brother, Hiring, was killed by the Northumbrians whilst Harald was king of Denmark. He would have been Swein's half-brother, and in the context of other events, must have been killed some four decades earlier, when Swein was a boy. The *ASC* record of events in the final decade of the tenth century seems to preclude the possibility of Æthelred refusing an exiled Swein refuge in England. William of Malmesbury wrote that the invasion of 1013/14 was motivated by Swein's desire for revenge after the massacre of Danes in England in 1002.[28]

That Swein did not invade England until the summer of 1013 may reflect the need to await suitable weather as well as the time required to gather an invasion force. However, during the period between the news of Thorkell's agreement with Æthelred and the departure of the invasion fleet, there was probably intense diplomatic activity preparing for Swein's successful invasion. The extent and nature of this activity may be deduced from the events that occurred during his first few weeks in England.

The annals for 1013 in the *ASC* commence:

In the year after the archbishop was martyred, the king appointed Bishop Lifing to the archbishopric of Canterbury.[29]

25 Andersson, 'The Viking Policy of Ethelred the Unready'.
26 Campbell, *Encomium*, Bk I, cc. 2, 3.
27 Lappenberg, *Mag. Adami*, Bk II, c. 49: 'Suein, rex Danorum atque Nortmannorum, veteres iniurias tam occisi fratris quam suae repulsionis ulturus, classe magna transfretavit in Angliam.'
28 Chapter 4, pp. 62–3, above.
29 *ASC* C D E *s.a.* 1013, Whitelock's translation in *EHD*.

Archbishop Ælfheah was killed in April 1012 and, allowing that the *ASC* annal year may have commenced during September, the annalist is indicating that the see remained vacant for at least five months and probably more. John of Worcester indicates at least eight months since he puts the event under his annal year 1013 and, for him, the year commenced in January. However, John may have made an assumption about the date for lack of information from another source. Perhaps the delay was due, in part, to the devastated state of Canterbury following its siege and capture in 1011.

ASC C D E says nothing more about the events of 1013 until Swein's invasion:

> And in this same year, before the month of August, King Swein came with his fleet to Sandwich, and then went very quickly round East Anglia into the mouth of the Humber, and so up along the Trent until he reached Gainsborough. And then at once Earl Uhtred and all the Northumbrians submitted to him, as did all the people of Lindsey, and then all the people belonging to the district of the Five Boroughs, and quickly afterwards all the Danish settlers ['here'] north of Watling Street, and hostages were given to him from every shire.[30]

John of Worcester says that the invasion started in July and adds that the fleet was 'powerful' ('valida classe'), Swein stayed a few days at Sandwich, and he made a camp ('castra') at Gainsborough.

On several occasions the chronicler, from whose account the C D E versions of the *ASC* are derived, ascribes English failures and defeats against Scandinavian forces to the behaviour of English leaders.[31] John of Worcester, following the *ASC*, frequently refers to treachery in relation to failures of the English leadership.[32] Yet, in his chronicle for the year 1013, John described the people living north of Watling Street swearing fealty to King Swein without any comment on the way they and their leaders were treacherously abandoning their pledges of loyalty to King Æthelred. Nor does the *ASC* make a comment about the behaviour of the English leadership at this time. Indeed, the *ASC* only names Uhtred, and he was already dead when work on *ÆE*, the exemplar from which the extant manuscripts derive their annals, commenced. Significantly, Uhtred had forsaken Edmund Ironside, the hero of the *ÆE* annals, and attempted to make a separate peace with Cnut. The deaths of Sigeferth and Morcar, in 1015, are assigned to the treachery of Eadric Streona and care is taken not to condemn them for their own treachery in 1013, probably because King Edmund had married into their family in a manner that, to another chronicler, might have been termed an act of rebellion against his father.[33] *ÆE* is positive in its praise of Ulfcytel of East Anglia who fought bravely against Scandinavian invaders,[34] making no mention

---

[30] Whitelock's translation, *EHD*, *s.a.* 1013. See Figure 12, opposite.

[31] *ASC* C D E *s.aa.* 992, 993, 998, 1003, 1009, 1011.

[32] For example: Ealdorman Ælfric in 992, Fræna and Godwine in 993, Eadric Streona in 1009.

[33] Chapter 7, below; also *ASC* C D E *s.a.* 1015.

[34] *ASC* C D E *s.aa.* 1004, 1010 and 1016.

Figure 12. Territories that recognised Swein's authority in August 1013

100 miles

 approximate area recognising Swein's authority in August 1013

------ Watling Street

① Gainsborough   ② Lincoln   ③ Nottingham   ④ Derby   ⑤ Leicester
⑥ Stamford   ⑦ Oxford   ⑧ Winchester   ⑨ London   ⑩ Greenwich

of his changes of allegiance although it may be argued that he probably transferred his allegiance to Swein Forkbeard in 1013, reverted to King Æthelred in 1014, supported Edmund Ironside against his father in 1015 and eventually died fighting for King Edmund in 1016. It would have been impossible for the peoples of the Danelaw to support Swein Forkbeard and, later, Edmund Ironside without the positive involvement of their leaders. Scandinavian sources show that forces loyal to King Æthelred probably fought against Ulfcytel on the king's return to England in 1014. Yet such is the propaganda influence of *ÆE* that Campbell and others have 'interpreted' these sources in an, arguably, unlikely manner in defending Ulfcytel's reputation.[35] Likewise, Professor Whitelock suggested that Archbishop Wulfstan was in York in 1014, a fortnight after King Swein died, with a view to persuading the people to change their allegiance back to King Æthelred.[36] The following points should be taken into account in opposition to Whitelock's interpretation of Wulfstan's actions:

Archbishop Wulfstan was in York to consecrate a bishop of London, replacing a man who had fled the country as a supporter of Æthelred;[37]

the Scandinavian fleet remained close to York;

the Northumbrians had accepted Swein as king and had no reason to desire the restoration of a king who would believe he had been betrayed by them;

Cnut had married into an important northern family and his wife was about to bear his child;[38]

Cnut had been acknowledged as his father's successor by Swein himself (*Encomium*), by the Danish fleet (*Encomium*, *ASC* C D E F), and by the English leaders (*ASC* F);[39]

Skaldic evidence (Sigvat) indicates that Swein's forces had garrisoned the fortifications at Canterbury and London (to which might be added Oxford, Winchester, Wallingford and Bath, though they are not named specifically);[40]

Cnut held hostages from all parts of England.

Archbishop Wulfstan was undoubtedly an astute politician and would not have advocated the restoration of Æthelred at a time when there was only one king (Cnut) present in England, and certainly he would not have done so at York, near where Cnut and his followers had concentrated their forces.

As described in the *ASC* and in John of Worcester's Chronicle, in 1013 there

---

35 Campbell, *Encomium*, pp. 76–8.
36 Whitelock, *Sermo Lupi ad Anglos*, p. 15.
37 Bishop Ælfhun was sent to Normandy by King Æthelred with the æthelings Edward and Alfred: *ASC s.a.* 1013, and Keynes, *Diplomas*, p. 267.
38 Howard, 'Swein Forkbeard's Invasions of England', pp. 140–41. The marriage took place in 1013 and there were two sons, born before 1017. The first son, Swein, was probably born in 1014 and the second son, Harald, in Denmark in 1015. See Chapter 7, p. 137, below.
39 *Encomium*, Bk I, c. 4. *ASC* C D E F *s.a.* 1014.
40 Hollander, *Heimskringla*, St Óláf's saga, pp. 251–6, cc. 12–15. *ASC* C D E *s.a.* 1013; also this chapter, pp. 120–2, below.

was deliberate treachery by the Northumbrians and the people of the Danelaw. Swein took his fleet far inland to make his camp at Gainsborough. It should have been a dangerous strategy to take his fleet into enemy territory without first inflicting a defeat upon the forces that ought to have been brought against him, so he could only have adopted this strategy if he had been reasonably confident that there would be no significant opposition. This indicates that agreements were already in place – and, consequently, hostages provided to him – before he sailed to the Humber estuary and up the river Trent. The *ASC* may be used as evidence. It says that Earl Uhtred, the Northumbrians and the people of Lindsey submitted 'at once' ('þa sona beah').[41]

The significance of this immediate submission is underlined by other evidence that Swein's triumph was pre-planned. King Swein's son, Cnut, was married to Ælfgifu of Northampton, the daughter of Ealdorman Ælfhelm whose death had been ascribed to Æthelred's chief adviser Eadric Streona and whose brothers, Wulfheah and Ufegeat, had been blinded on the orders of King Æthelred.[42] She was presumably under the protection of her uncle's heirs, Morcar and Sigeferth, who were the heads of the most influential family in the Danelaw and north-west England.[43] Morcar had been unaffected by the events of 1006 which led to the downfall of Ælfhelm and his sons. He had remained a minister of the king and had received substantial grants of land in Derbyshire in the years 1009, 1011 and 1012, suggesting that King Æthelred felt assured of Morcar's loyalty and that he remained in favour with the king until Swein's invasion.[44]

Cnut's marriage probably took place soon after Swein's arrival in England and before Swein led an army south to invade the country beyond Watling Street. This suggests that the details of a marriage settlement may have been agreed before Swein's arrival and that he had every intention of demonstrating his alliance with a leading northern family, an alliance which made it easier for many people to accept a change in their allegiance. In effect, it was a Danish – Mercian alliance and it is significant that the ætheling Edmund pursued an alliance with the same family when he rebelled against his father in 1015. It is likely that Æthelred and his chief adviser, Eadric, were taking revenge for this alliance with Swein, when Morcar and Sigeferth were killed and the king confiscated their lands, earlier in 1015.[45]

The political situation in England is discussed by Higham who suggests that dissatisfaction north of Watling Street with Æthelred and his advisers, may have

---

[41] *ASC* C D E *s.a.* 1013.

[42] Darlington and McGurk, *John of Worcester, s.a.* 1006. *ASC* C D E *s.a.* 1006. Figure 8, p. 69, and Chapter 4, pp. 70–1, above.

[43] Whitelock, *Anglo-Saxon Wills,* no. XVII. 'The Will of Wulfric', pp. 46–51, and notes pp. 151–60. For Ælfhelm's family connections, see Figure 8, p. 69, above; see also Higham, *Death of Anglo-Saxon England*, p. 46.

[44] S.922, 924, 928.

[45] *ASC* C D E *s.a.* 1015. See Stenton, *Anglo-Saxon England*, pp. 397, 405–6, 420–1, for further information about Ælfgifu of Northampton; also, Howard, 'Swein Forkbeard's Invasions of England', Part One, Section 8, pp. 140–1.

driven English leaders there to encourage Swein to undertake an invasion.[46] We do not know the terms that had been agreed with Earl Uhtred of Northumbria, which may have become evident had Swein lived longer. Uhtred's background is explained by Stenton:

> From the fall of the ancient Northumbrian kingdom until the conquest of England by Cnut, the country between the Tees and the Scottish border seems to have been ruled almost continuously by the successive heads of the same native Northumbrian family.
> . . . in 1006 Malcolm, Kenneth's son, led a great army through northern Northumbria and besieged Durham. Waltheof, the reigning earl, was too old to take action, but Uhtred, his heir, annihilated the Scottish army in a battle . . .
> On several occasions the head of this house was appointed earl of Yorkshire by the king, and when Swein of Denmark landed in 1013, Uhtred, son of Waltheof, was clearly in power to the south as well as to the north of the Tees.[47]

Along with the rest of the country, the Northumbrians had suffered heavy taxation and had witnessed the failures of the king's ministers in dealing with Scandinavian invasions. By the end of the year 1012, Æthelred was under the political influence of a man, Eadric, whom northerners had no cause to trust following the events of 1006, and was under the military 'protection' of a Scandinavian army. There was a long history of Scandinavian influence and control in Northumbria prior to 954 and it must have seemed to Uhtred that submission to Swein was a safer option than opposing the Scandinavian armies, which both he and King Æthelred appeared powerless to resist. No doubt, he negotiated promises from Swein to safeguard his own position and that of his family in Northumbria.

Other than that there was a marriage agreement whereby Cnut married Ælfgifu, we do not know the terms agreed with the leading family in the midlands, which was headed at that time by Morcar. He was probably related, directly or through marriage, with Ealdorman Ælfhelm who was killed in 1006 shortly after his sons had been blinded. He had inherited property from Ælfhelm's brother, Wulfric, and was an important landowner and one of Æthelred's ministers.[48] He seems to have increased in favour with Æthelred and, by implication, with the influential Ealdorman Eadric because he received grants of estates from the king.[49] However, as Morcar's influence increased, and with the example of what had befallen Ælfhelm and his sons before him, he may

---

[46] Higham, *Death of Anglo-Saxon England*, pp. 56–9.
[47] Stenton, *Anglo-Saxon England*, pp. 417–18; also Whitelock, 'The Dealings of the Kings of England', pp. 70–88.
[48] Morcar attests charters in 1001 (S.898), 1004 (S.906), 1005 (S.911), c. 1012 (S.926) and 1013 (S.931). He signed in second place in the list of ministers in 1013. Keynes, *Diplomas*, table 8.
[49] Morcar received estates at Weston, Morley, Smalley, Kidsley, Crich and Ingleby in Derbyshire in 1009 (S.922); 'Ufre' in 1011 (S.924); Eckington, Derbyshire, in 1012 (S.928).

have felt insecure because he might have aroused the jealousy of Ealdorman Eadric Streona.[50]

There remains the question of how far Æthelred, Eadric and Thorkell were aware of Swein's plans. It would have been impossible for Swein to disguise the fact that he was gathering an army and a fleet. Merchants would bring information of this nature to England. Æthelred and his ministers would have been particularly keen to know what was happening in Scandinavia and, thus, Æthelred should have been aware of the gathering threat in Denmark.

If Æthelred was aware of the threatened defection of Northumbria and the midlands, there is no record of any preparations to deal with it. Perhaps an attack on the south coast, the south-east, or London, was anticipated. Not since 993 had a Scandinavian army attacked Northumbria. Swein probably caused no surprise by sailing first to Sandwich, a port which provided harbour and other facilities ideally suited for marshalling a vast Danish fleet which presumably arrived over a period of several days. The fact that Swein then sailed to the Humber with his fleet rather than raiding inland seems to have surprised the English. Certainly, Thorkell, who had a fleet in the Thames defending the river approach to London, appears to have done nothing to prevent the enemy fleet sailing up the coast and past the mouth of the Thames. It seems that Earl Uhtred attended King Æthelred earlier in 1013 because he witnessed one of his charters.[51] This is further evidence that Æthelred had no suspicion of Uhtred's imminent defection. Morcar also attested a charter in 1013 and grants of land to Morcar as late as 1012 suggest that the king had no reason to suspect him. It must be concluded, therefore, that Æthelred was not aware of Swein's intentions.

Thorkell the Tall's position deserves some consideration. If, as is possible, he had acknowledged Swein's authority as recently as 1009 and again in c. 1011, it would be surprising if Swein had not included Thorkell in his diplomatic 'offensive'. Since Æthelred did not appear to know of Swein's intentions in the north, it may safely be presumed that, if Swein approached Thorkell, he did not reveal his detailed plans to him. Swein could have negotiated for Thorkell's support for an attack on London without revealing his plan to conquer the north first. There are no records suggesting negotiations with Thorkell, but there is some evidence in the *Gesta Normannorum Ducum* of William of Jumièges that Swein entered into negotiations with Richard II of Normandy,[52] so there may have been wide-ranging diplomatic contacts by Swein. In such negotiations, Swein was, no doubt, just as keen to misinform potential enemy allies as he was to gain their neutrality and friendship.

Whatever the details of Swein's diplomatic activity, nearly half the country had agreed to accept Swein as king soon after he appeared with his army. The

---

[50] It was commonly rumoured that Eadric had been responsible for the treacherous killing of Ælfhelm: Darlington and McGurk, *John of Worcester, s.a.* 1006.

[51] S.931.

[52] Brown, *Norman Conquest*, p. 5.

agreements were quickly put into effect so that Swein was in a position to lead an invasion of the country south of Watling Street, reinforced by the resources of the Danelaw.

The Chronicles of Croyland

The chronicles of Croyland Abbey (Lincs.) may be useful in providing some evidence of how Swein administered the territories that submitted to him initially and also information about his campaign itinerary.

The original chronicle is supposed to have been written by Ingulph of Croyland, who was abbot from 1075 to 1109.[53] It commences with a brief reference to the reign of the Mercian king, Penda. The first date mentioned is 664 when 'the monastery at Medeshamsted' was founded.[54] This monastery was known later as Burgh and subsequently Peterborough. The chronicle quotes in full a charter, dated 716, for the foundation of Croyland Abbey by King Æthelbald of Mercia and it quotes a charter, dated 793, in which King Offa confirmed the possessions of Croyland. The chronicle continues, recounting major historical events, relating them to local events and frequently quoting in detail charters of various kings confirming property rights. The chronicle terminates in 1091 but there are continuations by other writers until the year 1486. Parts of these records were mutilated and several sections were lost. The then earliest extant manuscript was destroyed in a fire in the Cotton Library in 1731 leaving a sixteenth-century transcript, and two printed editions dating from the late sixteenth and early seventeenth centuries.

In about 1415, the chronicle supposedly written by Ingulph was used as the basis for a successful court action in London establishing the property rights of Croyland Abbey in a dispute with the people of Spalding and others. The action took two years to prepare and it seems likely that Ingulph's chronicle was itself 'prepared' to some extent during this period for the purposes of litigation. The abbey no longer possessed all the charters necessary to support its legal claims, and the chronicle was produced as evidence of the existence and the terms of the charters and was accepted as such. Suspiciously, there are various anachronisms in Ingulph's Chronicle. Also, the continuations of the chronicle make no mention of the charters in Ingulph's Chronicle, although there are passages where it would have been appropriate to do so.[55] The charters, as they stand, are considered spurious by many historians and this casts doubt upon the value of the other material in Ingulph's Chronicle.[56] Although there is no firm evidence for the existence of an original manuscript by Ingulph, one may have existed

---

[53] Riley, *Ingulphus's Chronicle*, p. xvi.
[54] Riley, *Ingulphus's Chronicle*, p. 2.
[55] Riley, *Ingulphus's Chronicle*, p. x.
[56] The royal charters which relate to Croyland are recorded in S.82, 135, 162, 189, 200, 213, 538, 741, 965. S.1294 is a charter of Dunstan, though it is recorded as being signed by the king as well. Other charters are quoted that are of more general application, such as S.92 and S.314 and some donations by noblemen are supported by charters.

since the clerks preparing the evidence during the two years leading to the successful conclusion of litigation in 1415 must have had some written source available to them. The supposed chronicle of Ingulph records that, in 974, Abbot Turgar had a history of Croyland prepared covering the period from its foundation until the fourteenth year of the reign of King Edgar.[57] This local information, together with the *ASC* and other accounts of the time, presumably provided the basis for Ingulph's Chronicle in its extant version.

Ingulph's Chronicle provides an account of local events in 993 when the Vikings were attacking the east coast,[58] and of local events when Vikings were ravaging the 'wild fens' in 1010. These seem realistic and can be identified with accounts in *ASC* C D E. The chronicle describes high levels of taxation and a specific impost for building ships at all the ports. The description of how taxes were exacted suggests there may have been some imaginative addition to the extant record, but the underlying facts accord with the *ASC*. Of particular interest is an account in the chronicle of Swein's invasion in 1013. Obviously, it was written some time after the event, and it is relevant that the Abbot of Croyland was accused of being 'a traitor to his country' after Æthelred's restoration in 1014.[59]

In 1013, Croyland and its possessions were in territory that King Swein would have regarded as friendly and covered by the terms of the submissions made to him at Gainsborough. However, an army of several thousand men, even if 'friendly', would have had an impact on local communities and would have caused considerable damage to property, which they might have commandeered on a temporary basis. It was probably politic for the original chronicler to exaggerate the damage done by Swein's invasions and also to describe the taxes which they paid to Swein's representatives at Lincoln as fines and exactions.[60] The list of properties recorded as damaged during Swein's invasion belonged to the monasteries of Croyland, St Pega and Burgh and the properties are included in the chronicle in no particular order other than to relate them to an appropriate monastery. However, when all these properties are plotted on a map, it is quite clear that we have a record of a route and it may be that this was indeed part of the route taken by King Swein and his army; it is shown in Figure 13.

Swein Forkbeard's Campaign of Conquest

The *ASC* provides an account of Swein's invasion of southern England:

> When he perceived that all the people had submitted to him, he gave orders that his army should be provisioned and provided with horses, and then he

---

[57] Riley, *Ingulphus's Chronicle*, p. 97.
[58] Riley, *Ingulphus's Chronicle*, pp. 111–12. The editor's page heading suggests the year 992, but 993 seems the more likely date, to accord with *ASC* C D E *s.a.* 993.
[59] Riley, *Ingulphus's Chronicle*, p. 115.
[60] Riley, *Ingulphus's Chronicle*, p. 114.

**Figure 13. Initial stages of King Swein's campaign route
as indicated in the Chronicle of Croyland Abbey**

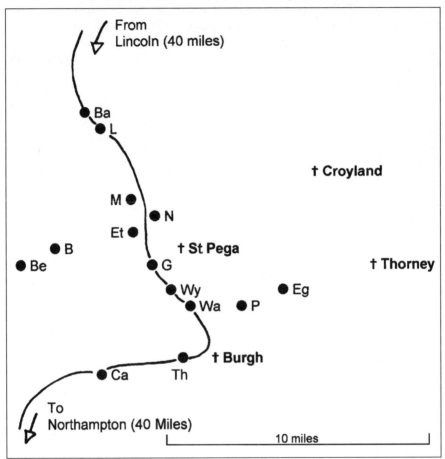

Possessions of Croyland
Ba Baston;   L Longtoft;   Croyland (Crowland)

Possessions of St Pega
M Makesey;   N Northumburtham;   Et Etton;   Peykirk (St Pega);
  G Glinton;   B Badyington;   Be Bernake

Possessions of Burgh (Peterborough)
Wy Wytheryngton;   Wa Walton;   P Paston;   Eg Ege;   Burgh (Peterborough)
*Didisthorp;   Th Thorpe;   Ca Castre

Spellings are from Riley, *Ingulph's Chronicle*, pp. 112–14

*Didisthorp is 'in' and Thorpe 'near' Peterborough: Mellows, *The Peterborough
Chronicle of High Candidus*, index

turned southward with his full forces ['fyrde' not *here*] and left the ships (and the hostages) in charge of his son Cnut.[61]

The words 'and the hostages' are omitted from *ASC* D, probably a copying error since versions C E F contain the phrase. John of Worcester adds that Swein turned south against the southern Mercians and indicates that Swein's army was reinforced from the areas which had submitted to him.[62] The use of the word *fyrd* to describe Swein's army supports John's account, since it is the word applied to an army raised locally.

Much may be learned about Swein's invasion of the south by following his campaign route, as shown in Figure 14, p. 114. Although Scandinavian forces were capable of travelling across country, the conduct of a major campaign required the movement of equipment and supplies on a large scale and it is safe to assume that Swein made good use of available roads. When the evidence in the *ASC* and in Ingulph's Chronicle is compared with the analysis of the Roman road network in Margary's *Roman Roads in Britain* and the roads known to have been used in Anglo-Saxon times in Hill's *An Atlas of Anglo-Saxon England*, there is sufficient information to map most of Swein's route with a reasonable degree of confidence.

Swein had stationed his fleet at Gainsborough whilst he awaited the submission of the leading nobles in the northern parts of the country. The *ASC* says that Cnut was left in charge of the ships and hostages. It was more than that of course. Figure 12, p. 105, shows the extent of the territory that had thrown off its allegiance to Æthelred and had recognised Swein as king. Cnut was left in charge of this territory, which was, arguably, larger, wealthier and politically more complex than the kingdom of Denmark. Through his marriage, Cnut was personally allied to the leading family in the midlands and his advisers presumably included Earl Uhtred and Morcar as well as Danish followers of King Swein. His remit would have been to retain control of the northern provinces, encourage loyalty to the new royal family and raise supplies and men to reinforce his father's campaign, which was aimed at the conquest of southern England. For a young man of about twenty-three it was a demanding undertaking. The alternative view of his date of birth would have made him about fourteen years old at this time.

Swein's route south took him through friendly territory. Using road and river transport he first made his way to Lincoln.[63] This important town, situated on the main north-south road, probably became his administrative headquarters. Cnut sent out messengers, in his father's name, demanding tribute and taxes that had to be paid at Lincoln.[64] Since Swein's army was in friendly territory, it was presumably kept outside the towns and the force protecting the ships would have

---

[61] *ASC* C D E *s.a.* 1013, my translation, though very close to Whitelock, *EHD*.

[62] 'sibi lectos auxiliarios de deditis sumens': Darlington and McGurk, *John of Worcester, s.a.* 1013.

[63] Figure 14, p. 114. Margary, *Roman Roads in Britain*, map 7 (a); Hill, *Atlas*, map 234.

[64] Riley, *Ingulphus's Chronicle*, p. 114. Lincoln was not the only administrative centre used by Cnut and Swein: see notes on Thetford in Hart, *The Danelaw*, p. 52.

Figure 14. King Swein's campaign route: 1013

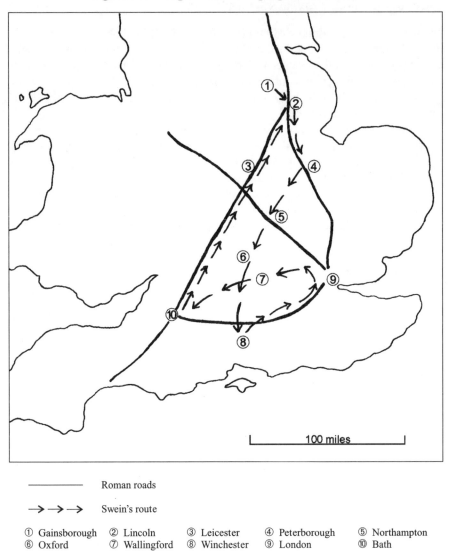

———————   Roman roads

→ → →   Swein's route

① Gainsborough ② Lincoln   ③ Leicester   ④ Peterborough ⑤ Northampton
⑥ Oxford   ⑦ Wallingford ⑧ Winchester   ⑨ London   ⑩ Bath

remained at Gainsborough. However, Cnut and his advisers, with a sufficient force of men for garrison and protection duties, would have had to operate from an urban centre to collect taxes and organise logistical support for the army.

From Lincoln, Swein's army travelled down Ermine Street towards Peterborough. At Ancaster, it turned off Ermine Street and followed King Street through Bourne, which was a more direct route to Peterborough, keeping closer to the fen land.[65] This part of the route is evidenced by Ingulph's Chronicle. The

---

[65] Figure 14. Margary, *Roman Roads in Britain*, map 8.

journey from Lincoln to Peterborough[66] would probably have taken about five days. Five days allows for the army, its equipment and supplies travelling at about ten miles a day. A lightly equipped vanguard, especially on horseback, could travel much more quickly; indeed, the whole army could have been moved more rapidly if occasion demanded, but this was the start of what might have been expected to be a long campaign.

At Peterborough, Swein was able to draw upon the resources of a monastery which was amongst the richest in the country[67] as well as upon nearby Stamford which had already sent hostages to him.[68] Although at first Swein's army travelled through friendly territory which had submitted to the Danish king, it does not mean that the Scandinavian army was welcomed nor does it mean that the army did not cause considerable fear and disruption. The account in Ingulph's Chronicle says that the abbot and brethren from the monastery of St Pega, which was on Swein's campaign route, sought refuge in the monastery at Croyland. Holy relics and other treasures were removed from the monastery at Peterborough and taken by the abbot to the monastery at Thorney for safe keeping whilst the prior, taking with him the arm of St Oswald, escaped to the island of Ely. The abbot was perhaps wise in being unavailable to greet King Swein: the outcome of the invasion could not be foreseen and disloyalty to King Æthelred might attract drastic punishment. This certainly seems to have been the case as regards the monastery of St Pega and, to a lesser extent, the monastery at Croyland where the abbot, according to the Croyland chronicle, remained behind and made substantial payments to King Swein – albeit unwillingly.[69] Godric, abbot of Croyland was in danger of being brought before King Æthelred accused of being a traitor. He avoided this, but the monastery had to bribe one of Ealdorman Eadric's followers to be its 'guardian and protector' at court.[70] The abbot of Peterborough moved on from Thorney and joined Æthelred's court. At the end of the year he went into exile with the royal family.[71]

At Peterborough, Swein was about a hundred miles from London[72] and so was in a position to mount an attack upon the city within a week. No doubt Æthelred and his advisers were making preparations to face a possible attack from the north at this stage.

However, Swein's immediate plans lay elsewhere. He planned an attack on Oxford, which was nearer and would encourage the submission of the south midlands.[73] The route chosen probably took Swein's army via Northampton,

---

[66] Hill, *Atlas*, map 231. Margary, *Roman Roads in Britain*, map 7 (a) and p. 190, for a description of this route.

[67] The Domesday valuation made it the eleventh richest in terms of gross income: Hill, *Atlas*, map 249.

[68] *ASC* C D E *s.a.* 1013; it was one of the 'Five Boroughs'.

[69] Riley, *Ingulphus's Chronicle*, p. 114. The monks of St Pega eventually lost the site of their monastery and their manors: *ibid.* pp. 113, 116, 126–8.

[70] *Ibid.* pp. 114–16.

[71] *ASC* C D E *s.a.* 1013.

[72] Hill, *Atlas*, maps 231, 229; Margary, *Roman Roads in Britain*, maps 7 (a), 7 (b) and p. 189.

[73] In 1066, Oxford had maybe over 5,000 inhabitants and 'it must then have been the largest and most prosperous town in midland England': Darby, *Domesday England*, p. 306.

which the bulk of his army should have been able to reach within five days. It was a route that followed the river Nene, through Castor, Irthlingborough and Irchester.[74] An alternative possible route was via Bedford, which would have taken longer and taken Swein away from friendly territory sooner and so must be considered less likely. Also, Swein had allied himself to an important land-owning family in Northamptonshire by the marriage of his son, Cnut, to the heiress Ælfgifu of Northampton. From there, Swein invaded the south and permitted his army to ravage at will:

> When he had crossed the Watling Street, they did the greatest damage that any army could do. He then turned to Oxford, and the citizens at once submitted and gave hostages; and from there to Winchester, where they did the same.[75]

John of Worcester describes the great damage done by the army after it crossed Watling Street and the fear inspired by Swein which made the citizens of Winchester submit quickly.

Within five days of leaving Northampton Swein's army could have been in force outside Oxford, which quickly submitted. A route from Northampton would have taken him across Watling Street near Towcester and then via Alchester to Oxford.[76] Swein's army inspired great fear by their actions and the citizens were no doubt influenced by the memory of the sacking of their town only four years earlier by a Scandinavian army.[77] From Oxford, Swein's army moved south against Winchester, a journey which could have been made in about five days. The route would have followed the north-south road, through Dorchester and Silchester.[78] It was a route that took the army past the important river crossing and fortified town of Wallingford. *ASC* C D E *s.a.* 1013 says that he went through Wallingford later in his campaign but does not mention it at this point. It would have been out of keeping with his strategy for Swein to have ignored Wallingford and the possibility that he captured the town at this stage in his campaign should be considered.[79] Whether or not he took Wallingford, he continued to Winchester, which, like Oxford, quickly submitted. At this point, Swein had gained the submission of much of southern Mercia and much of the West-Saxon heartland. At each stage on his campaign itinerary Swein's army was in a position to threaten London. Its route from Northampton (or possibly

---

[74] 'Five days' being about fifty miles at about ten miles a day. Hill, *Atlas*, map 231; Margary, *Roman Roads in Britain*, map 5 and pp. 187–8. There is little evidence of the route today, particularly around Northampton. The best guide is the *Ordnance Survey: Roman Britain South Sheet*, 4th edition (revised) 1994.

[75] *ASC* C D E *s.a.* 1013, Whitelock's translation in *EHD*.

[76] 'Five days' being about fifty miles at about ten miles a day. Hill, *Atlas*, map 231. Margary, *Roman Roads in Britain*, map 5 and pp. 162–5.

[77] *ASC* C D E *s.a.* 1009.

[78] 'Five days' being about 50 miles at about 10 miles a day. Hill, *Atlas*, map 228. Margary, *Roman Roads in Britain*, maps 5, 3, 4 and pp. 89–90, 163–6.

[79] The strategic position of Wallingford may be judged from Hill, *Atlas*, map 228, and from the Ordnance Survey, *Roman Britain South Sheet*, 4th edition (revised) 1994 (this version of the map superimposes Roman roads and places over a modern map). See also, Hill and Rumble, *Defence of Wessex*, pp. 219–21; and Darby, *Domesday England*, p. 307.

Bedford) to Winchester described the arc of a circle with London at its centre, so the army remained within a week's march of the city.

The Domesday survey indicates that, after London, the most populated towns in the country were Winchester, York, Lincoln, Norwich, Thetford and Oxford.[80] Other than London, all these major towns submitted quickly to Swein, four voluntarily and the other two under threat.

The information that Swein's army ravaged the country once it had crossed Watling Street implies that it treated the Danelaw as friendly territory. This is in keeping with what was said above about the agreements made between Swein and the northern leaders.

That Oxford and Winchester submitted quickly, although they were fortified towns,[81] is an indication of the fear that this army inspired, of its overwhelming power and of the expectation of the citizens that no English army was likely to come to their rescue.

There were good roads between Winchester and London, going through the important Roman centre of Silchester and crossing the Thames at Staines, and thus the army was within seven days of London.[82] Swein then led an attack on London. Only there did Swein meet substantial resistance:

> He then turned eastward to London, and many of his host were drowned in the Thames because they did not trouble to find a bridge. When he got to the fortified place the citizens would not yield, but resisted with utter valour, because King Æthelred was inside and Thorkell with him.[83]

This was the first major setback to Swein's campaign. The words of the *ASC* suggest that many of his men attempted, unsuccessfully, to ford the River Thames rather than use the bridge, or bridges since there may have been more than one, at Staines.[84] When he saw that London was well defended, Swein was not tempted into a long siege:

> Then King Swein turned from there to Wallingford, and so west across the Thames to Bath, where he stayed with his army ['fyrde']. Then Ealdorman Æthelmær came there, and with him the western thegns, and all submitted to Swein, and they gave him hostages.[85]

Determining this part of the army's journey presents some difficulties, because Wallingford would have been on a direct route for Bath only if the army had been going across country. It is possible, therefore, that Swein was leading his army north along Watling Street and then changed direction, going from

---

[80] See Darby, *Domesday England*, p. 303.
[81] Hill and Rumble, *Defence of Wessex*, pp. 211–13, 225–6.
[82] Hill, *Atlas*, maps 228, 229; Margary, *Roman Roads in Britain*, map 3, 4 and pp. 84–90; 'seven days' being about seventy miles at about ten miles a day.
[83] *ASC* C D E *s.a.* 1013, my translation.
[84] Margary, *Roman Roads in Britain*, pp. 85–6.
[85] *ASC* C D E *s.a.* 1013, my translation.

Dunstable to Wallingford, from where he could travel south or south-west to join the main Silchester to Bath route.[86]

Wallingford and Bath were important fortified sites,[87] but the *ASC* does not refer to resistance at either place. Wallingford may have already been under Swein's control, since his route from Oxford to Winchester may have taken him through the town. Swein remained at Bath until he had received the submission of the south-west provinces. The reference to Ealdorman Æthelmær leading the submission of the western thegns is significant. He seems to have retired from public life in the period 1005/6, when many other leading advisers of the king were replaced, causing Keynes to reflect upon the possibility of 'something approaching a palace revolution'.[88] That he was persuaded to leave his monastery at Eynsham and lead the submission to King Swein was a political and diplomatic coup. He was the king's kinsman, the son of Ealdorman Æthelweard, and very influential.

After this, the *ASC* says that Swein 'turned northwards to his ships'. Bath is on the old Roman Fosse Way which led directly to Lincoln. Swein could have used this route to return via Leicester, another friendly fortified town, to Lincoln.[89] The journey to Leicester was just over a hundred miles and the journey from Leicester to Lincoln was about fifty miles so the full journey, travelling at about ten miles a day, could have taken about a fortnight, depending upon whether or not his army stayed for any length of time at places such as Leicester. In Lincoln he was at Cnut's administrative headquarters and within easy reach of his fleet at Gainsborough:

> When he had thus overcome everything, he then turned northward to his ships, and all the nation regarded him as full king. And after that the citizens of London submitted and gave hostages, for they were afraid that he would destroy them. Then Swein demanded full payment and provisions for his army ['hære' or 'here'] that winter, and Thorkell demanded the same for the army ['here'] which lay at Greenwich, and despite that they ravaged as often as they pleased. Then nothing availed this nation, neither from the south nor from the north.[90]

The *ASC* refers to *here* in relation to payment and provisions, indicating it was only required for the *lið*s, which had invaded England with Swein. The native element of Swein's army presumably dispersed and returned home for the winter months. John of Worcester changes the order of information to describe the provisioning of Swein's fleet and Thorkell's fleet and their subsequent behaviour after saying how Æthelred and his family went into exile. The *ASC* suggests that provisions were demanded and supplied to both fleets whilst Æthelred was

---

[86] Hill, *Atlas*, map 228, noting the Icknield Way. Margary, *Roman Roads in Britain*, maps 3, 7 (b). This part of the route is best followed on the Ordnance Survey, *Roman Britain South Sheet*, 4th edition (revised) 1994.

[87] Hill and Rumble, *Defence of Wessex*, pp. 190–2, 219–21.

[88] Keynes, *Diplomas*, p. 211; also, Chapter 4, pp. 70–1, above.

[89] Hill, *Atlas*, maps 227, 231; Margary, *Roman Roads in Britain*, maps 5, 7 (a) and pp. 141–3, 150–3, 218–21; Collen, *Britannia Saxonica*, p. 10.

[90] *ASC* C D E *s.a.* 1013, my translation.

still in England, and this is more likely to have been the case since Æthelred did not leave until after Christmas and the armies would have needed supplying in their camps long before then. John adds some illustrative thoughts that explain the fears which impelled the Londoners to submit. He also makes an aside about Swein, saying he was a tyrant and implying that he was not a fit person to rule.[91]

Whether King Swein would have established himself as a successful king of England and whether annalists and skalds might have praised him and his rule over an empire of the north cannot be known. Equally, we cannot know whether John of Worcester's assessment of Swein as a tyrant who was unfit to rule would have proved justified. King Swein Forkbeard died in February 1014, only a few weeks after the submission of London and the exile of England's former king, Æthelred II.

The *ASC* account of events[92] following Swein's death suggests that his rule was not firmly established and that his son, Cnut, and Swein's army were driven from England with relative ease. According to this account, the leading nobles in England negotiated King Æthelred's return to England shortly after Swein's death. Æthelred said:

> that he would be a gracious lord to them, and reform all the things which they all hated; and all the things that had been said and done against him should be forgiven, on condition that they all unanimously turned to him without treachery. And complete friendship was then established with oath and pledge on both sides, and they [the nobles, 'ecclesiastical and lay'] pronounced every Danish king an outlaw from England for ever.[93]

Only the people of Lindsey continued to support the Scandinavian invaders. They and Cnut's army were surprised by the rapid advance of an army commanded by King Æthelred himself. Lindsey was:

> ravaged and burnt, and all the men who could be got at were killed; and Cnut put out to sea with his fleet, and thus the wretched people were betrayed by him.[94]

Although the *ASC* refers to King Æthelred's army it says nothing about its composition, whether it was a national *fyrd*, or a mercenary army, including the men of Thorkell's fleet and other *liðs*, perhaps under the leadership of St Olaf. The *ASC* says that the enemy forces were surprised and it makes no mention of a battle and no mention of having to recapture fortified towns from the Scandinavian forces.

In 1986, Professor Lund wrote about the *ASC* account:

> Soon after his final victory Swein died in Gainsborough and the fleet then elected Cnut king. The English witan, however, decided to recall Æthelred

---

91 Darlington and McGurk, *John of Worcester*, s.a. 1013: 'si iure queat rex vocari, qui fere cuncta tirannice faciebat'.
92 *ASC* C D E *s.a.* 1014.
93 Whitelock's translation in *EHD*.
94 *Ibid.*.

from Normandy rather than to transfer their loyalty (which they had previously sworn to Swein and for which they had given him hostages) to Cnut. In addition, they banished all Danish kings from England – and it is one of the ironies of history that to express this they had recourse to a Danish loanword: *and æfre ælcne denisc(n)e cyning utlagade of engla lande gewædon*. In constitutional terms, this, from an English point of view, reduced Cnut to being simply the leader of a Viking fleet which they would have to get rid of, one way or another. As far as the conquest of England was concerned Cnut had to start from scratch – and made an unsuccessful start, while Thorkell got his employer back and was paid handsomely: £21,000 were handed over to the army at Sandwich.[95]

However, it seems very possible that the *ASC* is disguising the truth by omitting important information. If the chronicler's purpose in writing the annals of the reigns of King Æthelred and King Edmund included emphasising the differences between an unfortunate father and a decisive, warlike son, it could not easily describe a successful campaign of conquest led by King Æthelred. Yet there are indications that there was such a campaign in 1014. The argument in favour of this is based on:

(a)   Swein had taken a firm control over the north and south of England,
(b)   written evidence for the campaigns of King Æthelred's army.

(a) Swein's control over England

Firstly, there is the evidence of the *ASC* that 'all the nation recognised him as full king' and that 'London submitted and gave hostages'.[96] Secondly, there is the evidence that the people north of Watling Street had submitted to Swein when he was at Gainsborough, so switching their allegiance from King Æthelred. The *ASC s.a.* 1013 only mentions the submission of the Northumbrian leader, Uhtred. However, it has been observed that Cnut married into the most influential family in the Danelaw and it has been argued that leaders, such as Morcar and Ulfcytel, would almost certainly have represented the people when submission was made to King Swein. The evidence that Archbishop Wulfstan of York was one of these leaders was examined above. Thirdly, there is evidence that the most important strategic strongholds had been garrisoned with men loyal to King Swein and his son, Cnut. This evidence is examined below in relation to King Æthelred's campaign to re-conquer England. Fourthly, there is evidence in *ASC* F and in the *Encomium* that Cnut was accepted, in succession to Swein, as king of England.[97]

(b) The campaigns of Æthelred's army

Events following King Swein's death are put in a different perspective by an account supplied by two skalds, Ottar and Sigvat, who knew St Olaf and who wrote verses about his early campaigns before he became king of Norway.

[95] Lund, 'Armies', p. 116.
[96] *ASC* C D E *s.a.* 1013, Whitelock's translation in *EHD*.
[97] Howard, 'Swein Forkbeard's Invasions of England', Part One, Section 2 for *ASC* F; Part One, Section 8 for the *Encomium*.

Whilst Campbell and others have acknowledged that Sigvat and Ottar were well placed to provide an accurate account of events, probably from St Olaf's personal recollection, doubt has been expressed about the chronology of their verses, largely, it seems to me, because the verses do not allow Olaf a fifteen-year reign in Norway. The length of Olaf's reign is stated to be fifteen years in *Heimskringla*, on the authority of Ari.[98] But *Heimskringla* is equally specific about time spans, such as the reign of King Cnut, which run concurrently with Olaf's reign, and these other time spans are demonstrably inaccurate by about five years. It is my belief, based on a detailed analysis of *Heimskringla*'s chronology,[99] that there is sufficient evidence to demonstrate the real possibility that Olaf's reign extended for between ten and eleven years and that his skalds' accounts of his participation in a reconquest of England by King Æthelred are therefore possible and realistic. It follows that Campbell's transposition of events, which are described in the verses, to an earlier period is unnecessary and there is a case for a re-examination of his conclusions.[100]

Given that London was the key to the rich Thames valley and that Scandinavian armies, including those commanded by Swein himself, had failed to take London over a period of twenty years since Swein's first attack on the town, it is to be expected that King Swein would have garrisoned London with men he knew to be loyal to him.

Following Sigvat and Ottar, therefore, it appears that London not only submitted to Swein but that the fortification in London and the fortification on the opposite bank of the Thames at Southwark were both garrisoned by Swein's men. Snorri uses these verses in *Heimskringla* to support his story of how King Æthelred returned to England and recaptured London from the Danes. St Olaf was only one of Æthelred's army commanders, but he and his *lið* volunteered to undertake the difficult mission of destroying London Bridge, an action which resulted in the capture of London by Æthelred's army.[101] It seems that the fortified London Bridge not only controlled the Thames but also provided access between the fortifications at Southwark and London This made it almost impossible for an attacking army to cut off the defenders of London from supplies and reinforcements. St Olaf's destruction of a section of the bridge removed these advantages from the defenders.

Since England north of Watling Street had submitted to Swein without a fight, their leaders would have had good reason to fear the restoration of a king they had betrayed. They might, therefore, have been expected to remain loyal, initially at least, to their allegiance to the Danish dynasty. The verses of Sigvat and Ottar tell us that King Æthelred's army had to fight and win a battle in East Anglia.[102] Snorri explains that King Æthelred's army had to fight against an

[98] See Appendix 1, below.
[99] See Appendix 1, below.
[100] Howard, 'Swein Forkbeard's Invasions of England', Part One, Section 8 regarding the chronology, and Part Two, Section 16 quoting Campbell's conclusions.
[101] Hollander, *Heimskringla*, cc. 12–13, pp. 251–4, including the verses.
[102] *Ibid.* c. 14, p. 254. Hollander says 'Ella's offspring' is a kenning for 'the English'. In this he is following Margaret Ashdown's interpretation. However, she noted that Ella was a

army commanded by Ulfcytel in East Anglia.[103] If the East Anglian leaders had declared their support for King Swein in 1013, Ulfcytel might have been expected to be foremost amongst them.

Snorri then tells us that:

> At that time large parts of England were brought under the sway of King Æthelred; still the Company of the Thingmen and the Danes occupied many strongholds, and wide stretches of land were still held by them.[104]

Snorri continues to explain how other towns and territory, including Canterbury, were recovered by St Olaf on behalf of King Æthelred. He supports his account with further verses from Sigvat and Ottar. Snorri concludes by telling us that St Olaf was in England for three years on this occasion, a reminder that, according to the *Heimskringla* account, St Olaf came to England whilst King Swein was alive. However, it is probable that he chose to join his old comrade in arms, Thorkell the Tall, at this time, evidence that Thorkell's *lið* remained in England during Æthelred's exile and that King Æthelred may have been planning a speedy return.

If 'the Danes occupied many strongholds', it may safely be assumed that Oxford, Winchester, Wallingford and Bath, as well as London, were among them. Swein would not have accepted the surrender of these places and then continued on his way without either destroying their fortifications or filling them with men who were entirely loyal to him. This would have been in addition to taking hostages.

From this perspective, Swein, who according the *ASC* was regarded by all the nation as full king, had conquered the south of England and secured the key strategic locations. He was prepared to deal with an invasion if King Æthelred chose to attempt to return supported by mercenary forces, such as St Olaf's *lið*, and by Thorkell's army ('here'). The *ASC* indicates that the latter had remained at Greenwich, but it may well have accompanied Æthelred to the Isle of Wight before Christmas 1013, since it would have been unsafe for King Æthelred to travel over land that had submitted to King Swein; so he and his family may have had to travel by sea under the protection of Thorkell's ships. Also, if London and the south-east had submitted to King Swein, it must mean either that they had obliged Thorkell and Æthelred to depart or that the old king had left of his own accord, leaving London little option but to sue for peace from Swein. In either event, Thorkell is unlikely to have remained with his fleet in enemy territory where he might have been trapped by Swein's fleet and army in the next campaigning season.

Given the evidence that the *ASC* may at times have been deliberately selective in what it said in order to present an account of the reigns of King Æthelred and his son, King Edmund Ironside, that was biased for political reasons, the

---

Northumbrian king who was killed by Scandinavian invaders. In context, this may be significant, since an army, fighting in East Anglia against a returning King Æthelred, might be expected to have included Northumbrians. See also, Fell, 'Víkingarvísur', p. 116.

[103] Hollander, *Heimskringla*, c. 14, pp. 254–5.

[104] *Ibid.* Hollander says that 'the Company of the Thingmen' was 'King Knút's bodyguard'.

possibilities that England was firmly under the control of King Swein by January 1014, and that the *ASC* was deliberately reticent about the extent of the fighting that took place before Æthelred was restored to his throne must be taken seriously. If true, they would indicate that Æthelred was able to return partly due to the ability of his generals, such as Thorkell and Olaf, and partly due to the inept handling of the defence of England by Cnut and his advisers. This would account for an apparent attempt in the *Encomium* to disguise the extent of Cnut's failure at this time, and also to explain why Cnut returned to Denmark with so few of the army which had originally accompanied Swein and Cnut in their invasion of England the previous year.[105]

---

[105] Howard, 'Swein Forkbeard's Invasions of England', Part One, Section 8.

7

Thorkell the Tall and the English Succession

Thorkell the Tall in 1014

Before his death, Swein Forkbeard had been acknowledged as king of England: 'all the nation regarded him as full king' and 'the citizens of London submitted and gave hostages'.[1] King Æthelred, with his family and supporters, had been driven into exile. They had taken valuables and money with them and were apparently being allowed to use Normandy as a base from which to mount an invasion to recover the throne. At some point, during his period of exile, King Æthelred seems to have come to an arrangement whereby St Olaf, a future king of Norway, and his *lið* agreed to support an invasion of England.

In England, King Swein disbanded his local levies for the winter season and commandeered money and provisions to sustain the Scandinavian *lið*s which were stationed on the River Trent, at Gainsborough.[2] In effect, the English nation was being asked to provide for the king's mercenary forces; an expensive undertaking, but not unique since King Æthelred had made similar demands on his subjects at various times during his long reign. However, such 'taxation' was particularly onerous coming at the end of a period of seven years during which the country had suffered at the hands of Scandinavian armies led by Tostig, Heming, Eglaf, Thorkell[3] and, finally, Swein Forkbeard, as well as suffering from national armies, raised on King Æthelred's orders, foraging for provisions.[4]

According to the *Anglo-Saxon Chronicle*, Thorkell remained in England during the winter/spring of 1013/14 and demanded similar payment and provisions for the army which lay at Greenwich as Swein had obtained for his army in the north.[5] It is likely that the *ASC* is being strictly accurate when it says that Thorkell required payment and provisions for his army when it lay at Greenwich. However, as on previous occasions, it is possible that the *ASC* is omitting significant information to imply that Thorkell's forces remained at Greenwich until King Æthelred returned to England. For reasons discussed in the previous

---

[1]   *ASC* C D E *s.a.* 1013, Whitelock's translation in Whitelock *EHD*.
[2]   *ASC* C D E *s.a.* 1013 and Chapter 6, pp. 118–19, above.
[3]   Tostig, Heming, Eglaf and Thorkell: Chapter 5, pp. 72–7, above.
[4]   *ASC* C D E *s.a.* 1006: 'and the English levy caused the people of the country every sort of harm so that they profited neither from the native army nor the foreign army', Whitelock's translation in *EHD*.
[5]   *ASC* C D E *s.a.* 1013.

chapter, it seems likely that Thorkell and his army went to the Isle of Wight, with King Æthelred, before Christmas, 1013. Thorkell could not have retained his position at Greenwich with any degree of safety after London had surrendered to King Swein unless he and his army had submitted to the Danish king. The events of 1014 and Thorkell's part in them seem to preclude this possibility, although an early version of the *Encomium* may have implied that Thorkell was loyal to Swein's son, King Cnut, during the period 1014 to 1015; the *Encomium*, a politically motivated account of events, is deliberately ambiguous about Thorkell's activities during the period immediately after King Swein's death.[6] The *ASC* implication that this army remained at Greenwich seems deliberate. In the annal for 1014, a no doubt grateful King Æthelred is said to have 'ordered 21,000 pounds to be paid to the army which lay at Greenwich'.[7] Again a strict interpretation of the words in the *ASC* may be deemed accurate, since Greenwich was a suitable place for Æthelred to maintain a mercenary army after his re-conquest of England, but this second reference to Greenwich, in context, carries the implication that it was Thorkell's army and that it had remained on the Thames throughout the period of Æthelred's exile.

Thorkell did not accompany his paymaster, King Æthelred, to Normandy and the evidence that St Olaf came to England in the autumn before Swein's death suggests that Thorkell and his Scandinavian army remained in England.[8] The Isle of Wight had long been regarded as a safe haven by the Scandinavians and the *ASC* account of Æthelred's stay there for the Christmas festival before he retired to Normandy is strong evidence that it was held by forces loyal to Thorkell.

Snorri Sturluson informs us that St Olaf and Thorkell the Tall had operated together off the Danish coast, making piratical attacks on shipping in that area.[9] This was in 1010 or 1011,[10] before Thorkell returned to England to avenge his brother's death. Since they had been allies so recently and since St Olaf opposed the regime that ruled his native Norway with Swein Forkbeard's support, he and his *lið* probably joined Thorkell's forces when they came to England. The likelihood of this being the case is reinforced by the fact that St Olaf and his *lið* fought on behalf of King Æthelred when he returned to England, after Swein's death, to regain his throne. The rapidity with which Cnut was driven from the country after his father's death suggests that preparations had been made during his father's lifetime for a renewal of the war by Æthelred's supporters.

Of course, Thorkell's position in the winter of 1013/14 was ambiguous. He remained in England, a land which had acknowledged Swein as king, but apparently he had not submitted to Swein. Given Swein's previous record of having gained as much through alliances and negotiations as through warfare, it seems likely that he would have tried to open talks with Thorkell. On the other hand,

---

6   Howard, 'Swein Forkbeard's Invasions of England', pp. 136–8; also Campbell, *Encomium*, Bk II, cc. 1–2.
7   *ASC* C D E *s.a.* 1014, Whitelock's translation in *EHD*.
8   Hollander, *Heimskringla*, Saint Ólafs saga, c. 12; also Chapter 6, p. 122, above.
9   Hollander, *Heimskringla*, Saint Ólafs saga, c. 10.
10 Appendix 1, below, Table 5.

Thorkell had good reason to fear Swein, whom he had betrayed; he had probably been joined by St Olaf, who was opposed to Swein; King Æthelred was across the Channel with considerable financial resources recruiting support for a return to England. Swein Forkbeard's death in February 1014 may have resolved matters for Thorkell or simply made his chosen course of action easier to follow.

King Swein died in February 1014.[11] All the manuscripts, *ASC* C D E F, agree that he died at Candlemas on 'iii nonas Februarii'.[12] Candlemas falls on 2 February, 'iii nonas Februarii' is 3 February.[13] Whitelock translates 'Candlemas, on 3 February' without comment. Garmonsway translates 'Candlemas [2 February]' and Swanton translates 'Candlemas, 2 February'; both have footnotes to the effect that the manuscripts are wrong and should read 'iiii nonas Februarii', which is 2 February. However, this supposition by Garmonsway and Swanton that an error in *ÆE* was transmitted to the fair copy, *ASC* D, and via intermediate exemplars to *ASC* C E F seems unlikely since at least six scribes, all churchmen who would have known the date of Candlemas and recognised an anomaly, must have accepted the date of Swein's death for it to appear as it does in all our extant manuscripts. The division of the day and night into periods, at this time, was a complex matter and it seems possible that there was no common agreement as to the hour on which a new day commenced.[14] It follows that the dating of Swein's death is unlikely to be an error; in context the annalist/scribe was probably indicating that Swein died in the afternoon or evening on 2 February. Subsequent scribes who copied the dates recognised that it was an acceptable dating of the event. Snorri Sturluson wrote that 'King Svein had suddenly died at night in his bed'.[15] The encomiast says that he had time to settle his affairs before he died, but generally is in agreement with Snorri.[16] More lurid accounts of his death prevailed in England and are to be found in some twelfth-century English chronicles. These accounts blame Swein for demanding enormous amounts of tribute; the martyred St Edmund intervened personally; Swein was run through with a spear by the saint and fell from his horse; 'tormented with great pain until twilight, he ended his life with a wretched death'.[17] As Snorri explains, this story had been associated in an earlier period with

---

[11] *ASC* C D E *s.a.* 1014.
[12] Written in full in *ASC* D and with various abbreviations in *ASC* C E F, but all are clear in their dating.
[13] Cheney, *Handbook of Dates*, pp. 45, 76.
[14] For the complexity, see Cheney, *Handbook of Dates*, pp. 9–10, including the footnotes. As regards inconsistency of timing the start of a day, I have observed that it is not uncommon for manuscript sources to appear to disagree within one day in recording a death or some other event.
[15] Hollander, *Heimskringla*, Saint Óláfs saga, c. 12.
[16] Campbell, *Encomium*, Bk I, c. 5.
[17] Darlington and McGurk, *John of Worcester*, pp. 476–7, *s.a.* 1014. William of Malmesbury, *s.a.* 1014, says that God intervened to save the people and adds a story of how St Edmund killed Swein, adding that the story is uncertain: Stevenson, *William of Malmesbury: The Kings before the Norman Conquest*. Henry of Huntingdon, *s.a.* 1014, simply says that he 'died suddenly': Forester, *Chronicle of Henry of Huntingdon*.

another villain and another saint,[18] and so we may discount it as unlikely in this instance.

Swein's death was a considerable setback to the Danish conquest of England. It can only be said that the Danish conquest was complete when King Cnut was acknowledged as king by the whole nation early in 1017. For a seven-year period from February 1014, it is arguable that Thorkell the Tall was the catalyst for the changes that established and consolidated Cnut's rule in England.

Thorkell and Æthelred

According to the *ASC*, the English invited King Æthelred to return to England as soon as they knew of Swein's death.

> Then all the councillors who were in England, ecclesiastical and lay, determined to send for King Ethelred, and they said that no lord was dearer to them than their natural lord, if he would govern them more justly then he did before.[19]

The words 'who were in England' is a late addition to the exemplar of *ASC* C. Presumably, a later scribe felt that there was a need to clarify who invited Æthelred to return. Certainly, the *ASC* seems simplistic and biased in making the above statement. Many of the leaders who continued to support Æthelred were in exile with him. Other English leaders, such as Uhtred, Morcar, Sigeferth, Ulfcytel and Archbishop Wulfstan appear to have thrown in their lot with Swein and had good reason to fear the return of Æthelred. In any case, they and others represented the 'Danelaw' interest in England and, on another plane, Swein's conquest represented the triumph of the increasingly populous and wealthy east of England over the southern England of Wessex and the Thames valley. London held the balance of power in this struggle, which was as much economic as political, and London was controlled by a Scandinavian force loyal to Swein Forkbeard and his son, Cnut.[20] Whether the citizens of London welcomed Scandinavian control of their burgh is a debatable point, of course. They had been amongst the last to surrender to Swein Forkbeard in 1013.

Once again, as in the annal year 1001, we are fortunate in having two nearly contemporary sources for events. The first source is the *Æthelredian Exemplar* (*ÆE*), which was probably written in the years 1016 to 1017 and from which the annals *s.aa.* 1014 and 1015 in *ASC* C D E are derived. The other version derives from the verses of the skalds Sigvat and Ottar the Black, who knew St Olaf personally and who wrote about his exploits in England and elsewhere. Sigvat's verses are in his *Ólafsdrápa* and Ottar's are in his 'Head-ransom' and his *Knútsdrápa*. The skaldic verses were collected by the Norse/Icelandic writer and politician, Snorri, in the early thirteenth century and they, together with

---

[18] Hollander, *Heimskringla*, Saint Óláfs saga, c. 12.

[19] *ASC* C D E *s.a.* 1014, Whitelock's translation in *EHD*.

[20] Chapter 6, p. 121, above.

explanatory enhancements, are to be found in *Heimskringla*, sagas of the kings of Norway produced by Snorri, and in *Knytlinga saga*, sagas of the kings of Denmark, which was probably produced by one of Snorri's relatives who had access to Snorri's sources and who assimilated Snorri's manipulation of chronology, described in Appendix 1, below.[21] Translations are to be found in *English Historical Documents*.[22] English historians have generally followed Professor Campbell and others in giving credence to the *ASC* where the sources appear to differ. Campbell, indeed, made significant alterations to Snorri's version of events to make them fit his perception of the chronology and the account of events in the *ASC*.[23] However, a careful analysis of the chronology of *Heimskringla* and *Knytlinga saga* reveals that there is no fundamental problem in aligning *Heimskringla* and these skaldic sources with the *ASC*.[24] When this is done, it is apparent that the *ÆE* version of the *ASC* for the period 1014 to 1017 is avoiding certain events and issues, as it does on more than one occasion in earlier annals. In doing this it emphasises the difference between the, apparently, lethargic policies of Æthelred's ministers and the dynamic actions of King Edmund.[25] The account of events, which follows, draws upon both sources.

When Swein Forkbeard died, the bulk of the Scandinavian army was based on the river Trent at Gainsborough, in winter quarters. Steps had been taken to provision this force, whilst Swein's Anglo-Danish allies had returned to their homesteads and villages in the Danelaw. Swein had asserted his control over the country by garrisoning important burghs, including that at London. He was making political arrangements to assert his civil authority as well. For instance, a new bishop of London was appointed to replace the bishop who had fled into exile with Æthelred's court:

> and in the same year Ælfwig was consecrated bishop of London at York, on St Juliana's day (16 February)[26]

This passage is in *ASC* D only. It must have been added to D's exemplar, *ÆE*, shortly after the annals for the reigns of Æthelred and Edmund were added to the exemplars of *ASC* C and E.[27] The consecration took place after Swein's sudden death, but the timing indicates that arrangements for the consecration must have been made before Swein died. The timing also indicates a smooth transition of authority to Swein's son, Cnut, and this is supportive of the account

---

[21] The analysis is complex, but the author of *Knytlinga saga*'s mistaken belief that Cnut was ten years old when his father died can be aligned with Snorri's chronology. The author of *Knytlinga saga* was probably the Icelander, Olaf Thordarson, Snorri's nephew.

[22] Whitelock, *EHD*, pp. 305–9. For the original wording and an analysis, see Jónsson, *Heimskringla*, including vol. IV, *Fortolkning til Versene*.

[23] Campbell, *Encomium*, appendix III. Also Campbell, *Skaldic Verse and Anglo-Saxon History*.

[24] See Appendix 1, below.

[25] Chapter 1, pp. 3–5, above.

[26] *ASC* D *s.a.* 1014, Whitelock's translation in *EHD*.

[27] 'shortly after' because *ASC* D was probably a fair copy of *ÆE*: Howard, 'Swein Forkbeard's Invasions of England', pp. 61–88.

in the *Encomium*.[28] The consecration of a bishop would indicate that there were bishops and abbots in attendance when Archbishop Wulfstan led the ceremony. It follows that *ASC* F, Latin version, is probably correct when it records:

> Here King Swein died; however, the king's chief men and those who had come with him to England elected Cnut to kingship.[29]

The 'king's chief men' would be the *witan*. The *ASC* C D E versions simply record that 'all the fleet elected Cnut king',[30] which must be less than the whole truth given the political situation in England at the time of Swein's death.

Swein's unexpected death must have been a great encouragement to King Æthelred and his supporters. It is likely that the south of England was willing to return its allegiance to Æthelred and that the *ASC* annal is referring to genuine negotiations between some English leaders and Æthelred in the passage quoted above. A large body of mercenary forces was already in England, probably on the Isle of Wight, if we accept the Norse/Icelandic evidence that St Olaf came to England during Swein's lifetime. It seems probable that these forces were already in the pay of King Æthelred. However, the *Heimskringla* version states that Æthelred hastened to England after Swein's death and sent word to all who wished to enter his service for pay to join him to regain possession of his kingdom.[31] It is clear that Æthelred's generals, chief amongst them being Thorkell, acted swiftly when news of Swein's death was known. Their army advanced inland. Strategically, one would have expected the army to have taken the burgh at Winchester to safeguard its lines of communication, but the sources are silent. Snorri informs us that the army attacked London and that St Olaf's *lið* distinguished itself in dividing the Scandinavian defenders of the burgh at London from their associated defensive positions across the river at Southwark when it destroyed London Bridge. The burgh at Southwark was attacked and captured and the burgh at London then surrendered, because the defenders no longer controlled the passage up the Thames.[32]

Again, Æthelred's forces moved quickly. They were in East Anglia and had inflicted a defeat on local forces, which may have been commanded by Ulfcytel, before King Cnut was able to move south with the bulk of his army. However, some Northumbrians may have been amongst the forces fighting alongside Ulfcytel's people according to the Norse/Icelandic sources.[33] *Heimskringla* only mentions St Olaf and King Æthelred as leaders of the army at this battle, but

---

[28] Campbell, *Encomium*, Bk I, c. 5; Bk II, c. 1.

[29] Swanton's translation: Swanton, *Anglo-Saxon Chronicle*, p. 144 n. 12; also Dumville, *MS F*, f. 65r, *s.a.* 1014.

[30] *ASC* C D E *s.a.* 1014, Whitelock's translation in *EHD*.

[31] See Hollander, *Heimskringla*, Saint Óláfs saga, c. 12.

[32] Hollander, *Heimskringla*, Saint Óláfs saga, cc. 12, 13.

[33] *Ibid.* c. 14. Note the Sigvat's reference to 'Ella's offspring': Ella was a king of Northumbria. Holland says that this kenning refers to 'the English' in general but, in context, it may signify a Northumbrian presence in the army opposing Æthelred. See also Fell, 'Vikingarvísur', p. 116.

there can be little doubt that Thorkell and his forces must have been present at what is described as a great battle.

Æthelred's army then moved against Lindsey, where they might have expected stiff opposition from King Cnut's forces. Their advance was rapid. The *ASC* annal informs us that Cnut was still at Gainsborough, with his army, at Easter 1014, 25 April. Although he had planned to join forces with the men of Lindsey, 'King Ethelred came there to Lindsey with his full force before they were ready'.[34] In undertaking the rapid advance into East Anglia and then into Lindsey, they had taken military risks. They had omitted to attack and capture some of the important burghs in the south which were still occupied by forces loyal to Cnut. However, in the event, their strategy was justified. Cnut's problems were such that, faced with their rapid advance, he chose to abandon England and sail to Denmark, an act recorded with some disdain by the *ASC*: 'and Cnut put out to sea with his fleet, and thus the wretched people were betrayed by him'.[35]

This left Æthelred as the only king in England, although *Heimskringla* states that 'the Company of the Thingmen', Cnut's retainers, still occupied many strongholds and controlled wide stretches of land.[36] Snorri, quoting skaldic sources, informs us that St Olaf drove the Scandinavian garrisons from such important burghs as Canterbury and from other places, which have not been identified.[37] Ottar's verses say that the English could not hamper St Olaf's progress through the land and that he extracted much tribute from the traitors.[38] The skaldic sources concentrate attention on their hero, St Olaf, who remained in England until King Æthelred's death, in Spring 1016.[39] No doubt, Thorkell also played an important part in bringing the whole of England back to its former allegiance. In fact, his position was very important in 1014. He was the leader of the mercenary army upon which the king was still dependent and, as a Dane of high birth, he represented a political bridge to the peoples of the Danelaw and their leaders. Many of the leaders in the Danelaw must have feared Æthelred's return since he must have regarded their ready acceptance of Swein Forkbeard as an act of betrayal and treason. However, Æthelred appears to have promised to forgive and forget, a point made emphatically by the *ASC*:

> [Æthelred said] all the things that had been said and done against him should be forgiven, on condition that they all unanimously turned to him without treachery.[40]

---

[34] *ASC* C D E *s.a.* 1014, Whitelock's translation in *EHD*.

[35] *Ibid.*

[36] Hollander, *Heimskringla*, Saint Óláfs saga, c. 14.

[37] Hollander, *Heimskringla*, Saint Óláf's saga, c. 15.

[38] Hollander, *Heimskringla*, Saint Óláfs saga, c. 15.

[39] *Ibid.* c. 16; also *ASC* C D E *s.a.* 1016. Snorri provides a time frame by saying that St Olaf stayed in England on this occasion for three years, thus confirming that he came to England in 1013.

[40] *ASC* C D E *s.a.* 1014, Whitelock's translation in *EHD*.

There is evidence of this conciliatory policy in a charter dated 1014. Sawyer records two charters under the year 1014.[41] They are S.932 and S.933, both regarded as authentic and both prepared after Æthelred's return to England in the spring of 1014. We only have the subscriptions of S.933 which was probably prepared after the death of the ætheling Æthelstan on 25 June.[42] In this charter the elder æthelings, Edmund and Eadwig, are given precedence over their half-brothers, Edward and Alfred; Wulfstan of York is given first place amongst the bishops, with Lyfing of Canterbury in second place, although northern and eastern bishoprics and monasteries are not represented, other than Ely; Uhtred features among the ealdormen; Ulfcytel and Sigeferth are the first two in the list of *ministri*, although Morcar is not included. It is interesting to note that the mercenary commanders, Thorkell and St Olaf, are not included among the *ministri*, although it is possible that Thorkell had been included in a witness list to a charter of 1012;[43] this indicates a limitation to their influence and that they were regarded as mercenary commanders rather than as part of a continuing political establishment. There is no bishop of London in the witness list. Bishop Ælfhun returned from exile and was reinstated as bishop of London by 1015 when he witnessed a charter.[44] It is not clear what happened to Bishop Ælfwig.

Unfortunately for Thorkell, English politics were in a state of flux. By the standards of the time, King Æthelred was an old man and he appears to have been seriously ill on more than one occasion.[45] Political thoughts turned towards the future and the possibility of a disputed succession. King Æthelred had fathered sons in two marriages. His eldest son, the ætheling Æthelstan, died in 1014. It is likely that he had been the king's designated successor for many years, a fact that was known beyond the shores of England, since Thietmar, bishop of Merseburg in northern Germany, had heard of him and knew his name, though he appears to have been ignorant of the names of any of the archbishops of Canterbury who had succeeded St Dunstan since 988.[46] Thietmar was writing shortly after the events of 1016/17 and was unaware that Æthelstan had died, so, in his chronicle, he confused the æthelings Edmund and Eadwig with Æthelstan and Edmund.

When Æthelstan died, his full brother, Edmund, clearly believed that he should succeed to his brother's claim to the throne. This claim was supported in the Danelaw, because, through his mother, he had family connections in the north. His claim to the throne was opposed by King Æthelred's wife, Emma, who was many years the king's junior, was an adept politician and had the support of the leading ealdorman, Eadric, for the succession of one of her sons, Edward and Alfred. Once more, Thorkell's position was ambiguous. As a Dane

---

41 Sawyer, *Anglo-Saxon Charters*.

42 Keynes, *Diplomas*, p. 267.

43 The charter of 1012 is S.926. See Keynes, 'Cnut's Earls', p. 55, and Campbell, *Encomium*, p. 75 n. 3.

44 S.934 and Keynes, *Diplomas*, p. 267.

45 He was unavailable to lead the *witan* to London in spring 1012; he 'lay sick at Cosham' in 1015; he died on 23 April 1016: *ASD* C D E *s.aa.*

46 Trillmich, *Thietmari Merseburgensis*, Bk VII, cc. 40, 42.

he may have sympathised with Edmund's supporters. However, he appears to have been a loyal friend to Æthelred and Emma and, as Æthelred himself seems to have favoured his sons by Emma,[47] Thorkell probably found himself opposed to Edmund's claims. His friendship with Æthelred and Emma may be deduced from his actions in protecting the king and his family in 1013, his working relationship with Emma between 1017 and 1021 and from the many references to him in the *Encomium*.

Presumably, Thorkell would have preferred to avoid the succession issue for as long as possible. But matters were brought to a head in 1015, when a royal council was convened in Oxford.[48] The *ASC* describes it as 'the great assembly' and it was probably intended to establish a settlement of outstanding issues between the king and the people of the Danelaw and the regulation of the laws affecting trade between English Mercia and the Danelaw. If so, the choice of Oxford was geographically significant.

Ealdorman Eadric of Mercia had re-established himself as the king's chief adviser and he was a man who traditionally supported a 'hard line' policy. Just as he had probably advocated the St Brice's Day Massacre, some thirteen years previously, so now he advocated that Æthelred should take action against leaders of the Danelaw who had proved themselves his enemies in the past. No doubt, Eadric was also looking to the future and supporting Emma and her young sons in the succession dispute, a support which would further his own ambitions. Eadric could have had few friends in the north following his involvement in the death of Ealdorman Ælfhelm in 1006[49] and there appears to have been no love lost between the ætheling Edmund and Eadric.

Having convinced the king that 'hard line' action was necessary, Eadric brought about the deaths of Sigeferth and Morcar, the chief men in the Danelaw. Æthelred condoned this action by confiscating their property,[50] thus, indicating a foreknowledge of the act and his acceptance that they were plotting against him. Whether they were plotting or not, another northern leader, Uhtred, quickly distanced himself from the king and he was soon joined by the ætheling Edmund, who had reason to fear for his life now that the party favouring Edward's succession was in the ascendant.

Thorkell remained with the king. But his master was clearly being led by Eadric and Emma at this stage and Thorkell must have felt that his own position was being undermined. Following the deaths of Sigeferth and Morcar, no Dane in an influential position at court could feel secure. Edmund was in open revolt

---

[47] The *ASC s.a.* 1016 suggests that King Æthelred was suspicious of the ætheling Edmund's intentions: the king left an army which was led by Edmund because he was 'informed that those who should support him wished to betray him'. The *ASC s.a.* 1014 says that Æthelred was represented at the negotiations for his return by his son, Edward.

[48] *ASC* C D E *s.a.* 1015.

[49] *ASC* C D E *s.a.*1006; Darlington and McGurk, *John of Worcester, s.a.* 1006. The charge against Eadric in John of Worcester's chronicle is from a 'Life' of King Edmund, which was probably written in the mid-eleventh century; it draws upon northern tradition. I discussed this in a paper 'Sources for the Life of Edmund Ironside' presented at the Leeds International Medieval Congress in July 2000.

[50] *ASC* C D E *s.a.* 1015.

against his father, having rescued and married Sigeferth's widow and taken possession of the property of the dead thanes, Sigeferth and Morcar.[51] Supported as he was by Uhtred, Edmund had effectively declared the north independent of King Æthelred's authority. Thorkell decided that there was no point in remaining in Æthelred's court. He left the mercenary army in England and, according to the *Encomium*, returned with nine ships to Denmark. There, he submitted to King Cnut and offered to help him re-conquer England, a country which was near the point of outright civil war.[52] St Olaf remained with his mercenary army in England at this time.[53]

Thorkell and Cnut

To understand Cnut's action in leaving England in 1014, it is necessary to consider the political situation in Scandinavia. In doing so we can only place a limited reliance upon the *Encomium* as a source. Intent upon delivering a political message about two brothers and the return of a queen from exile, which was apposite to the political situation in the mid-eleventh century, the *Encomium* is deliberately misleading about events in 1014.

When Swein Forkbeard died, his eldest surviving son was Cnut[54] and he was immediately recognised as king by the Scandinavian army in England. Cnut had coins struck as king of Denmark, using dies cut in Lincoln.[55] England was a newly conquered country and far from secure, whilst Denmark was Cnut's ancestral home and the source of men and wealth to support his position elsewhere. Swein's alliances with Earl Erik of Lade, ruler of Norway, and King Olof of Sweden were 'personal' arrangements and Cnut was needed in Denmark to secure his authority and to bolster Danish hegemony over Scandinavia. In Denmark Cnut had a younger half-brother, Harald,[56] who could have claimed the Danish throne if Cnut had died or failed to exercise royal authority. The *Encomium*, for political reasons of its own, says that this Harald became king of the Danes, a suggestion that is not supported by any of the Norse/Icelandic and Danish sources. The sources that mention the matter state that Cnut succeeded his father as king of Denmark; these sources include Saxo, Snorri and the writer of *Knytlinga saga*. All the thirteenth-century Danish king lists show that Cnut succeeded his father.[57] The *ASC* annals for 1015 and 1016 derive from *ÆE*, which was probably written in 1016–17; these annals refer to 'King Cnut' from

51 *Ibid.*
52 Campbell, *Encomium*, Bk II, c. 3.
53 Hollander, *Heimskringla*, Saint Óláfs saga, cc. 15, 16.
54 Chapter 1, pp. 9–11, above.
55 Jonsson, 'Coinage of Cnut', pp. 223–4 and n. 68.
56 Chapter 1, pp. 9–11, above.
57 Howard, 'Swein Forkbeard's Invasions of England', p. 139 n. 218, lists the evidence for Harald Sweinsson's existence and Cnut's immediate succession. The Danish king lists are in Gertz, *Scriptores Minores Historiae Danicae Medii Ævi*.

the time of his invasion in 1015 and whilst King Æthelred was still alive.[58] Unlike the *Encomium*, the *ASC* does not recognise that Cnut had a title to the throne of England until after Æthelred's death, so his title, 'king', is presumably given because the English regarded Cnut as king of Denmark from the time of Swein's death.

Despite attempting to mislead, the words of the *Encomium* do suggest something of the political problems which Cnut faced at this time. In 1014, Cnut had lost London, and possibly Winchester. Forces loyal to him had been defeated in East Anglia. The outcome of the new war in England was looking doubtful. He needed to assert himself in Denmark. Without the resources of Denmark and his Scandinavian allies he could not hope to be successful in England. Cnut was above all a realist and a ruthless egocentric, so he had no compunction in abandoning the local levies, people of Danish extraction, which had rallied to him in Lindsey. He also abandoned his Scandinavian followers who held the strategic burghs in southern England. Contemporaries did not necessarily condone his actions, of course, and the encomiast had some difficulty in explaining them away. The encomiast achieved this by implying that Scandinavian forces in England were left under Thorkell's command.[59]

Cnut's position in England may have been more desperate than the *ASC* and the *Encomium* suggest. *Heimskringla* and the skaldic verses contained therein describe the battle in East Anglia as a great battle and say that many were killed. If so, Cnut's ships, stationed far inland at Gainsborough, would have been in danger and a speedy retreat, at least as far as the Humber, would have been essential. Indeed some ships may have been abandoned since the *Encomium* tells us that Cnut returned to Denmark with no more than sixty ships.[60] The fact that Earl Uhtred, Ulfcytel and Sigeferth appear to have recovered their positions in Æthelred's court quickly,[61] suggests that they withdrew their support for Cnut at an early stage.

Cnut could have had no doubt, in his own mind, that he had been betrayed by people who had allied themselves to his father. Æthelred's army could not have advanced so rapidly and with so little regard for its lines of communication if the population had not been friendly. So, Cnut had no compunction in mutilating his hostages, an act which served as a warning for the future since he probably expected to return to England after securing his authority in Denmark:

> and there the hostages, who had been given to his father, were put ashore and [he] cut off their hands, ears and noses.[62]

---

[58] The *ASC* annals for 1015 and 1016, until the death of Æthelred, refer to Cnut as: 'Cnut cyng' twice, 'Cnut' three times, 'se cyng' once, 'se cyng Cnut' once.

[59] Howard, 'Swein Forkbeard's Invasions of England', pp. 126–44; Campbell, *Encomium*, Bk II, cc. 1, 2.

[60] Campbell, *Encomium*, Bk II, c. 1. The encomiast disguises any difficulty by saying that it was King Cnut's decision that not more than sixty ships should accompany him: 'rex non amplius quam sexaginta naues secum abire permisit'. This Latin quotation incorporates Campbell's corrections to the manuscript text.

[61] Chapter 7, pp. 130–1, above, and S.933.

[62] *ASC* C D E *s.a.* 1014, my translation; *ASC* E omits 'ears'.

For what happened next we have three sources that are independent of each other. The first is the *Æthelredian Exemplar*, which was probably written within a year of the events of 1015/16; the second is the contemporary chronicle of Thietmar of Merseburg; the third is the *Encomium*, which was written some thirty years later but which drew upon Emma's recollection of events and what Thorkell and others subsequently told her. In this context, it is relevant to note that Thorkell's name is mentioned more often in the *Encomium* than any other except for King Cnut.

In 1015, Cnut and Thorkell invaded England. They were later followed by Cnut's ally, the Norwegian ruler, Earl Erik of Lade.[63] Unlike his father, Cnut concentrated his invasion on Wessex rather than on the Danelaw. In this, he was probably following the advice of Thorkell who had local knowledge of the political situation. The encomiast says Thorkell made this point about local knowledge to Cnut when he returned to Denmark, together with the suggestion that Scandinavian mercenaries in England would join them when they invaded.[64] The explanation for the strategy was not just that Cnut had abandoned his northern allies the previous year when he had returned to Denmark. The reason for ignoring the north was that northern leaders had thrown their support behind the ætheling Edmund. They were fully committed to his cause and to fighting for his right of succession at that time.

Whilst Wessex might have been expected to have remained loyal to King Æthelred, there was a political situation which undermined that loyalty. The king was ill and, because of his age and health, not expected to reign for much longer. By remaining loyal to Æthelred, the people of Wessex were effectively supporting the ætheling Edward's (or Alfred's) succession. This, in turn, meant a royal council which would be dominated by the Norman queen, Emma, and the Ealdorman of Mercia, Eadric. The people of Wessex had reason to be wary of a Norman alliance with the English leadership, because it might threaten local interests in the Channel, interests which appear to have lead to major international disputes in the past.[65] Also, there was still some economic and political rivalry between the peoples of Wessex and those of Mercia. There had been a shift in comparative economic wealth and influence away from Wessex.[66] London was the economic and political key to England and it was geographically situated in a position which was important to both Wessex and Mercia. Control of London by the Mercian ealdorman and his friends might further reduce the economic and political influence of Wessex in the country as a whole.

This is the background that explains why Cnut and Thorkell chose to invade Wessex, where they met with success and some, though not total, support. The

---

[63] Erik was summoned to join Cnut in England: Appendix 1, below, Tables 3, 4, 5. This was probably in 1016. The *Encomium* is ambiguous on this point and its chronology is suspect but it first mentions Erik's presence in England after the battle of Sherston, which took place in 1016: see Campbell, *Encomium*, Bk II, cc. 6, 7.

[64] Campbell, *Encomium*, Bk II, c. 3.

[65] Chapter 4, pp. 55–6, above.

[66] See Chapter 2, pp. 21–2, above.

sources indicate some resistance and the *Encomium* says that Thorkell distinguished himself in overcoming that resistance.[67] This may well have been strictly true, though it should be remembered that the writer of the *Encomium* was briefed by Thorkell's friend, Queen Emma and that the details of events during the opening months of Cnut's campaign appear to be faulty.[68] The *ASC* version informs us that:

> King Cnut came to Sandwich, and then made his way at once around Kent into Wessex, until he came to the mouth of the Frome, and ravaged then in Dorset, in Wiltshire and in Somerset.[69]

Faced with Cnut's successful invasion of Wessex, an attempt was made to reconcile the two English factions. The ætheling Edmund and Æthelred's supporters, led by Ealdorman Eadric, agreed to combine forces in order to attack the invaders. This alliance soon foundered on the mutual distrust of the ætheling Edmund and Ealdorman Eadric, and the English forces were dispersed. The *ASC* says:

> The king [Æthelred] then lay sick at Cosham. Then Ealdorman Eadric collected an army ['fyrde'], as did the ætheling Edmund in the north. When they came together, the ealdorman wished to betray the ætheling and, because of this, they then dispersed without giving battle, and gave way to their enemies. And then Ealdorman Eadric seduced forty ships from the king and then submitted to Cnut. And the West Saxons submitted and gave hostages and supplied horses to the army ['here'] and then it was there until mid-winter [Christmas].[70]

In reading this passage, it should be remembered that the writer of the annal and his sponsor were almost certainly supporters of Edmund and were biased against Eadric.[71] The forty ships are usually supposed to represent the Scandinavian mercenary army which had gone over to King Æthelred in 1012. John of Worcester says that they were manned by Danes.[72] As noted above the *Encomium* suggests that the mercenary forces were expected to go over to Cnut because of their loyalty to Thorkell, so Eadric may not have played so positive a part in the defection as the *ASC* suggests. St Olaf and his *lið* left England a few weeks after this event, in the spring.[73]

---

[67] Campbell, *Encomium*, Bk II, c. 6.
[68] Campbell, *Encomium*, Bk II, cc. 5–6; the encomiast seems to have confused a battle at Sherston in Wiltshire with resistance to the Scandinavian landing at Sandwich.
[69] *ASC* C D E *s.a.* 1015, my translation.
[70] *ASC* C D E *s.a.* 1015, my translation.
[71] Chapter 1, pp. 3–6, above.
[72] Darlington and McGurk, *John of Worcester*, pp. 480–1.
[73] Hollander, *Heimskringla*, St Olaf's saga, c. 16, p. 256. The legendary saga of St Olaf may be read to indicate that St Olaf formed an alliance with Cnut, for a brief period, at this time. This interpretation depends upon the writer's alignment of Sigvat's verses with the chronology of events being faulty, and there is evidence to support this possibility. Either way, it seems that St Olaf made no attempt to defend London at this time and that he left England altogether in the spring of 1016.

The failure of the English alliance strengthened Cnut's position. His marriage to Ælfgifu of Northampton[74] meant that he had potential allies in the north. He already had a son, Swein, by Ælfgifu. The mother and her baby son had escaped to Denmark in dramatic circumstances when Cnut had left England in 1014.[75] Whilst in Denmark she gave birth to another son, Harald.[76] This meant that Cnut could guarantee that, through his sons, support for his cause would eventually bring the throne of England into the hands of a dominant northern family. The queen of England would be a member of that family. It may be considered certain that diplomatic negotiations were started between Cnut and these northern interests at this time.

The ætheling Edmund had also married a northern heiress[77] and was thereby allied to the same northern family that had married Ælfgifu to Cnut in 1013.[78] The north remained committed to Edmund who had the full support of Uhtred of Northumbria at this stage, an alliance which was later to cost Uhtred his life when he fell into Cnut's power.[79] Edmund already had sons by an earlier alliance, a weakness in his political position that may have been of increasing significance.[80]

Diplomacy was nothing without success on the battlefield, however. A civil war was by this time being fought between forces loyal to Ealdorman Eadric and forces loyal to Edmund and his chief supporter, Uhtred. The Anglo-Saxon Chronicle goes so far as to say that Ealdorman Eadric had betrayed Æthelred and made submission to King Cnut. Cnut and Thorkell decided to take advantage of the situation and attack the north. This proved to be a military masterstroke. Faced with military disaster in the north, Uhtred felt obliged to save himself and his people by submitting to Cnut. He, therefore, deserted Edmund and returned north to York. Cnut welcomed him, but he never allowed a former ally a second chance to betray him: Uhtred was killed shortly after his submission to Cnut. Whether or not the killing was ordered by Cnut may be debated but Uhtred's death met with his approval.[81]

---

[74] Chapter 6, p. 107, above.

[75] My researches suggest that she is the 'matrona', referred to by Thietmar (Trillmich, *Thietmari Merseburgensis*, Bk VII, c. 37) and by the encomiast (Campbell, *Encomium*, Bk II, c. 3). She and her baby son, Swein Forkbeard's grandson, were living proof of northern England's commitment to King Swein. This was an embarrassment to her family when Æthelred returned, so they organised her escape to Denmark, with her baby and the body of Swein Forkbeard.

[76] Howard, 'Swein Forkbeard's Invasions of England', pp. 140–1, discusses when her sons were born.

[77] *ASC* C D E *s.a.* 1015.

[78] See Figure 8, p. 69, above.

[79] *ASC* C D E *s.a.* 1016.

[80] He was married to Sigeferth's widow for a little over a year before he died. This makes it very unlikely that she was the mother of the sons who survived Edmund, since there is no reference to them being twins or babies when Edmund died.

[81] *ASC* C D E *s.a.* 1016. The annal in version C says that Earl Uhtred was killed 'by the advice of Ealdorman Eadric'; this late addition to the annal may come from an unreliable, because very biased, source. A later source adds that the killing was carried out by Thurbrand the Hold: see Higham, *The Death of Anglo-Saxon England*, pp. 64–5.

Cnut and Thorkell now decided to attack London. Once again, the ætheling Edmund agreed to ally himself with his father. He returned to his father in London, where preparations were being made for a siege.[82] The king was again seriously ill and, in fact, died on 23 April 1016, before Cnut's army reached London. The political and military situation was consequently extremely complicated. The burgh of London was held by forces loyal to Queen Emma following the death of her husband, Æthelred, and she wanted her son, Edward, to become king. For political reasons both the *ASC* and the *Encomium* ignore Queen Emma's involvement in politics at this time. It is only through the contemporary chronicle of Thietmar of Merseburg that we have confirmation that she was with her husband when he died and that she and the king's loyal forces continued to control the burgh of London.[83] The ætheling Edmund, with his northern contingents, was also in London and was not prepared to surrender his claim to the throne. The stakes were high, for if Edward or Edmund were successful in claiming the throne, the rival candidate might be considered too dangerous to be allowed to survive. Outside London, was a Scandinavian army, now reinforced by some English contingents, which supported Cnut's claim to the English throne.

Emma held the burgh of London and one must suppose that forces loyal to Edmund were outside the burgh. It was the economic and political key to the control of England. Emma was not in a position to have Edward made king in the face of opposition from the ætheling Edmund and from Cnut. Fearing for his life, she opened negotiations with Cnut. She had long been a friend of Thorkell and Eadric and these friendships must have paved the way for negotiations. Again, we have only the contemporary chronicle of Thietmar to explain these events. For political reasons the *ASC*, which wanted to avoid portraying Edmund as merely the leader of an English minority faction, and the *Encomium*, which wanted to avoid mentioning the fact that Queen Emma was prepared to sacrifice the English hero, her 'son' through marriage, the ætheling Edmund, both avoid an explanation of what was happening in London. Thietmar tells us that the queen was negotiating to win peace for herself by paying a substantial tribute, handing over the contents of the burgh's armoury, which was said to have contained 24,000 coats of mail,[84] and surrendering her (step) sons.[85]

Discovering what the queen was doing, the ætheling Edmund was placed in a dilemma. If he remained in London, he ran the risk of falling into the hands of Cnut and Emma, the consequences of which would have been fatal. He fled

---

[82] *ASC* C D E *s.a.* 1016.

[83] Trillmich, *Thietmari Merseburgensis*, Bk VII, c. 40 (28): 'Lundunam, ubi regina tristis nece viri suimet et defensoris cum filiis Ethelsteno ac Ethmundo . . .' Thietmar was mistaken when he named the sons 'Æthelstan and Edmund', presumably because he was unaware of Æthelstan's death: the two surviving sons of Æthelred's first marriage were Edmund and Eadwig.

[84] Cf. Chapter 5, pp. 78–9, above, for the provision of 'helmets and corselets' to the king in 1008/ 9.

[85] Trillmich, *Thietmari Merseburgensis*, Bk VII, c. 40.

from London, leaving Emma and Cnut to negotiate for political and military control of the city.[86]

Edmund's situation was critical. Cnut had effectively conquered the north and Edmund's former northern ally, Earl Uhtred, was dead. Edmund, therefore chose to go into Wessex. There the rivalry between Wessex and the Danelaw stood him in good stead and he was able to raise an army.[87] Cnut, fearing that he might be trapped between Emma's English forces, which held the burgh, and Edmund's English army from Wessex, decided to retire from London. There followed some inconclusive fighting between forces led by Edmund and Cnut's army. Cnut also attempted a siege of London during this period. Since there is no evidence that Emma gave up the burgh, it is likely that she and her forces also remained in London. Her position was ambiguous. Her friend and ally, Ealdorman Eadric, was with Cnut. She also had good reason to feel that she could trust Thorkell who had served her and her children well in the past. She had no reason to trust Edmund, who posed a threat to the lives of her children.[88]

Later in 1016, according to the *ASC*, Ealdorman Eadric withdrew his support from King Cnut and submitted to Edmund, acknowledging him as king. The *ASC* says that this was because Cnut's forces had suffered a defeat, but it also implies that Eadric was keen to protect Cnut from an overwhelming defeat. The political situation remained complex and it is possible that the ambiguity in the *ASC* account masks the likelihood that negotiations were taking place between Eadric, Emma and Edmund at this time. Cnut's continued presence in England meant that King Edmund needed to retain the support of Eadric and Emma. It is apparent that Eadric and Emma felt that they could not trust King Edmund, however.

The war continued and Edmund's forces suffered a significant defeat at Ashingdon. The *ASC* has a dramatic account of how Eadric's forces fled from the battlefield and so exposed Edmund's army to an overwhelming defeat.

> Thereupon Ealdorman Eadric did just as he had often done before; [he was] the first to start the flight with [the] Magesætan.[89] And so betrayed his liege lord and all the English nation.[90]

The *Encomium* adds to the story, saying that Eadric's withdrawal from the battle may have been a deliberate act of betrayal.[91] However, the *Encomium* was

---

[86] *Ibid.* c. 41. *ASC* C D E *s.a.* 1016, says that Edmund escaped from London before Cnut commenced a siege.

[87] *ASC* C D E *s.a.* 1016.

[88] This is an abbreviated account of events. I hope to expand on the events of the period, 1014 to 1017, in a future book. Incidentally, the description, in *ASC s.a.* 1016, of Cnut's strategy for the siege of London makes it evident that London Bridge had been repaired, and strengthened to protect it from an attack using St Olaf's methods.

[89] The *fyrde* raised in Herefordshire and south Shropshire.

[90] *ASC* C D E *s.a.* 1016, my translation.

[91] Campbell, *Encomium*, Bk II, c. 9. See also Darlington and McGurk, *John of Worcester, s.a.* 1016, pp. 490–1.

anxious to justify Cnut, who befriended and honoured Eadric and then had him killed.

These stories again mask the true political situation for, whatever the truth about Eadric's activities, it seems that his forces were deliberately kept from supporting either side in battle. With his army intact he was in a strong position to play a leading part in the negotiations between the kings, Edmund and Cnut, which followed the battle of Ashingdon. England was divided between them, though the terms of the division remain uncertain and there seems little doubt that neither of the kings regarded the agreement as a permanent settlement.

and Edmund succeeded to Wessex and Cnut to the north region[92]

This is the translation of *ASC* D. Versions C and E substitute 'Mercia' for 'the north region'.

Emma's situation remains unknown, as does the important question concerning the control of the burgh at London. The terms of the agreement seem to have allowed Cnut's ships to make use of facilities on the Thames at London. However, it seems that Edmund also went to London.[93] This has usually been taken as an indication that London was to be controlled by Edmund under the terms of the partition of England between him and Cnut. However, London's neutrality at this juncture seems the more likely explanation, with the queen maintaining control of the burgh. The *ASC* refers to the 'Londoners' making a separate peace with Cnut's army. The record of the country's partition takes no account of the political and strategic importance of an independent London, or more significantly of a London where the burgh was controlled by forces loyal to Queen Emma. Both the Danish fleet and King Edmund may have been in London with the permission of the queen and the citizens, a possibility which makes sense of a situation which would otherwise be difficult to explain.

The political and strategic situation was soon altered by King Edmund's sudden death on 30 November 1016. His brother, Eadwig, inherited his claims to the crown, since Edmund's sons by a marriage, which he must have contracted before that to the widow of Sigeferth in 1015, were too young to be immediate contenders. Edmund's position, after suffering a major military defeat, was not strong and Eadwig was not able to muster significant support. An agreement between Queen Emma and King Cnut resolved the political stalemate, leaving Eadwig with no effective support for his cause. It was this agreement to which the encomiast refers when he says in the *Encomium* that Queen Emma was instrumental in bringing peace to England at this time:

and perhaps there would scarcely or never have been an end of the fighting if he [Cnut] had not at length secured by the Saviour's favouring grace a matrimonial link with this most noble queen[94]

---

[92] *ASC* C D E *s.a.* 1016, my translation of MS D. See also Campbell, *Encomium*, Bk II, c. 13.
[93] Darlington and McGurk, *John of Worcester, s.a.*1016, pp. 492–3.
[94] Campbell, *Encomium*, 'Argument'.

Under the terms of the agreement, which Eadric and Thorkell were in an ideal position to broker, Queen Emma became Cnut's wife and so retained her title and authority as queen of England. Cnut thereby became the 'father' of her sons Edward and Alfred who were thus no longer a threat to Cnut and could be allowed to survive. Cnut, for his part, gained an undisputed title to the English crown, which he quickly consolidated by disposing of Eadwig and the future threat represented by King Edmund's young sons, who were driven into exile. As part of the agreement, Ealdorman Eadric, Emma's long-term supporter, was reinstated in his position as ealdorman of Mercia. However, Cnut was not prepared to leave so much authority in the hands of a man whom he could not completely trust. The occasion which led to Eadric being killed is not recorded; such information is usually omitted from the annals. What is certain is that Eadric was killed in 1017, probably on Cnut's direct command.

Cnut himself took personal control of Wessex and left the north to be administered by the Norse earl, Erik of Lade. This was an interesting decision since there was considerable Norse influence in the north of the country, especially around York. However, Cnut appears to have judged correctly that he could rely on the loyalty of Erik.

Regency and Death

With hindsight we know that Cnut's recognition as sole king in 1017 signalled the completion of the Danish conquest of England. However, there remained a need for consolidation and Thorkell again had an important part to play in political events. Thorkell was rewarded for his part in the conquest by being put in charge of East Anglia. In effect, 'the north region' which had been assigned to Cnut in the partition of the country was to be controlled for him by his two chief Scandinavian supporters, Erik of Lade in Northumbria and Thorkell in East Anglia. Wessex, which was to have been ruled by Edmund under the partition agreement, was ruled directly by Cnut himself during this initial period of his reign.

> Here in this year King Cnut ascended the throne of all England, and [he] divided it into four [parts], himself [taking] Wessex, and Thorkell East Anglia, and Eadric Mercia, and Erik Northumbria.[95]

It is uncertain who was responsible for Mercia during most of this initial period. Eadric's appointment was apparently no more than a political expedient. Shortly after the division of the country he was killed on Cnut's orders, an act which the *Encomium* justified by saying that it was a signal to others that treachery to a liege lord would not go unpunished. In this instance, according to the *Encomium*, the treachery in question was Eadric's betrayal of King Edmund.[96]

As well as his marriage to Emma and his organisation for the political control

---

95 *ASC* C D E *s.a.* 1017, my translation.
96 Campbell, *Encomium*, Bk II, c. 15.

of the country, Cnut consolidated his rule by disposing of people who might have threatened his authority.

> And in this year was Ealdorman Eadric slain, and Northman son of Ealdorman Leofwine, and Æthelweard son of Æthelmær the Stout, and Brihtric son of Ælfheah of Devonshire. And King Cnut exiled the ætheling Eadwig and afterwards had him killed.[97]

The above translation is taken from *ASC* C. Version E has Ælfgeat instead of Ælfheah of Devonshire. There is also a reference to Cnut having exiled 'Eadwig, king of the peasants' in versions D and E *s.a.* 1017 and in version C *s.a.* 1020. None of the *ASC* versions of the annals subsequent to 1016 are derived directly from the contemporary *Æthelredian Exemplar*.

As Ealdorman or Earl of East Anglia, Thorkell was also the king's chief adviser, effectively the power behind the throne and the regent in England when Cnut was absent in Scandinavia.

Despite the loss of her friend and adviser, Eadric, the queen seems to have remained on good terms with Cnut by whom she had two children, Harthacnut and Gunnhild. She probably continued to depend upon Thorkell for support in the early days of her new relationship, and he must have been party to the decision which allowed the æthelings Edward and Alfred to retire to the comparative safety of Normandy. The new political order was celebrated when Thorkell and Cnut attended the dedication of a minster, which was founded to commemorate the men who had fallen at the battle of Ashingdon.[98]

Unfortunately for Thorkell, the position he held in England was a dangerous one. His true power base was dependent upon his friendship with Cnut and yet he had to exercise authority as if he were king himself, during Cnut's absence from the country. Inevitably Cnut became suspicious of his power and Thorkell's enemies were able to play upon those suspicions. Matters came to a head in 1021, though we do not know what event brought about Cnut's anger and reaction.

> Here in this year, at Martinmas, King Cnut outlawed Earl Thorkell.[99]

Martinmas was on 11 November.

Thorkell was probably sufficiently aware of his danger to flee to his old safe-haven, the Isle of Wight, after which nothing certain is known about him. He was an old man by the standards of the time and may have died a natural death. However, Cnut was not the man to leave a potential rival untroubled and evidence that he manoeuvred a fleet off the Isle of Wight in 1022[100] suggests a show of strength. Under the new political regime, the inhabitants of the Isle would not have had any desire to defy the king, and one may presume that

---

[97] *ASC* C D E *s.a.* 1017, my translation of Version C.
[98] *ASC* D *s.a.* 1017. This annal was added to Version D in the mid-eleventh century so it does not have the same authority as the earlier annals. However, the dedication of the minster is confirmed by other versions of the *ASC* and Thorkell's presence is confirmed by Version C.
[99] *ASC* C D E *s.a.* 1021, my translation.
[100] *Ibid. s.a.* 1022.

Thorkell would have been given up to the king, dead or alive. Either way, Cnut would not have allowed him to live. Thorkell's removal from the scene marks the end of the period of conquest.[101] Cnut was firmly in control of an empire which stretched from Denmark to England and had pretensions to extend his authority in other parts of Scandinavia and the British Isles.

[101] Because a scribe seems to have confused a story about Ulf Thorgilsson with Earl Thorkell, it is sometimes thought that Thorkell and Cnut were reconciled. *ASC* C *s.a.* 1023 says: 'In this year King Cnut came back to England, and Thorkel and he were reconciled, and he entrusted Denmark and his son for Thorkel to maintain and the king took Thorkel's son with him to England. And afterwards he had St Ælfheah's relics moved from London to Canterbury' (Whitelock's translation in *EHD*). *Heimskringla* and other Scandinavian sources say that it was Ulf Thorgilsson, Cnut's brother-in-law, who was given custody of Cnut's son and made regent of Denmark. Furthermore, the chronology of the *ASC* account is suspect because Cnut's son is known to have been in England, not Denmark, in 1023 when St Ælfheah's relics were translated.

Conclusion

Three periods of Anglo-Saxon history are particularly well documented: the reigns of Alfred the Great, Æthelred (the Unready), and Edward the Confessor. Much has been written about the reigns of Alfred and Edward, but, by comparison, little attention has been paid to the reign of Æthelred.

An examination of the sources for Æthelred's reign shows that he and his councillors have been victims of much malign propaganda. In the period immediately after his death, Æthelred's failure to combat and defeat invading armies was contrasted unfavourably with the dynamic actions of his son, King Edmund Ironside, and it was suggested that God had used the invasions to punish the English nation because the murder of King Edward the Martyr, in 978, had gone unpunished. After the Norman Conquest, this suggestion was taken further. It was said that God had punished the English by allowing a Danish conquest and then a Norman conquest of the country because of the murder of King Edward the Martyr, a murder which had been instigated by his (step) mother Queen Ælfthryth, who wanted her son, Æthelred, to become king. This malign propaganda led to an assessment of the king and his reign which can be summarised in the words of Eadmer:

> The indolence of the King became known round about and the greed of those outside her borders, aiming rather at the wealth than the lives of the English, invaded the country by sea at one point after another and laid waste at first the villages and cities near the coast, then those further inland and in the end the whole province, driving the inhabitants in wretchedness from their homes. The King instead of meeting them in arms panic-stricken shamelessly offered them money sueing for peace; where-upon they accepted the price and retired to their homes, only to return in still greater numbers and still more ruthless, from renewed invasion to receive increased rewards.[1]

This assessment has been generally accepted over the centuries and it may have been the perceived failures of Æthelred, as a king and as a man, which made this period of history unattractive to historians. Because there has been comparatively little interest in the history of King Æthelred's reign, there have been relatively few scholars to challenge this common perception, a perception still to be found in the brief histories of the kings and queens of England which are sold to tourists.

Yet the assessment of the king is false. It ignores entirely more than a quarter of a century of progress and consolidation when Æthelred built successfully and prosperously upon the economic and political foundations left by his father, King Edgar. By tackling the subject of the invasions and Danish conquest of England largely from a Scandinavian perspective, this book goes to the heart of

---

[1] Bosanquet, *Eadmer's History of Recent Events in England*, p. 4.

the charges levelled against Æthelred and challenges them. It is based on a scientific analysis of the evidence, providing a more accurate chronology of events; an examination of the chronological order in which our sources, and amendments to our sources, were created; a consideration of the provenance of the evidence; and an investigation of the logical relationships between English and overseas sources. Also, the book has had regard to number. Today England is one of the most densely populated countries on earth; then it was sparsely populated: there may have been more sheep than people in England; a very substantial township might boast a population of 5,000. The impact of small-scale immigration and small-scale invasion on a sparsely populated country was relatively significant then, as it would not be now, following the massive population explosion of the nineteenth and twentieth centuries.

The analysis reveals that the impact on England of invasions during the so-called Second Viking Age has been misunderstood. England was a country enjoying increasing population, trade and wealth during most, if not all, of King Æthelred's 38-year reign. The king employed mercenary forces, mostly Scandinavians, as did many other rulers at this time. Although there were incursions into England over the land frontiers and there were piratical raids along the English coast, such incursions and raids also occurred during the reigns of Æthelred's predecessors and successors; they should not necessarily be regarded as a distinguishing feature of his reign.

In Chapter 1 a description of England's increasing prosperity during most of King Æthelred's long reign is in marked contrast to what we may glean from Eadmer's description of events. That Æthelred was no weak and indolent king is shown by the fact that many of the most famous warriors of the Second Viking Age were his allies, with Olaf Tryggvason, Thorkell the Tall and St Olaf showing a significant degree of loyalty to his cause. The Scandinavian sources refer to him with respect. It is true that the invasions developed from being coastal incursions into full-scale invasions and, finally, wars of conquest; but this book shows that the later invasions and the conquests by Swein and Cnut were largely possible because they were supported by the indigenous population. The support of Northumbria and the Danelaw for King Swein in 1013 is partly a reflection of a shift in economic and political power to the north and east of England and away from Wessex. Eadmer is mistaken about payments to invaders. Æthelred did not pay raiders to go away; he paid for winter truces or for the invaders to change their character and become mercenaries acting in his political interests. Though the biased account of events in the *Anglo-Saxon Chronicle* suggests that English forces were unsuccessful and badly led, there seems to be no doubt that armies and fleets were raised to combat the invaders and that they were probably, on occasion, more successful than the *ASC* would wish to allow – as, for example, in 1004/5 when Swein Forkbeard's army suffered heavy losses in battle and withdrew from England without having forced the English into any sort of negotiation or *gafol* payment, and also in 1014 when Æthelred's forces re-conquered England. Finally, a reconstruction of the chronology of events in our sources allows us to understand the nature of the marriage agreement between King Cnut and Queen Emma; in effect, Cnut's 'conquest' of England was based, in part, upon a negotiated settlement with members of the English establishment. Eadmer fails to recognise that it was civil conflict over the succession to the throne of an ailing king which brought about the final disasters of Æthelred's reign and allowed the Danish king, Cnut, an opportunity to establish himself as king of England.

A detailed analysis of the invasions and conquest allows us to develop a more balanced appreciation of Æthelred and his reign. This analysis opens up the way to a reappraisal of the period 978 to 1016 with greater emphasis on English political, economic and social developments, rather than in terms of foreign invasion and conquest.[2]

---

2   This is a task which I am undertaking in a forthcoming book, *The Reign of King Æthelred II (the Unready)*.

Appendix 1. *Heimskringla*

Snorri Sturluson's History of the Kings of Norway, usually known as *Heimskringla*, is an important source of information about events in Scandinavia during the period covered by this book.[1] It is also valuable for an understanding of some events in England. Its value to students of English history has been diminished by a difficulty in aligning some events, associated with the *Heimskringla* hero, St Olaf, with the chronology of events recorded in the *Anglo-Saxon Chronicle* (*ASC*). This difficulty has led some historians to interpret the *Heimskringla* sources in a manner that the present writer questions.

Professor Campbell was a very influential critic who agreed that Snorri's interpretation of his skaldic verse evidence, concerning St Olaf's exploits in England, should be amended. Although Campbell was not the instigator of some of the revised interpretations of the evidence in *Heimskringla*, he explains them in appendix III of his edition and translation of the *Encomium Emmae Reginae*.[2] It is convenient, therefore, to address the question, of whether Snorri's interpretation of events needed revision, by specific reference to Campbell's work. The chronological problem is best introduced in Campbell's own words:

> It is one of the most fixed elements in the northern chronology that Óláfr reigned fifteen years, but there is some doubt as to the point from which these were reckoned. If they are reckoned from his arrival in Norway, this must be placed in 1015, but if the first winter, before the defeat of Earl Sveinn, or the period after his flight to Russia in 1028, in which he was a king without power, be excluded from his reign, his arrival most be put in 1014.[3]

Campbell quotes discussion of the dates 1014 and 1015 by various authorities and concludes:

> I do not consider it possible to decide finally between these years. On the other hand, the fifteen years reign of Óláfr is a firm tradition, and is confirmed by a verse of Sigvatr – so it is manifestly impossible to make the period from the summer of 1030 back to the autumn of his arrival in Norway include *less* than fifteen winters; also, since he was present at Æthelred's restoration in 1014, it cannot include *more* than sixteen winters.[4]

As will be noted later, if St Olaf 'was present at Æthelred's restoration in 1014',

---

[1] Jónsson, *Heimskringla*; this provides variant readings and an analysis of the skaldic verses. English translations of *Heimskringla* include: Hollander, *Heimskringla*; Monsen, *Heimskringla*; Laing, *Heimskringla, the Norse King Sagas*; Laing, *Heimskringla, the Olaf Sagas*.
[2] Campbell, *Encomium*, appendix III.
[3] *Ibid.* p. 79 n. 8.
[4] *Ibid.* pp. 79–80 n. 8.

the chronology of subsequent events would preclude his arrival in Norway in either 1014 or 1015. The dates quoted by Campbell are derived by allowing St Olaf a reign of fifteen years before his death, which occurred in 1030. Neither of these dates allows St Olaf time to participate in the restoration of King Æthelred to the English throne in 1014 and then undertake the campaigns which Snorri, quoting his skaldic verse sources, relates to the period after Æthelred's restoration.

However, if the matter of King Æthelred's restoration is put to one side for the moment, the problem posed by the earlier parts of Campbell's observations will not easily go away. St Olaf is supposed to have reigned fifteen years because Snorri himself says so, quoting his mentor, Ari the Wise, and, as Campbell observes, quoting Sigvat the Scald.[5] It is evident that either Snorri's account of St Olaf's campaigns is suspect or the length of his reign must be less than fifteen years.

This appendix examines the chronology of Snorri's sagas in *Heimskringla* and concludes that St Olaf reigned for between ten and eleven years and that Snorri deliberately manipulated his history in order to accord with Ari's observation that St Olaf reigned fifteen years.

To allow St Olaf a reign of fifteen years, Campbell and others have felt obliged to transpose events described by Snorri to an earlier period in an arguably questionable manner. Campbell's justification for doing so is that Snorri must have misinterpreted the skaldic verses on which his account is based. On the subject of skaldic verses and their use as historical sources, Campbell wrote:

> It cannot be too clearly emphasised that the verses of the skalds, who composed for the kings of Norway and Denmark in the tenth and eleventh centuries, and occasionally for prominent noblemen, are preserved only in quotations in the Old Norse Sagas, particularly in *Heimskringla* and *Fagrskinna*. Hence, although the basic principle of the study of early Scandinavian history must always be to study the verses separately from the prose in which they are embedded, and to see if they necessarily bear the meaning which the prose alleges them to do, yet, even when this is done, the danger always remains that a verse may not be genuinely early, or may be early but not refer to the events with which the prose connects it. The verses in the Sagas of the kings seem to be given in good faith by the compilers, who appear to avoid the practice, which is not uncommon in other Sagas, of writing verses to fit their narrative, and alleging that characters in their story composed them.[6]

Given the highly stylised nature of the skaldic verse format,[7] it would be difficult to justify ignoring entirely the prose explanation which accompanies the verses in the sagas. Campbell's concern about Snorri's interpretation is

---

[5] Laing, *Heimskringla, the Olaf Sagas*, pp. 391–2, c. CCLX: it is convenient to follow Laing's translation because the editorial comment follows the chronology supported by Campbell.
[6] Campbell, *Encomium*, appendix III, p. 66 n. 3.
[7] To quote Campbell: 'Norse poets of that period aimed at the artistic decoration of facts known to their hearers rather than at giving information . . .', *Ibid.* appendix III, p. 66.

two-edged when he uses Snorri, quoting Sigvat's verse, to justify a fifteen-year reign especially when, as will be demonstrated below, Snorri's chronology of events and the fifteen-year reign cannot both be correct. Arguably, if Snorri had had access to the *ASC* he would himself have recognised the impossibility of a fifteen-year reign. It is perhaps fortunate that Campbell is generally able to rely upon the 'good faith' of Snorri's selection of early skaldic verses, since our knowledge of the Scandinavian history of this period would be greatly reduced without them. Snorri's veracity is discussed below. Campbell, who is an influential figure in the analysis of our sources for the period covered by the present book, fully understood what Snorri said about St Olaf's campaign in England on behalf of King Æthelred, but does not believe Snorri, dismissing his chronology with the following words:

> I refrain from comment on the wild chronology into which all this is fitted.[8]

Campbell was inclined to use rhetorical devises such as this to emphasis the validity of an interpretation of the sources which he favoured. This feature of his work is most apparent when, having re-interpreted verses quoted by Snorri to make them refer to an earlier period and different events, he wrote:

> It can, therefore, be concluded with a certainty almost as great as is ever possible in the study of Old English history, that Óláfr took part in Thorkell's campaign of 1009–11.[9]

The following analysis explains why St Olaf's participation in Thorkell's English campaign, which commenced in 1009, is far from likely and why Snorri's interpretation of the skaldic sources and events in England should not be dismissed because of his reference to a reign of fifteen years.

Heimskringla is a history of the rulers of Norway from the earliest times. In a series of sagas, it tells their histories and provides additional material which enhances those histories. Thus, we learn about many other historical figures and about geography, climate, customs, religion and other matters. *Heimskringla* touches upon the histories of Iceland, Scandinavia and parts of northern Europe in so far as they impact upon that of Norway. It acquired its name in a fortuitous manner which, no doubt, would have surprised its author, the Icelander, Snorri Sturluson.[10] The oldest known manuscript had lost its preface and opening words, leaving *Kringla heimsins* as the first words in the book. A name was derived for the book from these words.

Snorri probably wrote the sagas, incorporated in *Heimskringla*, between his return from a visit to Norway in 1220 and his death in 1241. Although his history may be regarded as distant in time from the events described, he drew upon contemporary sources such as skaldic verses. The skalds were contempo-

---

[8]   *Ibid.* appendix III, p. 82.
[9]   *Ibid.* appendix III, p. 77.
[10] For a summary of the evidence for Snorri's authorship of *Heimskringla* and the *Edda*, referred to below, see Whaley, '*Heimskringla*', pp. 276–9.

raries of the kings they praised and many claimed a close working relationship with them. Snorri also drew upon the writings of earlier Icelandic historians, including some that are no longer extant. A major influence was the work of Ari Thorgilsson, the Wise, who lived from 1067 until 1148. Snorri quotes Ari to support his chronology, and it is likely that Snorri's attempts to align his sagas with Ari's time-scale have led to a significant chronological confusion in his saga of Olaf Helgi. The sources, both verbal and written, which were available to Snorri greatly exceed those available to us.

Snorri quoted extensively from skaldic sources in *Heimskringla*, explaining their value in his preface. The verses are complex, with kennings which are not readily recognisable to a modern audience. It seems to the present writer doubtful whether a contemporary audience would have understand a verbal presentation of the verses any more than a modern audience would understand complex art forms such as opera and ballet without foreknowledge or assistance. A modern audience is often reminded of the story in the programme in order to enhance its appreciation of the performance and one may presume that skalds developed a tradition of explaining the story before delivering the verses. Snorri follows this pattern, first explaining the story and then quoting the supporting verses.

Snorri was a skald himself and wrote a definitive study about skaldic verses. It is relevant to Snorri's standing as a historian that his *Edda* demonstrates a deep understanding of the skaldic art since he claims skaldic verses as contemporaneous evidence of events and people. He makes this claim in his preface to *Heimskringla* in a passage which is often quoted:

> and we rest the foundations of our story principally upon the songs which were sung in the presence of the chiefs themselves or of their sons, and take all to be true that is found in such poems about their feats and battles: for although it be the fashion with skalds to praise most those in whose presence they are standing, yet no one would dare to relate to a chief what he, and all those who heard it, knew to be a false and imaginary, not a true account of his deeds; because that would be mockery, not praise.[11]

Snorri, as an Icelander, may be considered distant from the location of the events he describes. However, the lives of the leading Icelanders of his time, and indeed before his time, were closely bound up with events in Norway and Snorri himself visited Norway and spent much time there. In effect, he was practically a native of Norway and had a good knowledge of neighbouring Scandinavian countries. It is relevant that he and his sources made sea voyages and travelled extensively. No doubt they met other travellers and discussed the history and geography of parts of the world they had not visited themselves. As a result, Snorri's knowledge of the geography and history of the British Isles is demonstrably greater and more realistic than that of north German chroniclers such as Thietmar of Merseburg and Adam of Bremen. Arguably, this is also true of his knowledge of Scandinavian geography and history, despite the fact that Adam of

---

[11] Laing, *Heimskringla, the Norse King Sagas*, Snorre's Preface, p. 4.

Bremen claimed the much-travelled king of Denmark, Swein Estrithsson, as his principal informant.

Unlike most chroniclers, Snorri was himself a leading political figure and his book was not particularly influenced by the dictates of a sponsor. This is not to say that he did not seek the political favour of powerful men. In Norway, these included King Hakon and Duke Skuli and his skaldic verses, in *Hattatal*, are written in their praise. However, he was, in a sense, himself a sponsor. It is to be expected that he used some of his resources to employ others to collect skaldic verses and their accompanying stories and, although there need be no doubting Snorri's authorship of *Heimskringla*, it is likely that his work was dictated to scribes and that their discussions and comments helped him to enhance his work. There is no written acknowledgement of the mechanics of production, though it is entirely logical that a rich and powerful statesman, with many responsibilities and many friends and servants eager to please him, would conduct an onerous project in a manner which devolved much of the detailed work upon others.

Snorri was undoubtedly a self-centred man of strong personality. However, he gives little reason to suspect biased manipulation of his histories. We should, of course, make allowance for the nature of his interests and the influence of the times in which he lived and one should expect an element of bias in one particular direction. Snorri and his contemporaries lived in communities that had a close relationship with farming and the land. Breeding, ancestry and continuity were important to them and the pedigrees of many important families are noted in *Heimskringla* together with stories enhancing their family pride and reputation. We are too far removed to question much of the detail and, for that matter, the family pedigrees, but, because these matters were important to his contemporaries, we should expect that Snorri would have shown some bias in the inevitable selectivity which is required of any author faced with a superfluity of information.

Snorri's source information, only part of which is extant, was varied and of disparate value. It is a measure of the man's considerable intellect that he was able to evolve a series of sagas which, individually and together, maintain a logic and credibility. This recognition of Snorri's achievement is not an acknowledgement that he was always correct in his interpretation and presentation: mistakes are discernible, but, because of Snorri's intellect and endeavour, they are difficult to spot.

Only occasionally is it possible to fault Snorri and evidence an error of fact or chronology. There are two reasons for this. Firstly, and very importantly, the written evidence which we have for Scandinavian history at that time, to compare with *Heimskringla*, is sparse and of relatively poor quality, often suffering from similar time and distance objections without the saving qualities of Snorri's careful analysis. Secondly, Snorri was a man of considerable intellect who was able to make chronological sense of a complex story. He advanced a history of different people in different places and, although he sometimes needed to move backwards in time to catch up with events in different places, he usually achieved this without causing confusion. It may be considered self-evident that he 'interpreted' his sources in order to achieve this end, but it is rarely apparent, from a reading of his book, where he has introduced his own interpretations to maintain the flow and sense of the story. Thus, it is difficult to distinguish and evidence Snorri's mistakes as we can those of Adam of Bremen[12] and, although there are different and sometimes contradictory accounts of what happened, it is difficult to use them, as we can in the case of John of Worcester,[13] to highlight probable errors.

Some errors, discrepancies and imaginative addition are evident in *Heimskringla*, but if we were to ignore Snorri's work in order to avoid error, our modern scholarship would be greatly the poorer. Snorri was selective about what he described and was most interested in the activities of Norwegian rulers, tending to view the world through their eyes. However, they had dealings with other Scandinavian countries and further afield and Snorri wrote sympathetically about events in those countries, especially Denmark whose kings often had a suzerainty over part or all of Norway in the late tenth and early eleventh centuries. Although Snorri was a Christian, he was not particularly biased against the pagan rulers of Norway, tending to the view that they represented an old order whose time was past rather than condemning them out of hand. This understanding of Norway's pagan rulers did not extend to pagan practitioners or 'wizards' and he describes, without apparent concern, how kings such as Olaf Tryggvason tortured and killed them.

During the period covered by this book Snorri provides no dates. Yet some of his sources contained dates and his chronology within each saga is realistic, demonstrating that he had dates for certain events before him. Snorri's chronology was influenced by the work of Ari the Wise, who was born in 1067, and in his preface, Snorri explains how Ari:

> reckoned the years first to the time when Christianity came to Iceland and thereafter right down to his own days. Thereto he added many happenings in the lives of the kings in Norway and Denmark and likewise in England . . .[14]

An assessment of Snorri's veracity is a matter closely related to a study of the chronology of events in *Heimskringla*. Although Snorri may not have intended to deceive his audience, he was not writing to provide an accurate analysis of events suited to the needs of the modern scientific historian. He was an excellent raconteur whose work must be used with caution as an historical record. In the *Heimskringla* sagas about kings Harald Greyskin, Olaf Tryggvason and Olaf Helgi there are some chronological faults which demonstrate that Snorri was prepared to manipulate his sources to produce a coherent story. This evidence of manipulation must put us on warning.

We are indebted to Snorri, and others like him who incorporated the extant skaldic verses in their books, but it should not be overlooked that our understanding of skaldic verse is much influenced by Snorri's choice of verses and

---

[12] I. Howard, 'Adam of Bremen's History of the Archbishops of Hamburg-Bremen', unpublished paper.
[13] Howard, 'Swein Forkbeard's Invasions of England', pp. 102–17.
[14] Monsen's translation: Monsen, *Heimskringla*, p. xxxvi.

also by his book, *Edda*, which explains how to write and interpret them. This may be regarded as a quibble compared with the fact that, in *Heimskringla*, we have the views of a man with access, directly or indirectly, to written sources otherwise unavailable to us and who understood thirteenth-century interpretations of skaldic verses.

In forming an appreciation of Snorri's chronology and consequently his veracity, the following features should be considered:

good internal chronology in the *Heimskringla* sagas;

Heimskringla being out of phase with 'real' time over a period of years whilst remaining consistent within itself;

the manner in which dates may be extrapolated from *Heimskringla*;

the use of seasons in *Heimskringla* to mark the passage of time.

Examples of realistic internal chronology can be identified in three chronological tables derived from Snorri's references to the number of years elapsing between events. They demonstrate that Snorri had a strong sense of the passage of time and the time relationship between events. It seems likely that he noted the dates of some events and arranged his stories in a logical sequence before writing or dictating them. He probably omitted dates because that was his concept of the saga format. Also, their complete omission precluded debate; an advantage since he could not have had exact dates for many of the events he described.

In the following chronological tables the chapter references are from Laing's edition of *Heimskringla*. Saga references are 'H.G.' for 'Hakon the Good'; 'E.' for 'The Sons of Eric'; 'E.H.' for 'Earl Hakon'; 'O.T.' for 'Olaf Trygvesson'; 'O.H.' for 'Olaf Helgi'; 'M.G.' for 'Magnus the Good'. Laing's edition is preferred because the editorial comment agrees with the 'Campbell' interpretation of chronology. Laing's edition may be compared with the translations by Monsen and by Hollander.

Snorri leaves a degree of doubt about the chronology in the final years in Table 1. The likely timescale overlaps with that in Table 2. Although Snorri provided no reference point where a positive alignment of the two can be agreed, nothing in them precludes a near agreement for historical analysis purposes.

The significance of the chronology in Tables 1 and 2 may be better appreciated if they are related to 'real' time dates. This can be done for Table 1 by assuming that the 'year 0' is 961, a generally accepted date for the death of King Hakon the Good. 'Year 0' in Table 2 may be 969. This birth date for Olaf Tryggvason is extrapolated: Snorri says he was born after his father's death and a probable date for King Tryggvi's death is derived from the first table.

Based on information in some German annals, Olaf Tryggvason may have accompanied his father-in-law, Boleslav Mieszko, on an expedition in 985 or 986.[15] If this expedition occurred in the middle of Olaf's three-year stay in

---

[15] Pertz, *Annales Quedlinburgenses*, and Pertz, *Annales Hildesheimenses*, *s.aa.* 985, 986.

Table 1. Chronology of events: the twenty-year period from the death of Hakon the Good

Year

0	Fall of King Hakon the Good. [H.G. XXXII]
0	The sons of Eirik and Gunnhild succeed. [E. I]
2	Earl Sigurd of Lade was killed. (See below for confirmation of the year.) [E. III]
5	Earl Hakon (Sigurdsson) fought the sons of Eirik for three years. ('Years' 3,4,5.) [E.H. I]
8	There was peace between Earl Hakon and the sons of Eirik for three years. ('Years' 6,7,8.) [E.H. I]
(8)	King Tryggvi was killed, probably just before the end of the period of peace. He was killed following a meeting with Earl Hakon which made the sons of Eirik suspicious of their intentions. The sons of Eirik then killed Tryggvi and their army attacked Earl Hakon. [E.H. IV and VII]
14	There was war between Hakon and the sons of Eirik for six years. ('Years' 9 to 14, but see next line. The timescale is wrong by one year.) [O.T. XIII]
15	Correction: Snorri, quoting Ari, says that King Harald Greyskin was killed fifteen years after the fall of King Hakon the Good and thirteen years after the fall of Earl Sigurd of Lade. [O.T. XIII]
15	Harald Grenski was eighteen years old in this year. [O.T. XV]
(18)	Eirik Hakonarson was ten or eleven years old and he quarrelled with the brother of Earl Hakon's new wife. Since Eirik was born in the period of peace in 'years' 6, 7 or 8 and Snorri says he was now ten or eleven, this 'year' lies between 16 and 19 and is nearer to 18 or 19 to allow for the events leading up to Hakon's wedding. (18) and subsequent figures are, therefore, extrapolations and also subject to an error of +/– one year. [O.T. XX]
(19)	Eirik Hakonarson killed Tidings-Skofti, Earl Hakon's brother-in-law, and escaped to Denmark. [O.T. XX]
(20)	Eirik Hakonarson was made an earl by King Harald of Denmark. [O.T. XX]

The 'years' in brackets are not identified exactly by Snorri.

Table 2. Chronology of events: the 25-year period from the birth of Olaf Tryggvason

Year

0	Birth of Olaf Tryggvason. [O.T. I]
3	Olaf was captured by pirates when he was three winters old. [O.T. V]
9	Olaf was a slave in Estonia for six years. [O.T. V]
18	Olaf was nine winters old when he went to Gardariki and he stayed a further nine years. [O.T. VII]
21	Olaf went to Vendland and remained there for three years. [O.T. XXX]
25	Olaf harried in northern Europe and the British Isles for four years before he went to the Scilly Isles. [O.T. XXXI]

Vendland, the second chronological table provides a date of 988, so there may be an anomaly in Snorri's chronology at this point.

Olaf Tryggvason attacked London and harried other parts of England in the autumn of 993.[16] He was probably at peace in England, under the terms of a treaty, for the greater part of the years 994 and 995. On this basis, Snorri's chronology seems to be in agreement with 'real' time and Table 2 accords with the opening point in Table 3. The tables cannot be amalgamated, however, because Snorri provides no timescale, such as the length of time Olaf stayed, at peace, in England.

Table 3 provides an excellent example of *Heimskringla* being out of phase with 'real' time over a period of years whilst remaining consistent within itself. It warrants a detailed analysis because the anomalies in it have caused considerable confusion to translators, editors and historians.

Although Table 3 is derived from three sagas, there is evidence that Snorri was working to one chronological sequence of events. The battle of Svold has a chronological position in the Olaf Tryggvason Saga. This event is referred to in the Olaf Helgi Saga as 'the fall of Olaf Tryggvason' and is used as a reference point for establishing relative chronology. The length of Cnut's reign over his kingdoms is in the Saga of Magnus the Good, chapter 5, a chapter which is sequentially close to the chapter in the Olaf Helgi Saga which gives the length of Olaf Helgi's reign.

The problem in Table 3 is best illustrated by repeating relevant parts of the chronological sequence assuming the year '0' to be 995. This is done in Table 4.

Comparing the length of Cnut's Danish and English reigns with *ASC* 'real' time, it is reasonable to assume that we are dealing with inclusive 'years'. Swein Forkbeard died in February and Cnut succeeded him to the throne of Denmark, according to Snorri. Cnut was acknowledged as king by all the English early in 1017. Since Cnut died in the month of November, it is reasonable to count both the opening and closing years in counting the number of years that he reigned. However, Cnut's seven-year reign in Norway, which is entirely outside the chronological problem period, accords with sequential time.

Having said that, we must return to the major problem. The beginning and end of Snorri's chronological sequence is in accord with 'real' time but in the middle of the sequence there is a discrepancy of up to five years against 'real' time as measured by the *ASC*. Thus:

King Swein died in February 1014, not in autumn 1009;

King Æthelred returned to England in 1014, not 1009;

Eirik Hakonarson joined Cnut in England in 1016 (assuming that he did not accompany him in 1015), not in 1012 or 1011;

King Cnut became king of all England early in 1017 and reigned for nineteen years, inclusive; he did not become king in 1012 and reign for twenty-four years, inclusive;

Olaf Helgi must have been in Normandy with Æthelred's exiled sons in 1018, not in 1013.

[16] Chapter 3, pp. 42–6, above.

Table 3. Chronology of events: the forty-year period from Olaf Tryggvason becoming king of Norway

Year

0	Olaf Tryggvason invaded Norway and became king. [O.T. LII–LVII]
0	Earl Hakon was killed. [O.T. LV]
0	Earl Eirik Hakonarson went to Sweden. [O.T. LVII]
0	Olaf Helgi was born. (See 'years' 3 and 35 below for supporting evidence. It is possible to extrapolate an earlier birth date elsewhere in *Heimskringla*.)
2	Thangbrand the priest was sent to Iceland two years after Olaf Tryggvason became king. [O.T. LXXX]
2	Eirik Hakonarson went to Denmark and married Gytha. [O.T. XCVII]
3	When he had been king for three years, Olaf Tryggvason was godfather to Olaf Helgi who was three years old. [O.T. LXVII]
4	Next year Olaf Tryggvason quarrelled with Queen Sigrid. [O.T. LXVIII]
4	Thangbrand returned from Iceland after two years. [O.T. LXXX]
4	After he had been king for four years, Olaf Tryggvason defeated Gudrod Ericsson's invasion and killed him. [O.T. XCIV]
5	Eirik Hakonarson harried in Russia for five years. [O.T. XCVII]
5	BATTLE OF SVOLD AND FALL OF OLAF TRYGGVASON. [O.T. CXI–CXXII]
5	Eirik Hakonarson became joint ruler of Norway. [O.T. CXXIII]
12	Olaf Helgi first went on a warship when he was twelve years old. [O.H. IV] (See 'years 0 and 3' for Olaf's date of birth.)
14	Swein Forkbeard died *in the autumn* and King Æthelred returned to England; Olaf Helgi, who had recently gone to England, joined King Æthelred. [O.H. XI] (This 'year' is derived from the sequence of events leading up to the 'year 18', below, where Snorri provides a reference point to the fall of Olaf Tryggvason. Using Snorri's references to seasons, it is possible to extrapolate either that Olaf had two campaigning seasons, 'years' 12 and 13, or three, 'years' 12, 13, 14.)
14	Cnut became king of Denmark. [M.G. V]
17	Olaf Helgi stayed in England for three years. [O.H. XIV]
17	King Cnut summoned Eirik Hakonarson to join him in England. Eirik had ruled over Norway for twelve years. ('twelve years' may be inclusive of the opening and closing years, making this 'year' 16.) [O.H. XXIII.]
17	Cnut became king of England three years after becoming king of Denmark. [M.G. V]
18	Olaf Helgi went harrying in western Europe for two summers and one winter. This was thirteen years after the fall of Olaf Tryggvason. [O.H. XIX]
18	Olaf Helgi wintered in Normandy. [O.H. XIX]
19	In the winter between the years 18/19, Olaf Helgi was in Normandy with Æthelred's sons. [O.H. XXV]
19	Olaf Helgi and Æthelred's sons failed in an attack on England. [O.H. XXVI]
19	Olaf Helgi sailed to Norway. [O.H. XXVII]
33	Olaf Helgi was in Norway for fifteen years inclusive: 19 + 15 inclusive of opening and closing years = 33. (Snorri quoted Ari.) [O.H. CLXXXIX]
33	Cnut became king of Norway. (M.G. V implies that this happened in 'year' 34. 'Year' 33 is preferred here to coincide with Olaf's departure from Norway.)
35	Olaf Helgi was killed on his return to Norway. It is not clear from Snorri's chronology whether this was one or two years after his flight from Norway. Snorri reckons in O.H. CLXXXIX and in O.H. CCLX that there were sixteen years between Olaf's arrival in Norway and his fall. He quotes Sigvat as saying that Olaf ruled for fifteen years until his fall and adds a year for the time when Earl Swein was in the land and Olaf was only recognised as king by the people of the Uplands. To coincide with other records (*ASC* C) and a reported eclipse of the sun, it is assumed that the sixteen years are sequential and that he died in the 'year' (19 + 16 =) 35. Snorri, quoting Ari, says that Olaf was thirty-five years old. [O.H. CCLX]

40   King Cnut died after being king of Denmark for twenty-seven years, of England for twenty-four years and of Norway for seven years. These are inclusive dates since Cnut died five years after Olaf. [M.G. V] However, the seven years of Cnut's reign in Norway appear to have been sequential.

Table 4. Chronology of events: the forty-year period from Olaf Tryggvason becoming King of Norway in 995

Year

995	Olaf Tryggvason invaded Norway and became king.
995	Earl Eirik Hakonarson went to Sweden.
995	Olaf Helgi was born.
997	Eirik Hakonarson went to Denmark and married Gytha.
998	When he had been king for three years, Olaf Tryggvason was godfather to Olaf Helgi who was three years old.
999	After he had been king for four years, Olaf Tryggvason defeated Gudrod Ericsson's invasion and killed him.
1000	Eirik Hakonarson harried in Russia for five years. (Between 995 and 1000.)
1000	BATTLE OF SVOLD AND FALL OF OLAF TRYGGVASON.
1000	Eirik Hakonarson became joint ruler of Norway.
1007	Olaf Helgi first went on a warship when he was twelve years old.
1009	Swein Forkbeard died *in the autumn* and King Æthelred returned to England; Olaf Helgi, who had recently gone to England, joined King Æthelred.
1009	Cnut became king of Denmark.
1012	Olaf Helgi stayed in England for three years. (1009 to 1012.)
1012	King Cnut summoned Eirik Hakonarson to join him in England. Eirik had ruled over Norway for twelve years. (Twelve years inclusive would be the year 1011.)
1012	Cnut became king of England.
1013	Olaf Helgi went harrying in western Europe for two summers and one winter. (The summer of 1012 – after the death of King Æthelred in the spring of that year – until the summer of 1013.) This was thirteen years after the fall of Olaf Tryggvason.
1013	Olaf Helgi wintered in Normandy.
1014	In the winter of year 1013/1014, Olaf Helgi was in Normandy with Æthelred's sons.
1014	Olaf Helgi and Æthelred's sons failed in an attack on England.
1014	Olaf Helgi sailed to Norway.
1028	Olaf reigned in Norway for fifteen years, inclusive. (Snorri quoted Ari and Sigvat.)
1028	Cnut became king of Norway.
1030	Olaf Helgi was killed on his return to Norway. Snorri, quoting Ari, says he was thirty-five years old.
1035	King Cnut died after being king of Denmark for twenty-seven years, of England for twenty-four years and of Norway for seven years.

Table 4 allows three years, 1007, 1008 and 1009 for Olaf Helgi's activities and battles before he went to England in 1009. Snorri quotes Sigvat and other skalds for Olaf's activities but the chronology is his own. Using dates from the above table, Snorri has Olaf Helgi and his foster father, Rani, voyage to Denmark, harry in Sweden, fight a first battle near the Sota Skerry, harry as far as Sigtuna, escape a trap set by the Swedish king and then voyage to Gotland where they took tribute and, presumably, spent the winter months. Because of some uncertainty about whether Snorri was referring to one or two autumns in his passages about these events, they may all have occurred either in the one year 1007 or in the two years 1007 and 1008. Next, Olaf Helgi harried Eysysla, fought his second battle there, harried in Finland, lost many men in a third battle there, joined Thorkell the Tall and together attacked Viking ships off Suderwick (i.e. a fourth battle off the west coast of Jutland), fought a fifth battle in Friesland and then arrived in England before the autumn where he helped King Æthelred's army capture London Bridge and force the surrender of the city, before winter. These events, according to Snorri, occurred in one year and relate to the year 1009 in Table 4.

Since there is evidence in the *ASC* and John of Worcester's Chronicle that Thorkell the Tall invaded England in August 1009, Campbell and others have assumed that Olaf and Thorkell were together in England and that Olaf Helgi took part in the English campaigns ascribed to the great army which invaded England in 1009 and finally made peace with King Æthelred's government in 1012.[17] Such an inference makes nonsense of the skaldic evidence and Sigvat's careful numbering of Olaf's battles, since his sixth battle is in support of King Æthelred at the taking of London Bridge.

Returning to the list of discrepancies against 'real' time, the clue to resolving the problem is in the statement that Cnut's reign in England lasted for twenty-four years. We know that the 24-year reign commenced some three years after Swein Forkbeard's death because of the reference to Cnut being king of Denmark for twenty-seven years. Snorri clearly intended us to understand that Cnut became king in 1012.[18] If we 'correct' Snorri's chronology to agree with *ASC* 'real' time, it is necessary to advance the date of Cnut's succession by about five years and reduce the length of his reign by five years. If we do the same for Olaf Helgi, the alignment of events in which both Cnut and Olaf participated is retained. In other words, Olaf Helgi became king of Norway in c. 1019 and he reigned for ten years, inclusive, not the fifteen which Snorri, following Ari, records.

To follow his mentor, Ari, and force a fifteen-year reign into his chronology, Snorri had to conflate events in the middle of the chronological table. It is realistic to suppose that Olaf's early campaigns were spread over a longer period than Snorri allowed. His chronology indicates an extensive campaign in 1007 and 1008 in Sweden, followed by a voyage to Gotland. It seems wise not to suggest any amendment to this. However, the multiplicity of campaigns in 1009 seems unrealistic and we should distinguish the campaign against the island of Eysysla and Finland in the eastern Baltic from a campaign in the company of Thorkell the Tall in which booty was taken from Viking ships off the west coast of Jutland. We should then distinguish, as a separate campaign, the fifth battle at Kinnlima side, in Friesland, which was followed by Olaf's voyage to England and his destruction of London Bridge. There is no mention of Thorkell's continued alliance with Olaf after the battle with the Vikings off Jutland and pre-

---

17 Campbell, *Encomium*, appendix III, p. 77.
18 Campbell gives no reference for his (questionable) statement that '*Heimskringla* also gives the length of his [Cnut's] reign in England correctly': *Ibid.* appendix III, p. 83 n. 1.

sumably the two leaders returned to a safe place to share the booty and divide forces.

This division of events into three distinct campaigns allows the chronological table to be adjusted so that the campaign in the eastern Baltic took place in 1009; the campaign off Jutland, in the company of Thorkell the Tall took place in 1010 or 1011; and the campaign which took Olaf to Friesland and London took place in 1013. After campaigning in England for three years, Olaf left in the summer of 1016, following King Æthelred's death in April of that year, and harried western Europe for two summers and one winter, bringing him to Normandy where he spent the winter of 1017/18 with King Æthelred's sons. In 1018, he attacked England again and then sailed to Norway.

Some comments are required about the above amendments. It is suggested that Olaf joined Thorkell the Tall for an expedition against Viking shipping in either 1010 or 1011 although it is generally supposed by Campbell and many others that Thorkell was in England during that time. In fact there is evidence, in *ASC* and in John of Worcester, that he was in England in 1009 and there is evidence, in *ASC*, that he was in England in 1012. There is evidence, in John of Worcester, that the Scandinavian army in England was led by Thorkell's brother, Hemming, in 1009. He was killed in England and the *Encomium* informs us that King Swein Forkbeard of Denmark granted Thorkell permission to go there, with an army, to avenge his brother's death.[19] It follows that Thorkell must have returned to Scandinavia at some time during the years 1010 and 1011.

The suggestion that Laing, Monsen and others have made that a future saint, Olaf, assisted at the destruction of churches, and at the capture, humiliation and martyrdom of the archbishop of Canterbury is remarkable. It is almost as remarkable to suppose that the Christian king, Æthelred, should ally himself with Thorkell the Tall immediately after he had participated in these events. Thietmar of Merseburg has an account, given him by a traveller from England, that Thorkell attempted to save the archbishop;[20] such a story would be more fitting if it was accepted that he had not participated in his capture and humiliation in the first place.

There remains a problem with Snorri's chronology because he believed that Swein Forkbeard died in the autumn. In fact, he did not die until February and there is no indication of what Olaf was doing in England until the return of King Æthelred in 1014. It may be supposed that he allied himself with Viking forces which were loyal to Thorkell rather than to Swein at this time, but there is no evidence.

Finally, there is a chronological difficulty with regard to Olaf's Helgi's return to Norway. If he was in Norway for ten years, inclusive, he did not arrive until 1019. That is eighteen years after the fall of Olaf Tryggvason. If he arrived in 1018, as suggested above, then he was there for eleven years inclusive (ten years sequential) until his departure in 1028. Given the evidence that Snorri was fudging the chronology in order to align himself with Ari, this must be

---

[19] Campbell, *Encomium*, Bk I, c. 2, p. 11.
[20] Trillmich, *Thietmari Merseburgensis*, Bk VII, c. 42 (29).

Appendix 1

Table 5. Revised chronological table of events

Year

995	Olaf Tryggvason invaded Norway and became king.
995	Earl Eirik Hakonarson went to Sweden.
995	Olaf Helgi was born.
997	Eirik Hakonarson went to Denmark and married Gytha.
998	When he had been king for three years, Olaf Tryggvason was godfather to Olaf Helgi who was three years old.
999	After he had been king for four years, Olaf Tryggvason defeated Gudrod Ericsson's invasion and killed him.
1000	Eirik Hakonarson harried in Russia for five years. (Between 995 and 1000.)
1000	BATTLE OF SVOLD AND FALL OF OLAF TRYGGVASON.
1000	Eirik Hakonarson became joint ruler of Norway.
1007	Olaf Helgi first went on a warship when he was twelve years old.
1008	*Olaf campaigned for two years in Sweden and Gotland.*
1009	*Olaf campaigned in the eastern Baltic.*
1011	*In 1010 or 1011, Olaf campaigned off Jutland with Thorkell the Tall.*
1013	*Olaf campaigned in Friesland and then went to England.*
1014	Swein Forkbeard died *in February* and King Æthelred returned to England; Olaf Helgi, who had recently gone to England, joined King Æthelred.
1014	Cnut became king of Denmark.
1016	Olaf Helgi stayed in England for three years. [*1013 to 1016.*]
1016	King Cnut summoned Eirik Hakonarson to join him in England. Eirik had ruled over Norway for *seventeen* years. (*Seventeen* years inclusive.)
1017	Cnut became king of England.
1017	Olaf Helgi went harrying in western Europe for two summers and one winter. (The summer of *1016* – after the death of King Æthelred in the spring of that year – until the summer of *1017*.) This was *eighteen* (*recte* seventeen) *sequential* years after the fall of Olaf Tryggvason.
1017	Olaf Helgi wintered in Normandy.
1018	In the winter of year *1017/18*, Olaf Helgi was in Normandy with Æthelred's sons.
1018	Olaf Helgi and Æthelred's sons failed in an attack on England.
1018	Olaf Helgi sailed to Norway.
1028	Olaf reigned in Norway for *ten* years.
1028	Cnut became king of Norway.
1030	Olaf Helgi was killed on his return to Norway. Snorri, quoting Ari, says he was thirty-five years old.
1035	King Cnut died after being king of Denmark for *twenty-two* years, of England for *nineteen* years and of Norway for seven years.

accounted a minor quibble. However, it may act as a reminder that it is dangerous to 'amend' a source whatever the justification. The above explanation of events is, therefore, put forward as the best available and as a necessary antidote to explanations which are now too readily accepted. Hopefully, further evidence will one day be forthcoming to further justify the 'amendment' or to advance the debate.

Meanwhile, it is possible to re-schedule the events in the chronology to accord with *ASC* 'real' time; see Table 5.

It will have been noted that in the above analyses dates have occasionally been extrapolated from Snorri's text by relating events to each other. It is very easy to undertake this exercise because Snorri was working to a chronological pattern and signposted the passage of time by reference to the passing seasons. Often the word 'winter' is synonymous with 'year' in the sense of the passage of time. Thus, Snorri may write that a person was a number of winters old or a number of winters has passed since an event. In other passages, therefore, it is tempting to count the years according to the number of winters which pass in Snorri's account and demonstrably the result is realistic.

It is apparent that Snorri's chronological database consisted mainly of relationships between events and few dates, if any, for the period under review. As well as the chronological fault line between 'real' time and 'Ari' time there are two chronological anomalies that should be considered.

The chronological fault line occurred in order to amend 'real' time to allow Olaf Helgi a fifteen year reign to accord with 'Ari' chronology. This was achieved by the conflation of three campaigns into one year. However, the required result might have been achieved if Olaf Helgi had been born five years earlier, in 990 rather than 995. Snorri's chronological database allowed for this possibility. In the Saga of Olaf Tryggvason, Snorri records that Olaf was born after the death of his father, Harald Grenski, who, he says, was killed in the winter after the Jomsvikings fought at Hjorungavag, thus aligning Olaf's birth with c. 990. A birth-date in 990 could not stand, however, because it contradicted the timing of other events in Olaf's life, so 'real' time continues. However, Snorri allowed the anomaly in his database to remain in the saga and this has caused some confusion. As an example, the chapter heading in Laing, *Heimskringla*, records that Harald Grenski was killed in 994–995; thus this edition accepts a 995 date for Olaf's birth and 'moves' the events leading to the battle of Hjorungavag. This 'move' is not possible because Swein Forkbeard, who instigated the events leading to the battle, was in England at the relevant time.

The second anomaly concerns the death of Eirik of Lade. It can be demonstrated that Snorri was writing in 'real' time until after the year 1007. It is less certain when 'Ari' time ended although it is clear that 'real' time appertains by 1028. It seems likely that Snorri's database made a transition back to real time about the year 1018: it cannot have been earlier because Cnut commenced his reign in England in 'Ari' time. The year 1018 seems likely because Snorri was confused about the date of Eirik of Lade's death. According to Snorri, he joined Cnut, who was already campaigning in England, in c. 1011 ('Ari' time). We know from diploma evidence that Eirik remained in England for some six or seven years.[21] This takes us to c. 1018 'Ari' time (or 1023 in 'real' time). According to Snorri, Eirik was in England no more than two years before he died.[22] It has long been apparent that Snorri was mistaken; he should have said that Eirik was in England for six or seven years (inclusive or sequential). It can be seen how Snorri's mistake came about: at the point where his database was

---

[21] Keynes, 'Cnut's Earls', p. 58.
[22] Laing, *Heimskringla, the Olaf Sagas*, c. XXIII.

switching from 'Ari' time to 'real' time he became confused. Having followed Snorri through this labyrinth the reader may feel some sympathy for him.[23]

The two anomalies serve as another warning that we should be cautious in the manner in which *Heimskringla* is used as an historical record. Like Snorri's statement that Swein Forkbeard died in the autumn, which can be disproved by reference to the *ASC*, this is further evidence, if it were needed, of manipulation.

However, the demonstrable errors are rare and the error forced upon Snorri by his attempt to align himself with Ari is by far the greatest. It is, perhaps, a measure of the confidence that Snorri has inspired in his editors and historians, that his chronological error in the Olaf Helgi Saga is not commonly noted as such and that so many attempts have been made to explain it away. Considering that Snorri set out to explain the history of the Norwegian kings to the best of his ability and did not intend his sagas to be analysed as if they were dated chronicles, his work withstands analysis remarkably well.

---

[23] An anomaly, concerning the length of Eirik's rule in Norway and the length of time between his departure and Olaf's invasion, that troubled Campbell disappears if the revised chronology in Table 5 is accepted: see Campbell, *Encomium*, appendix III, pp. 68–70.

Appendix 2. The *Anglo-Saxon Chronicle*
A reconstruction of the annal for the year 1008

The annal for the year 1008, in *ASC* C D E and F, appears to have used a taxation schedule as a source. As transmitted, it is deficient and has caused problems for the editors and translators of these versions of the *Anglo-Saxon Chronicle*.[1]

There are actually five versions of this annal since *ASC* F has both an Old English and a Latin version.[2] Each version of the annal agrees except in a phrase, which in the original version cannot have exceeded fifteen words. Each version differs slightly in its transmission of this phrase. Version F, Latin version, also differs from the others in that it adds a gloss explaining one of the words in the annal.

The problem phrase is highlighted in Analysis I, below, where the four extant Old English versions and the Latin version of the annal for 1008 are compared side by side. The Old English versions are taken from Thorpe's edition of the *ASC* and the Latin version is taken from a facsimile of *ASC* F.[3] This analysis demonstrates that there is a 'problem area' where no two versions are in agreement about the words to be copied. Both before and after the 'problem area' the five versions of the *ASC* are in agreement except that *ASC* F, Latin version, adds a gloss explaining the word 'sceзð'. Agreement might be expected throughout since all versions are derived from the same source, the *Æthelredian Exemplar* (*ÆE*).[4] The disagreement is evidence that, at this point, the annal in *ÆE* was deficient in some way.

ASC C has only three words in the 'problem area' but it makes grammatical sense. *ASC* C has been transmitted to us via an intermediate exemplar and, since the other extant manuscripts have more words, it is likely that a scribe has amended the original phrase, in the exemplar, to achieve this grammatical sense. Whitelock translated this version of the annal for 1008 as:

> In this year the king ordered that ships be built unremittingly over all England, namely a warship from 310 hides and a helmet and corselet from eight hides.[5]

However, as Professor Whitelock explained, in a footnote to the annal, '310 is an unusual unit'. Hides were usually dealt with as units of 100 for administrative and fiscal purposes. There is specific evidence of this practice applying to

---

[1] Howard, 'Swein Forkbeard's Invasions of England', pp. 65–73, discusses these problems and earlier attempts to make sense of the annal.

[2] *ASC* A: Cambridge, Corpus Christi College 173; *ASC* B: BL, Cotton Tiberius A vi; ASC C: BL, Cotton Tiberius B i; *ASC* D: BL, Cotton Tiberius B iv; ASC E: Bodleian Library, Laud 636; ASC F: BL, Cotton Domitian A viii.

[3] Thorpe, *The Anglo-Saxon Chronicle*; Dumville, *MS F.*

[4] The relationship of the extant versions of the *ASC* and *ÆE* is explained below.

[5] Whitelock, *EHD*, p. 219, *s.a.* 1008.

Analysis I. Annal 1008: problem area

WORDS IN:

ASC C	*ASC* D	*ASC* E	*ASC* F	*ASC* F	LATIN
þ	þæt	þ	þ	hoc	
is	is	is	ys	est	
ðonne	þonne	þonne			
.		.	.		
of	of		of	de	
þrim	þrym	þrym	CCC.	CCC.	
hund	hund	hund			
hidum		hidum	hidum	hidis	

	scipum				
	.				Problem
7	7	7	7	et	
of		of			Area
	x.	x.	x.	x.	
		hidon	hidum		
	be				
tynum	tynum				

ænne	anne	ænne	anne	unam	
scegð	scægð	scegð	scegð	scegð	
.	.	.	.	.	
7	7	7	7	et	
of	of	of	of	de	
viii.	viii.	viii.	viii.	viii.	
hidum	hydum	hydum	hidum	hidis	
helm	helm	helm	helm	galeam	
7	7	7	7	et	
byrnan	byrnan	byrnan	byrnan	loricam	
.	.	.	.	.	

ship-scot (*scypesce*[*ote*]) and based upon 300 hides in a writ of Bishop Æthelric of Sherborne.[6] It is difficult, therefore, to follow Professor Whitelock's acceptance of *ASC* C's interpretation of the 'problem area'.

ASC E, which is copied, with the omission of one word, by *ASC* F, fails to make sense. It has '300 hides', words which are not related to ships or any other objects, followed by 'and from ten hides one big ship'.

ASC D has the greatest number of words in the 'problem area' and it is a fair

6　S.1383 and Harmer, *Anglo-Saxon Writs*, Stamford, 1989, pp. 266–70.

copy of *ÆE*.[7] The annal does not make grammatical sense but this lack of sense in a fair copy, coupled with its greater number of words, suggests that it reflects most of what was readable in *ÆE*, a manuscript that had been miscopied from the taxation schedule or had been damaged in some way.

With these clues before us, it is possible to use the comparative words from each version of the *ASC*, in Analysis I, to reconstruct the words of the original taxation schedule. This reconstruction is provided in Analysis II, below.

The words in the reconstructed annal may be translated:

(a)   selected units of three hundred hides should provide a ship plus [a helmet and corselet] for every ten hides
and

(b)   selected units of ten hundred hides should provide a large warship plus a helmet and corselet for every eight hides.

Following the *ASC* D line in the reconstruction, it can be seen that after the words 'three hundred' ('þrym hund') it omits 'hides' ('hidum') and says 'a ship' ('an scip.'). Thus, it is deduced that the original required one ship from 300 hides, a statement that accords with the ship-scot in Bishop Æthelric's writ. *ASC* E F provide support for this interpretation because they have 'three hundred hides' ('þrym hund hidum') in the first phrase.

Next, *ASC* D has the Roman numeral 10 ('x.'); *ASC* E F have '10 hides' ('x. hidum'). Hence, it is deduced that there is a reference to the three hundred hides also providing a helmet and corselet for every ten hides to arm the men on their ship. The words 'helmet and corselet' do not appear in any of the extant versions, but it is clear that some object(s), of which there were ten, are missing from the phrase. Provision is made for helmets and corselets to arm the men on the large ships, in the next part of the annal, so it is logical to suppose that 'helmets and corselets' are the objects missing from this earlier part of the annal. The translation, above, includes the words 'a helmet and corselet' in square brackets at the appropriate place in the annal.

Next, in *ASC* D, come the words and 'for ten a large ship' ('be tynum ænne scægð'). All versions of the *ASC* agree on the words 'ænne scægð'. *ASC* C, which omitted the Roman numeral 10 ('x.'), has the word 'tynum' and this is supportive of the phrase in *ASC* D. There can be no doubt about the translation of the word 'scægð' as a large ship, and in context a 'large warship'. The Latin version of *ASC* F has a gloss to make the meaning quite clear: 'unam magnam nauem quae Anglice nominatur scægð'. In context, and because it is a repetitive phrase, the word 'hundred' (*hund*) after ten ('tynum') must be assumed. We are meant to understand that every ten hundred hides should provide a large ship. There can be no doubting this meaning, since ten hides could not supply a large

---

[7]   *ASC* D is the only extant fair copy of *ÆE*. *ÆE* was also copied into exemplars, which, following some amendments, were copied into our extant versions C and E of the *ASC*. *ASC* F draws upon versions of *ASC* E and A for its annals. A brief description of the likely history of the *ÆE* manuscript is provided later in this appendix.

Analysis II. Annal 1008: reconstruction

WORDS IN:	C	D	E	F	
þæt	✳	✳	✳	✳	
is	✳	✳	✳	✳	
þonne.	✳	✳	✳		
of	✳	✳		✳	
þrym	✳	✳	✳	✳	
hund	✳	✳	✳	✳	
hidum	✳		✳	✳	
an					
scip.		✳			was 'scipum.'
7	✳	✳	✳	✳	
of	✳		✳		
x.		✳	✳	✳	
hidum			✳	✳	
*					* ? perhaps
7					'helm 7
be		✳			byrnan.'
tynum	✳	✳			
hund					
hidum					
anne	✳	✳	✳	✳	
scægð.	✳	✳	✳	✳	
7	✳	✳	✳	✳	
of	✳	✳	✳	✳	
viii.	✳	✳	✳	✳	
hidum	✳	✳	✳	✳	
helm	✳	✳	✳	✳	
7	✳	✳	✳	✳	
byrnan.	✳	✳	✳	✳	

ship, so the original taxation schedule probably omitted the word *hund* deliberately.

Finally, all versions of the *ASC* agree that a 'helmet and corselet' ('helm 7 byrnan') should be provided for the ship from every eight hides, again, as in the earlier phrase using a Roman numeral ('viii. hidum'). There is a balanced phraseology in which Old English is used ('þrym' and 'tynum') before the larger units of hundreds and Roman numerals ('x.' and 'viii.') are used before the subdivision of those units for the provision of helmets and corselets. 125 helmets and corselets were required for a large warship and 30 for other ships.[8]

---

[8] The significance of the number of corselets and the different types of ships which would make up a fleet is discussed in Howard 'Swein Forkbeard's Invasions of England', p. 71.

It will be observed that *ASC* D has the most complete wording of the taxation schedule and that it is an extant fair copy of the *Æthelredian Exemplar* (*ÆE*). Because the history of *ÆE* is not generally known, a synopsis is provided here. The detailed evidence that supports this synopsis is provided elsewhere.[9]

The *Æthelredian Exemplar* (*ÆE*)

In 1016, Archbishop Wulfstan of York ordered the creation of this new version of the *Anglo-Saxon Chronicle*, at a time when he was supporting King Edmund's efforts to make himself king of all England in succession to his father, King Æthelred.[10]

Annals were prepared for *ÆE* using the Mercian annals, northern annals, the exemplar of *ASC* E and the exemplar for *ASC* C to provide the material for the period before King Æthelred's accession in 978. The schematic in Figure 1, p. 4, above, shows how this material was brought together for the compilation of *ÆE*. Archbishop Wulfstan may have added some homiletic passages to the exemplar of *ASC* E, which were subsequently copied into *ÆE*.[11]

Material, from several distinct sources, was gathered to provide the annalistic material covering the reigns of King Æthelred and his son, King Edmund.[12]

---

[9] The evidence is incorporated in discussion of the extant versions of the *ASC* in Howard, 'Swein Forkbeard's Invasions of England', pp. 50–101.

[10] See pp. 3–5, above, for an explanation of why Archbishop Wulfstan sponsored *ÆE* to assist King Edmund's cause.

[11] The annals for 959 and 975 include material that is recognised as being in the style of Archbishop Wulfstan. See Whitelock, *EHD*, pp. 205, 209; Bethurum, *The Homilies of Wulfstan*, p. 47 and her quotation from Jost, 'Wulfstan und die angelsächsische Chronik', *Anglia* xlvii, 1923, pp. 105ff. The words in Wulfstan's style in the annal for 959 are in versions D and E of the *ASC* (and, via E, they are in version F). The words in Wulfstan's style in the annal for 975 are in version D only; an abbreviation of the passage is in version E (and, via E, in version F). To these observations I would add that, because of its provenance (though not on stylistic grounds), the homiletic passage about King Edward the Martyr's death in the annal for 979 (*recte* 978) should also be linked to Archbishop Wulfstan.

[12] The sources are discussed in Howard, 'Swein Forkbeard's Invasions of England', pp. 85–8. Due to a misunderstanding of his sources the scribe of *ÆE*, and also Archbishop Wulfstan, believed that King Edward the Martyr had been killed on 18 March 979. Edward the Martyr was commemorated on 18 March (the date of his translation and, therefore, his commemoration at Shaftesbury) but the scribe probably assumed that he was commemorated on the day of his death. King Æthelred's consecration was on 4 May 979 and the scribe probably assumed that Æthelred's accession occurred shortly before the consecration. Hence, he wrote that Edward the Martyr was killed on 18 March 979. Our earliest source, *ASC* A, which does not appear to have been available to the scribe who wrote this annal, states that Edward was killed in 978. Another earlier source, a *Life of Saint Oswald*, states that he was killed, in the evening, ten days after the ninth or the fifth month. The ninth or fifth month is May and this hermeneutic phrase is telling us that he was killed on 10 June (ten days after the month of May). So our earliest sources are saying that King Edward the Martyr was killed, in the evening, on 10 June 978. These matters were explained in a paper which I read to the Manchester Centre for Anglo-Saxon Studies in April 2002 entitled 'King Edward the Martyr: When, How and Why did he Die? The Problem and a Proposed Solution'.

Immediately after the compilation of *ÆE*, the new annals covering the reigns of
Æthelred and Edmund were added to the exemplar for *ASC* E before the manuscript was returned to York. An interesting anomaly in *ASC* E is that the scribe
who copied the annals into its exemplar attempted to maintain an existing *caput
anni* (year commencement) for his annals. This explains why the 'annal year' in
ASC E sometimes differs from that in *ASC* C and D for annals between 978 and
991. Subsequently, some further amendments were made to this exemplar and,
as was normal practice, this exemplar was replaced by a fair copy, *ASC* E.

Immediately after the compilation of *ÆE*, the new annals covering the reigns of
Æthelred and Edmund were added to the exemplar for *ASC* C before the manuscript was returned to Abingdon. A significant amendment was then made to the
exemplar of *ASC* C. Most of the words from the *ÆE* annals for the years 978 and
979 were erased and new annals, unique to this version of the *ASC*, were substituted. Subsequently, some further amendments were made to this exemplar and,
as was normal practice, this exemplar was replaced by a fair copy, *ASC* C.

Two small amendments were made to *ÆE* before the fair copy, *ASC* D, was
created.[13] Then the chronicle was continued with annals covering events in the
year 1017. Subsequently, the leaves containing the annals for 1017 were
removed, with a consequential loss of part of the annal for the year 1016. In the
mid-eleventh century, the annal for the year 1016 was restored and further
annalistic material was added to *ASC* D, probably on the orders of Bishop
Ealdred of Worcester.[14] The leaves which were removed from *ASC* D were
retained at Worcester until the twelfth century, when they were used as a source
for the Chronicle of John of Worcester.[15]

---

[13] It is likely that Archbishop Wulfstan made the amendments himself. One of them, in the
annal for 1014, says that Ælfwig was consecrated Bishop of London, at York, on 16 February:
an event at which the archbishop must have officiated.
[14] Cubbin, *MS D*, Introduction, pp. lxxviii–lxxxi. But see Howard, 'Swein Forkbeard's Invasions of England', for the sponsorship of the *ASC* annals to 1016.
[15] Howard, 'Swein Forkbeard's Invasions of England', pp. 77–8.

Bibliography

Primary Sources

Manuscript
London, BL, Cotton Tiberius B iv: *Anglo-Saxon Chronicle* MS D

Printed
Alexander M. (trans.), *Beowulf: A Verse Translation*, Harmondsworth: Penguin Books, 1973
Ashdown M. *English and Norse Documents relating to the Reign of Ethelred the Unready*, Cambridge: Cambridge University Press, 1930
Bately J. M. 'The Anglo-Saxon Chronicle', in *The Battle of Maldon AD 991*, ed. D. Scragg, Oxford: Basil Blackwell, 1991, pp. 37–50
Bauer A. and R. Rau (eds), *Liudprandi Opera: Quellen zur Geschichte der Sachsischen Kaiserzeit*, in Ausgewählte Quellen zur Deutschen Geschichte des Mittelalters, in Verbindung mit vielen Fachgenossen, ed. R. Buchner and F-J. Schmale, Band 8, Darmstadt: Wissenschaftliche Buchgesellschaf, 1977
———— and R. Rau (eds), *Widukindi Res Gestae Saxonicae: Quellen zur Geschichte der Sachsischen Kaiserzeit*, in Ausgewählte Quellen zur Deutschen Geschichte des Mittelalters, in Verbindung mit vielen Fachgenossen, ed. R. Buchner and F-J. Schmale, Band 8, Darmstadt: Wissenschaftliche Buchgesellschaf, 1977
Bethurum D. (ed.), *The Homilies of Wulfstan*, Oxford: Clarendon Press, 1957
Blake E. O. (ed.), *Liber Eliensis*, Camden 3rd series, vol. XCII, London: Royal Historical Society, 1962
Blake N. F. (trans.), *The Saga of the Jomsvikings*, London: Thomas Nelson and Sons Ltd, 1962
Bosanquet G. (trans.), *Eadmer's History of Recent Events in England*, London: The Cresset Press, 1964
Brown R. A. *The Norman Conquest*, Documents of Medieval History 5, London: Edward Arnold, 1984
Campbell A. (ed.), *Encomium Emmae Reginae*, Camden 3rd series, vol. LXXII, London: Royal Historical Society, 1949; reissued with a supplementary introduction by Simon Keynes, Cambridge: Cambridge University Press, 1998
Christiansen E. (ed.), *Saxo Grammaticus, Danorum Regum Heroumque Historia, Books X–XVI: the text of the first edition with translation and commentary in three volumes*, vol. I, *Books X, XI, XII, and XIII*, British Archaeological Reports, International series 84, Oxford, 1980
———— (ed.), *Saxo Grammaticus, Danorum Regum Heroumque Historia, Books X–XVI: the text of the first edition with translation and commentary in three volumes*, vol. III, *Books XIV, XV, and XVI, Introduction and Commentary, General Index*, British Archaeological Reports, International series 118(ii), Oxford, 1981
———— (trans.), *The Works of Sven Aggesen, Twelfth-Century Danish Historian*, London: Viking Society for Northern Research, University College, 1992
Conner P. W. (ed.), *The Anglo-Saxon Chronicle, a Collaborative Edition, Volume 10: The Abingdon Chronicle, AD 956–1066 (MS C, with reference to B D E), a reconstructed edition with introduction and indices*, Cambridge: D. S. Brewer, 1996

Cubbin G. P. (ed.), *The Anglo-Saxon Chronicle, a Collaborative Edition, Volume 6: MS D, a semi-diplomatic edition with introduction and indices*, Cambridge: D. S. Brewer, 1996

Darlington R. R. and P. McGurk (eds), *The Chronicle of John of Worcester*, Volume II, *The Annals from 450 to 1066*, Oxford: Clarendon Press, 1995

Dasent G. W. (trans.), *The Story of Burnt Njal*, London: J. M. Dent & Sons Ltd, 1911

Davidson H. E. and P. Fisher, *Saxo Grammaticus, The History of the Danes, Books I–IX*, vol. I, *English Text*, Cambridge: D. S. Brewer, 1979

Driscoll M. J. (ed.), *Agrip af Noregskonungasogum*, London: Viking Society for Northern Research, University College, 1995

Dumville D. (ed.), *The Anglo-Saxon Chronicle, a Collaborative Edition, Volume 1: Facsimile of MS F: The Domitian Bilingual*, Cambridge: D. S. Brewer, 1995

—— and M. Lapidge (eds), *The Anglo-Saxon Chronicle, a Collaborative Edition, Volume 17: The Annals of St Neots with Vita Prima Sancti Neoti*, Cambridge: D. S. Brewer, 1985

Faulkes A. (trans.), *Snorri Sturluson: Edda*, London: J. M. Dent, 1987 (reissued 1995)

Flower R. and H. Smith (eds), *The Parker Chronicle and Laws (Corpus Christi College, Cambridge, MS 173): A Facsimile*, Early English Text Society, original series no. 208, London: Oxford University Press, 1941 (for 1937)

Forester T. (trans.), *The Chronicle of Henry of Huntingdon, Comprising the History of England from the Invasion of Julius Caesar to the Accession of Henry II. Also, the Acts of Stephen, King of England and Duke of Normandy*, London: Henry G. Bohn, 1853

Garmonsway G. N. (trans.), *The Anglo-Saxon Chronicle*, London: J. M. Dent & Sons Ltd, 1972 (first published 1953)

Gertz M. Cl. (ed.), *Scriptores Minores Historiae Danicae Medii Ævi*, vols I and II, København: J. Jørgensen & Co., 1917–20

Giles J. A. (trans.), *Roger of Wendover's Flowers of History, formerly ascribed to Matthew Paris*, vol. I, *Part One, 447 to 1066 AD*, Felinfach: Llanerch Publishers facsimile reprint, 1993 (first published London: Henry G. Bohn, 1849)

—— (trans.), *William of Malmesbury's Chronicle of the Kings of England from the Earliest Period to the Reign of King Stephen*, London: Henry G. Bohn, 1847

Greenway D. (ed. and trans.), *Henry, Archdeacon of Huntingdon, Historia Anglorum, The History of the English People*, Oxford: Clarendon Press, 1996

Harmer F. E. *Anglo-Saxon Writs*, Manchester, 1952, reissued Stamford: Paul Watkins, 1989

Hearn E. H. *The Sagas of Olaf Tryggvason and of Harald the Tyrant (Harald Haardraade)*, London: Williams and Norgate, 1911 (English translation of Gustav Storm's edition)

Hollander L. M. (trans.), *Heimskringla: History of the Kings of Norway by Snorri Sturluson*, Austin: University of Texas Press, 1964

Jack G. (ed.), *Beowulf: A Student Edition*, Oxford: Clarendon Press, 1995 (revision of 1994 publication)

Jónsson F. (ed.), *Heimskringla, Nóregs Konunga Sogur af Snorri Sturluson*, vols I to IV including *Fortolkning til Versene*, København: S. L. Møllers Bogtrykkeri, 1893–1901

Kemble J. M. *Codex Diplomaticus Aevi Saxonici*, vol. III, London: English Historical Society, 1845

Keynes S. 'King Æthelred's Treaty with the Viking Army (994)', appendix to 'The Historical Context of the Battle of Maldon' in *The Battle of Maldon AD 991*, ed. D. Scragg, Oxford: Basil Blackwell, pp. 103–7

Laing S. (trans.), *Heimskringla, the Norse King Sagas: Snorre Sturlason*, London: J. M. Dent & Sons Ltd, 1951
—— (trans.), *Heimskringla, the Olaf Sagas by Snorre Sturlason*, London: J. M. Dent & Sons Ltd, 1930
Lappenberg J. M. (ed.), *Chronicon Breve Bremense*, MGH VII, Hannover, 1846, pp. 389–92
—— (ed.), *Mag. Adami Gesta Hammenburgensis Ecclesiae Pontificum*, MGH VII, Hannover, 1846, pp. 267–389
—— (ed.), *Thietmari . . . Chronicon*, MGH III, 1889, pp. 723–871
Lattin H. P. (trans.), *The Letters of Gerbert with his Papal Privileges as Sylvester II*, New York: Columbia University Press, 1961
Luard H. R. (ed.), *Annales Monasterii de Wintonia (AD 519–1277), Annales Monasterii de Waverleia (AD 1–1291)*, Annales Monastici, vol. II, Rolls Series, London: Longman, Green, Longman, Roberts, and Green, 1865
Lund N. (ed.), *Two Voyagers at the Court of King Alfred: The Ventures of Ohthere and Wulfstan together with the Description of Northern Europe from the Old English Orosius*, York: William Sessions Limited, 1984
Mellows W. T. (ed.), *The Chronicle of Hugh Candidus, a Monk of Peterborough*, London: Oxford University Press, 1949
Mills S. M. (trans.), *The Saga of Hrolf Kraki*, Oxford: Basil Blackwell, 1933
Monsen E. (ed.), *Heimskringla or the Lives of the Norse Kings by Snorre Sturlason*, Cambridge: W. Heffer & Sons Ltd, 1932
Pálsson H. and P. Edwards (trans.), *Egil's Saga*, Harmondsworth: Penguin Books, 1976
—— and P. Edwards (trans.), *Knytlinga Saga: The History of the Kings of Denmark*, Odense: Odense University Press, 1986
—— and P. Edwards (trans.), *Orkneyinga Saga: The History of the Earls of Orkney*, London: Penguin Books, 1981
Pertz G. H. (ed.), *Annales Corbienses* in MGH III, Hannover, 1839, pp. 1–18
—— (ed.), *Annales Hildesheimenses* in MGH III, Hannover, 1839, pp. 52–97
—— (ed.), *Annales Quedlinburgenses* in MGH III, Hannover, 1839, pp. 52–78
Plummer C. (ed.), *Two of the Saxon Chronicles Parallel with supplementary extracts from the others*, vol. I: *Text, Appendices and Glossary*, Oxford: Clarendon Press, 1892
Riley H. T. (trans.), *Ingulphus's Chronicle of the Abbey of Croyland with the Continuations of Peter of Blois and Anonymous Writers*, London: Henry G. Bohn, 1854
Robertson A. J. (ed. and trans.), *Anglo-Saxon Charters*, Cambridge: Cambridge University Press, 1939
Sawyer P. H. *Anglo-Saxon Charters: An Annotated List and Bibliography*, London: Royal Historical Society, 1968
—— (ed.), *Charters of Burton Abbey*, Anglo-Saxon Charters 2, Oxford: Oxford University Press, 1979
Scragg D. G. (ed.), *The Battle of Maldon*, Manchester: Manchester University Press, 1981
Sephton J. (trans.), *The Saga of King Olaf Tryggwason who reigned over Norway AD 995 to AD 1000*, London: David Nutt, 1895
Stevenson J. (ed.), 'The Chronicle of Florence of Worcester' in *The Church Historians of England*, vol. II, part I, London: Seeleys, 1853
—— (trans.), *Simeon of Durham: A History of the Kings of England*, Felinfach: Llanerch Enterprises facsimile reprint, 1987 (first published in 1858 in *The Church Historians of England*)
—— (trans.) *William of Malmesbury: The Kings before the Norman Conquest*,

Felinfach: Llanerch Publishers, 1989 (facsimile reprint from *The Church Historians of England*)

Swanton M. (trans.), *The Anglo-Saxon Chronicle*, London: J. M. Dent, 1996

Taylor S. (ed.), *The Anglo-Saxon Chronicle, a Collaborative Edition, Volume 4: MS B*, Cambridge: D. S. Brewer, 1983

Thorpe B. (ed.), *The Anglo-Saxon Chronicle according to the Several Original Authorities*, vol. I, *Original Texts*, Rolls Series, London: Longman, Green, Longman and Roberts, 1861

—— (ed.), *Florentii Wigorniensis Monachi, Chronicon ex Chronicis* vol. I, London: English Historical Society, 1848

Trillmich W. (trans.), *Thietmari Merseburgensis Episcopi: Chronicon*, Berlin: Rütten & Loening; in *Ausgewählte Quellen zur Deutschen Geschichte des Mittelalters, in Verbindung mit vielen Fachgenossen*, ed. R. Buchner, IX, Darmstadt, 1974

Tschan F. J. (trans.), *Adam of Bremen: History of the Archbishops of Hamburg-Bremen*, New York: Columbia University Press, 1959 (an English translation of Schmeidler's 1917 edition)

Vigfusson G. (ed.), *Sturlunga Saga including The Islendinga Saga of Lawman Sturla Thordsson and Other Works*, Oxford: Clarendon Press, 1878

Waitz D. G. (ed.), *Widukindi Res Gestae Saxonicae* in *MGH* III, Hannover, 1839, pp. 408–67

Whitelock D. (ed. and trans.), *Anglo-Saxon Wills*, Cambridge: Cambridge University Press, 1930

—— (ed.), *English Historical Documents*, vol. I, *c. 500–1042*, London: Eyre & Spottiswoode, 1955

—— (ed.), *Sermo Lupi ad Anglos*, University of Exeter, 1976

——, D. C. Douglas and S. I. Tucker (eds), *The Anglo-Saxon Chronicle*, London: Eyre and Spottiswoode, 1961

Williams Ab Ithel J. (ed.), *Brut Y Tywysogion or The Chronicle of the Princes*, Rolls Series, London: Longman, Green, Longman, and Roberts, 1860

Secondary Sources

Abels R. 'English Tactics and Military Organization in the Late Tenth Century' in *The Battle of Maldon AD 991*, ed. D. Scragg, Oxford: Basil Blackwell, 1991, pp. 143–55

—— *Lordship and Military Obligation in Anglo-Saxon England*, Berkeley, Los Angeles, London: University of California Press, 1988

Andersson T. M. 'The Viking Policy of Ethelred the Unready' in *Anglo-Scandinavian England: Norse-English Relations in the Period before the Conquest*, ed. J. D. Niles and M. Amodio, University Press of America, 1989

Banton N. 'Monastic Reform and the Unification of Tenth-Century England' in *Religion and National Identity*, ed. S. Mews, Studies in Church History 18, Oxford: Basil Blackwell, 1982

Barraclough G. (ed.), *The Times Atlas of World History*: revised edition, London, 1986

Bately J. M. 'The Anglo-Saxon Chronicle' in *The Battle of Maldon AD 991*, ed. D. Scragg, Oxford: Basil Blackwell, 1991, pp. 37–50

—— 'Manuscript Layout and the Anglo-Saxon Chronicle', *Bulletin of the John Rylands University Library of Manchester* 70, 1988, pp. 21–43

Bates D. *Normandy before 1066*, London and New York: Longman, 1982

Bennett M. 'The Medieval Warhorse Reconsidered' in *Medieval Knighthood V, Papers from the Sixth Strawberry Hill Conference*, ed. S. Church and R. Harvey, Woodbridge: The Boydell Press, 1995

————'The Myth of the Military Supremacy of Knightly Cavalry' in *Armies, Chivalry and Warfare in Medieval Britain and France: Proceedings of the 1995 Harlaxton Symposium*, ed. M. Strickland, Stamford: Paul Watkins, 1998

Binns A. 'Ships and Shipbuilding' in *Medieval Scandinavia: An Encyclopedia*, ed. P. Pulsiano, New York and London: Garland Publishing Inc., 1993, pp. 578–580

Brooks N. *The Early History of the Church of Canterbury Christ Church from 597 to 1066*, London: Leicester University Press, 1984

———— 'Weapons and Armour' in *The Battle of Maldon AD 991*, ed. D. Scragg, Oxford: Basil Blackwell, 1991, 208–19

———— 'Arms, Status and Warfare in Late-Saxon England' in *Ethelred the Unready: Papers from the Millenary Conference*, ed. D. Hill, British Archaeological Reports, British series 59, 1978, pp. 81–104

Brown M. P. *Anglo-Saxon Manuscripts*, London: The British Library, 1991

Campbell A. *Skaldic Verse and Anglo-Saxon History: The Dorothea Coke Memorial Lecture in Northern Studies delivered at University College London, 17 March 1970*, London: H. K. Lewis, 1970

Cheney C. R. (ed.), *Handbook of Dates for Students of English History*, London: Royal Historical Society, 1978

Clapham J. H. 'The Horsing of the Danes', *EHR* XXV, 1910, pp. 287–93

Clark C. 'The Narrative Mode of the Anglo-Saxon Chronicle before the Conquest' in *England before the Conquest: Studies in Primary Sources presented to Dorothy Whitelock*, ed. P. Clemoes and K. Hughes, Cambridge: Cambridge University Press, 1971, pp. 215–35

Clemoes P. and K. Hughes (eds), *England before the Conquest: Studies in Primary Sources presented to Dorothy Whitelock*, Cambridge: Cambridge University Press, 1971

Collen G. W. *Britannia Saxonica*, London: William Pickering, 1833

Crumlin-Pedersen O. 'Ships, Navigation and Routes in the Reports of Ohthere and Wulfstan' in *Two Voyagers at the Court of King Alfred*, ed. N. Lund, York: William Sessions Limited, 1984, pp. 30–42

Darby H. C. *Domesday England*, Cambridge: Cambridge University Press, 1977

Davidson H. E. and P. Fisher, *Saxo Grammaticus, The History of the Danes, Books I–IX*, vol. II, *Commentary*, Cambridge: D. S. Brewer, 1980

Davis R. H. C. *A History of Medieval Europe from Constantine to Saint Louis*, London: Longmans, Green and Co., 1957

———— *The Medieval Warhorse: Origin, Development and Redevelopment*, London: Thames and Hudson, 1989

———— 'The Warhorses of the Normans', *Anglo-Norman Studies* 10, 1988, pp. 67–82

De Hamel C. *Scribes and Illuminators*, Medieval Craftsmen Series, London: British Museum Press, 1992

Demidoff L. 'The Death of Sven Forkbeard – in Reality and Later Tradition', *Medieval Scandinavia* 11, 1978–9, pp. 30–47

Dixon P. *The Making of the Past: Barbarian Europe*, London, 1976

Dodgson J. McN. 'The Site of the Battle of Maldon' in *The Battle of Maldon AD 991*, ed. D. Scragg, Oxford: Basil Blackwell, 1991, pp. 170–9

Dolley M. 'An Introduction to the Coinage of Æthelred II' in *Ethelred the Unready: Papers from the Millenary Conference*, ed. D. Hill, British Archaeological Reports, British series 59, 1978, pp. 115–33

Dronke U., G. P. Helgadottir, G. W. Weber, H. Bekker-Nielson (eds), *Speculum Norroenum*, Odense: Odense University Press, 1981

Fell C. 'Víkingarvísur', in *Speculum Norroenum*, ed. U. Dronke *et al.*, Odense: Odense University Press, 1981

Fellows Jensen G. 'The Vikings in England: A Review', *ASE* 4, 1975, pp. 181–206

Fillis J. *Breaking and Riding*, London: J. A. Allen & Company Limited, 1902, reprinted 1986

Frank R. 'King Cnut in the Verse of his Skalds' in *The Reign of Cnut, King of England, Denmark and Norway*, ed. A. R. Rumble, London: Leicester University Press, 1994, pp. 106–24

Friis-Jensen K. (ed.), *Saxo Grammaticus: A Medieval Author between Norse and Latin Culture*, Copenhagen: Museum Tusculanum Press, 1981

Gillingham J. 'Chronicles and Coins as Evidence for Levels of Tribute and Taxation in Late Tenth- and Early Eleventh-Century England', *EHR* 105, 1990, pp. 939–50

––––––– ' "The Most Precious Jewel in the English Crown": Levels of Danegeld and Heregeld in the Early Eleventh Century', *EHR* 104, 1989, pp. 373–84

Gordon E. V. 'The Date of Æthelred's Treaty with the Vikings: Olaf Tryggvason and the Battle of Maldon', *Modern Language Review* XXXII, 1937, pp. 24–32

Graham-Campbell J. (ed.), *Cultural Atlas of the Viking World*, London, 1994

Gransden A. *Historical Writing in England c. 550 to c. 1307*, London: Routledge & Kegan Paul, 1974

Griffith P. *The Viking Art of War*, London: Greenhill Books, 1995

Harrison K. *The Framework of Anglo-Saxon History to AD 900*, Cambridge: Cambridge University Press, 1976

Hart C. *The Danelaw*, London: The Hambledon Press, 1992

Heaton P. *Sailing*, Harmondsworth: Penguin Books, 1978

Higham N. J. *The Death of Anglo-Saxon England*, Stroud: Sutton Publishing, 1997

Hill D. (ed.), *An Atlas of Anglo-Saxon England*, Oxford: Basil Blackwell, 1981

––––––– (ed.), *Ethelred the Unready: Papers from the Millenary Conference*, British Archaeological Reports, British Series 59, 1978

––––––– 'Trends in the Development of Towns during the Reign of Ethelred II' in *Ethelred the Unready: Papers from the Millenary Conference*, ed. D. Hill, British Archaeological Reports, British series 59, 1978, pp. 214–26

––––––– and A. R. Rumble (eds), *The Defence of Wessex: The Burghal Hidage and Anglo-Saxon Fortifications*, Manchester: Manchester University Press, 1996

Hinton D. A. 'Late Saxon Treasure and Bullion' in *Ethelred the Unready: Papers from the Millenary Conference*, ed. D. Hill, British Archaeological Reports, British Series 59, 1978

Holmes G. (ed.), *The Oxford Illustrated History of Medieval Europe*, London: Guild Publishing, 1988

Holtzmann R. *Geschichte der sächsischen Kaiserzeit, 900–1024*, Munich, 1943

Howard I. 'Swein Forkbeard's Invasions of England: a thesis submitted to the University of Manchester for the degree of Ph.D. in the Faculty of Arts', 2000 (copies lodged with the John Rylands University Library, Manchester)

John E. 'The Encomium Emmae Reginae: A Riddle and a Solution', *Bulletin of the John Rylands Library* 63, 1980, pp. 58–94

––––––– 'War and Society in the Tenth Century: The Maldon Campaign', *TRHS* 5th series 27, 1977, pp. 173–95

Jonsson K. 'The Coinage of Cnut' in *The Reign of Cnut, King of England, Denmark and Norway*, ed. A. R. Rumble, London: Leicester University Press, 1994, pp. 193–230

Kennedy A. 'Byrhtnoth's Obits and Twelfth-Century Accounts of the Battle of Maldon' in *The Battle of Maldon AD 991*, ed. D. Scragg, Oxford: Basil Blackwell, 1991, pp. 59–78

Ker N. R. *Catalogue of Manuscripts Containing Anglo-Saxon*, Oxford: Clarendon Press, 1957

Keynes S. *Anglo-Saxon History: A Select Bibliography*, 10th and 11th editions, Cambridge: University of Cambridge, 1996

—— 'Cnut's Earls' in *The Reign of Cnut, King of England, Denmark and Norway*, ed. A. R. Rumble, London: Leicester University Press, 1994, pp. 43–88

—— 'Crime and Punishment in the Reign of King Æthelred the Unready' in *People and Places in Northern Europe 500–1600*, ed. I. Wood and N. Lund, Woodbridge: The Boydell Press, 1991, pp. 67–81

—— 'The Declining Reputation of King Æthelred the Unready' in *Ethelred the Unready: Papers from the Millenary Conference*, ed. D. Hill, British Archaeological Reports, British series 59, 1978, pp. 227–53

—— *The Diplomas of King Æthelred 'the Unready' 978–1016: A Study in their Use as Historical Evidence*, Cambridge Studies in Medieval Life and Thought, 3rd series, vol. 13, Cambridge: Cambridge University Press, 1980

—— 'The Historical Context of the Battle of Maldon' in *The Battle of Maldon AD 991*, ed. D. Scragg, Oxford: Basil Blackwell, 1991, pp. 81–113

—— 'A Tale of Two Kings: Alfred the Great and Æthelred the Unready', *TRHS* 5th series 36, 1986, pp. 195–217

—— 'The Vikings in England' in *The Oxford Illustrated History of the Vikings*, ed. P. Sawyer, Oxford, 1997, pp. 48–82

Lapidge M. 'The Life of St Oswald' in *The Battle of Maldon AD 991*, ed. D. Scragg, Oxford: Basil Blackwell, 1991, pp. 51–8

Lawson M. K. *Cnut: The Danes in England in the Early Eleventh Century*, London: Longman, 1993

—— 'Danegeld and Heregeld Once More', *EHR* 105, 1990, pp. 951–61

—— ' "Those Stories Look True": Levels of Taxation in the Reigns of Æthelred II and Cnut', *EHR* 104, 1989, pp. 385–406

Leyser K. J. *Rule and Conflict in an Early Medieval Society: Ottonian Saxony*, London: Edward Arnold, 1979

Lot F. *Les Derniers Carolingiens, Lothaire, Louis V, Charles de Lorraine (954–991)*, Paris, 1891

—— *Études sur le règne de Hugues Capet*, Paris, 1903

Loyn H. *The Vikings in Britain*, Oxford: Blackwell Publishers Ltd, 1994

Lund N. 'The Armies of Swein Forkbeard and Cnut: Leding or Lið?', *ASE* 15, 1986, pp. 105–18

—— 'Cnut's Danish Kingdom' in *The Reign of Cnut, King of England, Denmark and Norway*, ed. A. R. Rumble, London: Leicester University Press, 1994, pp. 27–42

—— 'The Danish Perspective' in *The Battle of Maldon AD 991*, ed. D. Scragg, Oxford: Basil Blackwell, 1991, pp. 114–42

—— *Lið, Leding og Landeværn: Hær og samfund i Danmark i ældre middelalder*, Roskilde: Vikingeskibshallen, 1996

—— 'Sven Haraldsson (Forkbeard)' in *Medieval Scandinavia: An Encyclopedia*, ed. P. Pulsiano, New York and London: Garland Publishing Inc., 1993, p. 627

—— 'Viking Age' in *Medieval Scandinavia: An Encyclopedia*, ed. P. Pulsiano, New York and London: Garland Publishing Inc., 1993, p. 693

Macgowen K. *Clonmacnois*, Dublin: Kamac Publications, 1998

Margary I. D. *Roman Roads in Britain*, London: John Baker, 1973

Mayr-Harting H. *The Coming of Christianity to Anglo-Saxon England*, 3rd edition, Pennsylvania: Pennsylvania State University Press, 1991

Meaney A. L. 'Scyld Scefing and the Dating of Beowulf – Again', *Bulletin of the John Rylands University Library of Manchester* 71, 1989, pp. 7–40

Metcalf D. M. 'Can we believe the very large figure of £72,000 for the geld levied by Cnut in 1018?' in *Studies in Late Anglo-Saxon Coinage in Memory of Bror Emil Hildebrand*, ed. K. Jonsson, Stockholm: Svenska Numismatiska Föreningen, 1990

———— 'The Ranking of the Boroughs: Numismatic Evidence from the Reign of Æthelred II' in *Ethelred the Unready: Papers from the Millenary Conference*, ed. D. Hill, British Archaeological Reports, British series 59, 1978, pp. 160–90

Mills A. D. *A Dictionary of English Place-Names*, Oxford: Oxford University Press, revised 1996

Nightingale P. 'The Ora, the Mark, and the Mancus: Weight-Standards and the Coinage in Eleventh-Century England, Part 2', *Numismatic Chronicle* CXLIV, 1984, pp. 234–48

Niles J. D. and M. Amodio, *Anglo-Scandinavian England: Norse-English Relations in the Period before the Conquest*, University Press of America, 1989

Noonan T. S. 'The Scandinavians in European Russia' in *The Oxford Illustrated History of the Vikings*, ed. P. Sawyer, Oxford: Oxford University Press, 1997

Oman C. *A History of England before the Norman Conquest*, London: Bracken Books, 1994

Poole R. 'Sighvatr Þórðarson' in *Medieval Scandinavia: An Encyclopedia*, ed. P. Pulsiano, New York and London: Garland Publishing Inc., 1993, pp. 580–1

———— 'Skaldic Verse and Anglo-Saxon History: Some Aspects of the Period 1009–1016', *Speculum* 62/2, 1987, pp. 265–98

———— *Studies in Chronology and History*, Oxford: Clarendon Press, 1934

Pulsiano P. (ed.), *Medieval Scandinavia: An Encyclopedia*, New York and London: Garland Publishing Inc., 1993

Rafasson S. 'The Atlantic Islands' in *The Oxford Illustrated History of the Vikings*, ed. P. Sawyer, Oxford: Oxford University Press, 1997, pp. 110–33

Richards J. D. *English Heritage Book of Viking Age England*, London: B. T. Batsford Ltd, 1991

Ritchie A. and D. J. Breeze, *Invaders of Scotland: An Introduction to the Archaeology of the Romans, Scots, Angles and Vikings, Highlighting the Monuments in the Care of the Secretary of State for Scotland*, Edinburgh: HMSO, 1991

Ritchie R. L. *The Normans in England before Edward the Confessor, An Inaugural Lecture delivered in the University College of the South West of England on 3rd May 1948*, 1948

Roesdahl E. *The Vikings*, London: Penguin Books, 1992

Rumble A. R. (ed.), *The Reign of Cnut, King of England, Denmark and Norway*, London: Leicester University Press, 1994

Sawyer P. 'Cnut's Scandinavian Empire' in *The Reign of Cnut, King of England, Denmark and Norway*, ed. A. R. Rumble, London: Leicester University Press, 1994, pp. 10–22

———— 'The Density of the Danish Settlement in England', *University of Birmingham Hist. Jnl* 6, 1958

———— 'Ethelred II, Olaf Tryggvason, and the Conversion of Norway' in *Anglo-Scandinavian England: Norse-English Relations in the Period before the Conquest*, ed. J. D. Niles and M. Amodio, University Press of America, 1989

———— *Kings and Vikings: Scandinavia and Europe AD 700–1100*, New York: Barnes & Noble, 1994

—— (ed.), *The Oxford Illustrated History of the Vikings*, Oxford: Oxford University Press, 1997

—— 'Swein Forkbeard and the Historians' in *Church and Chronicle in the Middle Ages: Essays presented to John Taylor*, ed. I. Wood and G. A. Loud, London: The Hambledon Press, 1991

—— 'The Wealth of England in the Eleventh Century', *TRHS* 5th series 15, 1965, pp. 145–64

Scragg D. (ed.), *The Battle of Maldon AD 991*, Oxford: Basil Blackwell, 1991

Smyth A. P. *King Alfred the Great*, Oxford: Oxford University Press, 1995

Southern R. W. *The Making of the Middle Ages*, London: Arrow Books, 1959

Stafford P. 'The Reign of Æthelred II: A Study in the Limitations on Royal Policy and Action' in *Ethelred the Unready: Papers from the Millenary Conference*, ed. D. Hill, British Archaeological Reports, British series 59, 1978, pp. 15–46

—— *Unification and Conquest: A Political and Social History of England in the Tenth and Eleventh Centuries*, London: Edward Arnold, 1989

Stenton F. M. *Anglo-Saxon England*, 3rd edition, Oxford: Clarendon Press, 1971

—— *The Early History of the Abbey of Abingdon*, Oxford: Blackwell, 1913, reissued Stamford: Paul Watkins, 1989

Storey R. L. *Chronology of the Medieval World 800 to 1491*, Oxford: Helicon Publishing Ltd, 1994

Thomson R. *William of Malmesbury*, Woodbridge: The Boydell Press, 1987

Todd M. *The Barbarians: Goths, Franks and Vandals*, London: B. T. Batsford Ltd, 1972

Wätjen R. L. *Dressage Riding: A Guide for the Training of Horse and Rider*, London: J. A. Allen & Co., translated from the German 5th revised edition, 1958, reprinted 1988

Welch M. *English Heritage Book of Anglo-Saxon England*, London: B. T. Batsford, 1992

Whaley D. *Heimskringla: An Introduction*, London: Viking Society for Northern Research, University College, 1991

—— 'Heimskringla' in *Medieval Scandinavia: An Encyclopedia*, ed. P. Pulsiano, New York and London: Garland Publishing Inc., 1993, pp. 276–9

Whitelock D. 'The Dealings of the Kings of England with Northumbria in the Tenth and Eleventh Centuries' in *The Anglo-Saxons: Studies in Some Aspects of their History and Culture presented to Bruce Dickins*, ed. P. Clemoes, London: Bowes & Bowes, 1959

Whitton D. 'The Society of Northern Europe in the High Middle Ages' in *The Oxford Illustrated History of Medieval Europe*, ed. G. Holmes, London: Guild Publishing, 1988

Williams A. ' "Cockles Amongst the Wheat": Danes and English in the Western Midlands in the First Half of the Eleventh Century', *Midland History* 11, 1986, pp. 1–22

Wilson D. M. 'Danish Kings and England in the Late Tenth and Early Eleventh Centuries – Economic Implications', *Anglo-Norman Studies* 3, 1981, pp. 188–96

Wood I. and N. Lund (eds), *People and Places in Northern Europe 500–1600: Essays in Honour of Peter Hayes Sawyer*, Woodbridge: The Boydell Press, 1991

Wormald P. 'Æthelred the Lawmaker' in *Ethelred the Unready: Papers from the Millenary Conference*, ed. D. Hill, British Archaeological Reports, British series 59, 1978, pp. 47–80

—— *The Making of English Law: King Alfred to the Twelfth Century*, vol. I, *Legislation and its Limits*, Oxford: Blackwell, 1999

Index

Adam of Bremen's *Chronicle*
  Swein Forkbeard 8, 9, 32–3, 51, 103
  Scandinavian invasion of Saxony:
    994 48
  Cnut's mother 101
  Sawyer's opinion about Adam's
    Chronicle 34, 99
  comparison with Snorri Sturluson's
    Heimskringla 150–1, 152
Abingdon 168
*ÆE see Anglo-Saxon Chronicle,
  Æthelredian Exemplar*
Æfice 87
Ælfgeat *see* Ælfheah of Devonshire
Ælfgifu of Northampton 107, 108, 116,
  137
Ælfheah, archbishop of Canterbury 46–7,
  70, 95–7, 104
Ælfheah of Devonshire 142
Ælfhelm, ealdorman 69 fig. 8, 70–1, 107,
  108, 132
Ælfhun, bishop of London 96, 97, 106
  n.37, 131
Ælfmær of Canterbury 95
Ælfmær, abbot 95
Ælfmær, archdeacon *see* Ælfmær of
  Canterbury
Ælfred, king's reeve, *see also* Ælfweard,
  king's reeve 96
Ælfric, abbot of Eynsham 16
Ælfric, archbishop of Canterbury 70–1
Ælfric, ealdorman of Hampshire 38, 39,
  40, 42, 63–4, 65
Ælfric, ealdorman of Mercia 40, 77
Ælfstan, bishop 39
Ælfthryth, queen 144
Ælfweard, king's reeve 95–6
Ælfwig, bishop of London 128, 131, 168
  n.13
Æscwig, bishop 39
Æthelbald, king of Mercia 110
Æthelmær, ealdorman 71, 117, 118
Æthelmær the Stout 142
Æthelred II, king of England
  parents 6, 12, 14, 16
  succeeds Edward the Martyr as
    king 5–6, 15 fig. 3, 16
  economic features of reign 16, 19–22,
    70, 145

payments of tribute 37, 46, 60–1, 75–6,
    91–2, 96–7, 145
  relations with Norman court 55–6,
    60–1, 70, 124
  St Brice's Day massacre 13, 61–4, 70
  children 3, 5, 131–3, 135, 136, 138
  his fleets 38–9, 52–3, 77–82, 145
  his armies 28–9, 32, 52–3, 75, 84–5,
    89–90, 106, 119, 121–2, 130, 134,
    145
  uses mercenary forces 13, 19, 28, 46–9,
    54–7, 58, 60–1, 70, 106, 124
    mercenaries led by Thorkell the
      Tall 97–8, 100, 102–3, 109, 117,
      122–3, 124, 129–30
    mercenaries led by St Olaf 94, 119,
      121–3, 124, 125, 129–30, 133
  invasion: 1013 109, 113, 115, 117
  exile 11, 13, 49, 61, 115, 118–19, 122,
    124, 126
  restoration 111, 119, 120, 121–3, 127,
    129–31
  Council of Oxford 132
  illness and death 3, 96, 131, 134, 136,
    138, 146
  ministers 3, 5, 64, 68, 70–1, 77, 128,
    131, *see also* witan
    influence of Eadric Streona 85,
      96–7, 108, 132
    ministers withdrawal of
      allegiance 104–9, 127
  charter evidence 37, 43–6, 52
    nn.105–6, 61, 64, 131
  adverse propaganda 3–7, 120, 122–3,
    144–5
  chronological analysis of
    Heimskringla 147–9, 155–60
*Æthelredian Exemplar see under
  Anglo-Saxon Chronicle*
Æthelric, bishop of Sherborne 164, 165
Æthelric of Bocking 37
Æthelstan, son of King Æthelred II 68,
  131
Æthelstan, king of England 15, 53
Æthelstan, relative of King Æthelred 87,
  88
Æthelweard, ealdorman 46, 47, 118
Æthelweard, son of Æthelmær the
  Stout 142

Alchester 116
Alfred, son of King Æthelred and Queen
   Emma 131, 135, 141, 142
Alfred the Great 29, 144
Ancaster 114
Andover 47
Anglo-Saxon Chronicle
   significance as a historical source for this
      period 1–3
   Archbishop Wulfstan's influence 3–5,
      167–8
   Æthelredian Exemplar
      a source for the annals in *ASC*
         CDEF 3–5, 3 nn. 9–10, 142,
         167–8
      a biased source 3–5, 52, 57–9,
         104–7, 127–8
   ASC A: a source independent of the
      Æthelredian Exemplar 57–9
   ASC CDEF annal for 1008:
      reconstruction 163–7
Ari the Wise
   Snorri uses his chronology 121
   chronological analysis of
      Heimskringla 148–62
Ashingdon, battle of 139, 140, 142

Baltic Sea 8, 9, 11, 23, 35, 50, 63, 72, 83,
   158–60
Bamburgh 42–3, 44, 49
Bath 106, 117, 118, 122
Bayeux Tapestry 29
Bedford 88, 116, 117
Bedfordshire 91
Benno, duke of Saxony 48
Berkshire 75, 82, 84, 91
Boleslav, king of the Wends 8, 9, 153
Bourne 114
Brihtric, brother of Eadric Streona 79–81
Brihtric, son of Ælfheah of
   Devonshire 142
Buckinghamshire 88, 91
Burgh monastery *see* Peterborough
Byrhtnoð, ealdorman 35–6, 44
Byzantium 17

Calne 52
Cambridge 88
Cambridgeshire 87, 91
Campbell, Alistair *see under* Snorri
   Sturluson
Cannings Marsh 90
Canterbury
   commercial importance 22, 38
   attacks by Scandinavian armies 82,
      91–2, 94, 95–7, 104

   garrisoned by Swein Forkbeard's
      forces 106, 122, 130
caput anni 42–3, 49, 168
Castor 116
Celts 11, 38, 57
Channel (English) 35, 55, 67, 70, 84, 135
Cheshire 57
Chilterns 86
Clyst 58
Cnut the Great
   mother 8, 67, 101
   brothers 10–11, 67, 100, 133
   invades England: 1003–1005 67, 101–2
   invades England: 1013–1014 27,
      100–2, 113–14, 118–20, 123, 125,
      128–30, 134
   becomes king of Denmark 106, 129,
      133–4
   conquest of England: 1015–17 1, 3, 5,
      12, 27, 31–32, 101, 104, 127, 133,
      135–40
   marriages and children 106–8, 116,
      120, 137, 140–1, 142, 145–6
   establishes his authority in England 5,
      12, 73, 98, 140–3, 145–6
   chronological analysis of
      Heimskringla 94, 121, 155–61
coins / coinage
   English coinage 14–15, 15 n. 14, 19, 22
   Swein Forkbeard's Danish coins 51
   Cnut's Danish coins 133
Cookham 52, 81
Cornwall 57
Cosham 96, 136
Council of Enham 79, 81
Croyland Abbey 110–11, 115
Croyland Chronicle see Ingulph's Chronicle
Cumberland *see also* Strathclyde 18, 49,
   52, 54–6

Danelaw
   long-standing Scandinavian presence in
      eastern England 12
   submission to the West Saxon kings 12
   increase in population and wealth 21–2,
      127, 145
   St Brice's day massacre 61
   local leaders 68, 69 fig. 8, 70–1,
      104–7, 132
   supports Swein Forkbeard 13, 106–7,
      109–10, 117, 120, 128, 145
   re-conquest by King Æthelred's
      forces 129–30
   supports the Ætheling Edmund
      (Ironside) 131–2, 135, 137
   Cnut's military success 137, 139

attitude of twelfth-century writers 44 n. 68
Danish king lists 133
Dean 58
Derbyshire 107
Denmark
ruled by Harald Bluetooth (Gormsson) 8, 32
Swein Forkbeard's succession 8, 13, 32
control of Denmark: 990–995 9, 13, 33–4, 50
conflict and siege of Hedeby 9, 34, 48, 50–1, 103
Swein's authority: 995–1013 9, 51, 63, 66–8, 72–3, 83–4, 94–5, 98, 99–100, 102–3, 109
wealth and political stability 66–7, 72, 102, 113
Cnut's succession and authority 133–4, 143
chronological analysis of *Heimskringla* 148–60
Devon, *see also* Devonshire 57–8, 63, 64
Devonshire 54, 57–8
Domesday Book 2
population figures 21, 23, 23 n.43
most populated towns 117
Dorchester 116
Dorset 136
Dublin 50
Dunstable 118
Dunstan, saint, archbishop of Canterbury 6, 7, 131
Durham 108

Eadmer 6–7, 144, 145, 146
Eadnoth, bishop 96, 97
Eadric Streona,
ealdorman of Mercia 77
brother *see also* Brihtric 79
influence over the king 6, 71, 85, 96–7, 108–9, 115, 132, 136
Fabian strategy 85
succession dispute: 1016 3, 131–2, 135, 137, 138, 139–41
'treacherous' conduct 5, 71, 84–5, 104, 107, 132, 136, 139–40
relationship with Cnut 136, 137, 138, 139, 140, 141
death 5, 141–2
Eadwig, brother of Æfice 87
Eadwig, king of the peasants 142
Eadwig, son of King Æthelred, brother of Edmund Ironside 131, 140, 141, 142
Ealdred, bishop of Worcester 168

East Anglia
ships 40–2
Scandinavian attacks 62, 66–8, 70, 86–8, 91, 104
Æthelred's campaign 121–2, 129–30, 134
Earl Thorkell 141–2
Edda 150, 153
Edgar, king of England
'the Peaceable' 12, 14
coronation and authority 57
economic expansion and reform of the coinage 14–15, 16, 144
use of mercenaries 28
dispute over his successor 16
Edith, daughter of Earl Godwine 73
Edith, daughter of King Æthelred 85
Edmund Ironside
given precedence over his half brothers 131
dispute over his title to the throne 3, 6, 131–2, 137, 138–9
rebellion against his father 106, 107, 132–3
marriages 104, 107, 133, 137, 140
support of Earl Uhtred 104, 133, 135, 137
Eadric's treachery 136, 139–40
battles fought against Cnut 39, 106, 139
division of England and death 140
Edmund's sons 140–1
supported by Archbishop Wulfstan 3, 5, 47, 167–8
favourable propaganda 3–6, 47, 120, 122, 144, 167–8
lost *Life of King Edmund Ironside* 5–6
Edward the Confessor
son of Queen Emma and King Æthelred 3
precedence given to Edmund Ironside in charter S.933 131
succession dispute 131–2, 135, 138, 141
retires to Normandy 142
abolishes heregeld tax 19
Edward the Martyr 5, 6, 16, 144
Eglaf 76, 82–3, 94, 124
Elbe, River 48
Ely 88, 115, 131
Emma, queen of England
sister of Richard II, duke of Normandy 60, 70
marriage to Æthelred 60, 70

known as Ælfgifu in England   60
children by Æthelred   3, 131, 141
control of Exeter   64, 70
friendship with Eadric Streona   3, 131,
    132, 138, 139, 141
succession dispute   3, 131–2, 135, 138
friendship with Thorkell the Tall   98,
    132, 135, 136, 138, 139, 141
controls the burgh of London   138, 139,
    140
negotiates with Cnut   138–9, 140–1,
    145–6
children by Cnut   142
sponsor of *Encomium Emmae*
    Reginae   99, 135, 136, 140
Encomium Emmae Reginae
provenance   1, 99
propaganda purpose   5, 123, 139–40,
    141
selective information   33, 50, 138
credible information   34, 99, 126
manipulated information   67, 123, 125,
    133, 138, 139–40
evidences how armies used horses   27
evidences that Thorkell was in Denmark
    c. 1011   84, 92–3, 95
Thorkell's relations with King
    Swein   94–5, 98, 103
King Swein's invasion and conquest of
    England   98
Cnut's accession   106, 120, 128–9, 134
Cnut's return to Denmark   134
Cnut's invasion and conquest of
    England   135, 136, 139–40, 141
Thorkell's relations with Queen
    Emma   132, 135, 136
Thorkell's relations with King
    Cnut   133
Cnut's marriage to Queen Emma   140
chronological analysis of
    Heimskringla   147, 159
English Channel *see* Channel
Enham *see* Council of Enham
Erik Hákonarson of Lade
alliance with Swein Forkbeard   9–10,
    63, 72–3, 133
support for Cnut   135, 141
chronological analysis of
    Heimskringla   154–61
Erik the Victorious, king of Sweden   9, 34,
    50–1, 67
Ermine Street   114
Essex   32, 35, 36–7, 42, 44, 46, 84, 85, 91
Estonia   154
Estrith, daughter of Swein Forkbeard   10
Exe, River   57–8

Exeter   57–9, 60, 63–4
Eynsham monastery   118
Eysysla   158

Fagrskinna   148
Finland   158
Five Boroughs   104
Fosse Way   118
France   35
Friesland *see* Frisia
Frisia   23, 32, 33, 35, 158–60
Frisians   30, 38
Frome, River   136
Fyn   8
fyrd   17, 19, 32, 60, 87, 90, 113, 117, 119,
    136

Gainsborough   104, 107, 111, 113, 114,
    118, 119, 120, 124, 128, 130, 134
Garda   35, 154
Gardariki, *see* Garda
gafol ɫ metsung   17–18, 76, 77, 83, 86, 91,
    92, 94, 96, 97, 145
Gerbert d'Aurillac   26
Gesta Normannorum Ducum see William of
    Jumièges's Chronicle
Godric, abbot of Croyland
    accused of treachery   111, 115
Godwine, bishop   95
Godwine, earl of Wessex   73
Gotland   157, 158, 160
Greenwich   85, 88, 90, 98, 102, 118, 122,
    124–5
Gross Domestic Product   21, 23
Gudrod Ericsson   156, 157, 160
Gunhild, daughter of Earl Godwine   73
Gunnhild, daughter of King Cnut and Queen
    Emma   142
Gunnhild, sister of Swein Forkbeard   62
Gunnhild, wife of Swein Forkbeard   8, 9,
    10, 67
Guthmund, Steita's son   36–7, 47
Gyrth, son of Earl Godwine   73
Gytha, daughter of Swein Forkbeard   8, 9,
    156, 157, 160
Gytha, daughter of Jarl Thorgils   73

Hakon IV, king of Norway   151
Hákon, earl of Lade   8, 9, 50, 153, 154, 156
Hakon the Good, king of Norway,   153,
    154
Hampshire   46, 52, 56, 58, 59, 63–4, 65,
    75, 79, 82, 84, 91
Hampton *see* Northampton
Harald Bluetooth, king of Denmark   8, 32,
    33, 50, 51, 103, 154

Harald Fairhair, king of Norway 50
Harald Grenski 154, 161
Harald Greyskin, king of Norway 152, 154
Harald, son(s) of Swein Forkbeard 10, 67, 100, 133
Harald, son of Cnut and Ælfgifu of Northampton, grandson of Swein Forkbeard 137
Harold II, king of England 28, 73
Harthacnut 142
Hastings 91
Hastings, battle of 29
Hattatal 151
Head-ransom of Ottar the Black 127
Hebrides 48
Hedeby 9, 34, 35
Heimskringla, history of the kings of Norway
    value as a source based on contemporary or early tradition 7
    late tenth century ships and sea battles 29–30
    Swein Forkbeard's raiding activities and first invasion of England 32
    how the *lið*s came to England 35
    Scandinavian activity in the Irish Sea 48–9
    Olaf Tryggvason's claim to the throne of Norway 50
    Swein Forkbeard's wives 67, 101
    skaldic verse and accompanying explanations 93–4
    validity of some explanations questioned 94
    St Olaf's support for King Æthelred 121–2, 129–30
    chronological analysis 94, 121, 128, 147–62
Heming 76, 82–3, 84, 92, 93, 94, 124, 159
Hemming *see* Heming
Henry of Huntingdon's Chronicle 6, 39–40, 72
Henry the Fowler 25, 26
here 19, 76, 86, 87, 104, 113, 118, 122, 136
heregeld 17–19, 19 n.26, 48, 52
Hertfordshire 91
Hiring 103
History of the Archbishops of Hamburg-Bremen see Adam of Bremen
Hjorungavag, battle of 161
Horik I, king of Denmark 31
Hugh, Norman reeve of Exeter 64
Hugh Capet 26
Humber, River 42, 44, 49, 104, 107, 109, 134

Hungarians, *see also* Magyars 25
Huntingdonshire 91

Iceland 149, 152, 156
Ingulph, abbot of Croyland 110
Ingulph's Chronicle 110–11, 113, 114, 115
Ipswich 45, 86, 88, 90
Irchester 116
Ireland 11, 16, 48, 50
Irish Sea 12, 17, 32, 48, 49, 50, 52, 57
Irthlingborough 116

John of Worcester's Chronicle
    value as a source 1, 5–6
    distortions 38
    additional facts or chroniclers' interpretations? 43, 47, 54, 64–5, 66, 68, 71, 74, 79–80, 81, 82, 84–5, 86, 88, 90, 95–6, 97, 104, 113, 116, 118–19, 136
    sometimes more accurate than the *ASC* 88, 96–7, 168
    indicates 'missing' *ASC* annals 91–3, 94
    the battle of Maldon 36
    the invasion in 1006 76, 82–3
    the invasion in 1013 104, 106–7
    chronological analysis of *Heimskringla* 152, 158, 159
Jomsborg 8, 9
Jomsvikings 161
Jomsvikings saga 8
Jostein, 35, 36–7, 46, 47, 48
Justin *see* Jostein
Jutland 8, 35, 48, 77, 93, 158, 159, 160

Kaupang 35
Kenneth 108
Kent 35, 37, 38, 46, 78, 84, 85, 86, 91, 136
King Street 114
Kinnlima side 158
Knútr *see* Cnut
Knútsdrápa 101, 102, 127
Knytlinga saga 7, 100, 128, 133
Kringla heimsins see also Heimskringla 149

landfyrd 17–18
Laws
    II Æthelred 19, 35, 36, 47, 48, 49, 51, 52, 57, 61, 98
    V Æthelred 78, 79
Lechfeld, battle of 24–25
leding 12, 31–2, 74, 100
Leicester 118
Leo, bishop of Trèves 55

Leofrun, abbess   95
Leofwine, abbot   95
Leofwine, ealdorman   87, 142
Leofwine, son of Earl Godwine   73
Life of King Edmund Ironside   5–6
Lifing, archbishop of Canterbury *see*
    Lyfing
lið: definition   31–2
Limfjord   35
Lincoln   22, 111, 113, 114, 115, 117, 118,
    133
Lindsey   44, 102, 104, 107, 119, 130, 134
Listven, battle of   26
London
    economic, strategic and political
        importance   21–2, 86, 109, 115–17,
        121, 127, 135, 138
    disruption of trade   38, 81–2, 85–6,
    harboured English fleets   38–40, 81
    attack by Olaf and Swein: September
        993   25, 42–3, 44, 46, 47, 49
    Ealdorman Ealdred and the *witan*: Easter
        1012   96–7
    Archbishop Ælfheah buried in St Paul's
        Minster   96–7
    two bishops: 1014   106, 128–9, 131
    the burgh   106, 121, 122, 127–8, 129
    Swein's campaign: 1013   115–17
    Submission to Swein Forkbeard   13,
        118–19, 120, 122, 124–5
    Æthelred recaptures the burgh   121,
        129, 134
    Queen Emma controls the
        burgh   138–40
London Bridge   121, 129, 158
Lyfing, archbishop of Canterbury   103, 131

Magasætan   139
Magnus the Good, king of Norway   153,
    155
Magyars   24, 26
Malcolm   108
Maldon   36–7, 45
Maldon, battle of   33, 35–7, 44
Man, isle of   48, 49, 51, 52, 54–6
Medeshamsted monastery *see* Peterborough
Mercia   21, 22, 72, 74, 77, 91, 102, 116,
    132, 135, 140, 141
Mercian annals   167
Middlesex   91
Morcar   104, 107, 108, 109, 113, 120, 127,
    131, 132, 133

Nene, River   116
Nigel, vicomte of the Contentin   56
Norman Conquest   6, 144

Normandy
    mounted warriors used in battle   28
    English enmity   55–6
    peace agreement: 991   55
    'visit' by 'enemy fleet': 1000   52, 54–6
    Scandinavian army returns to
        England   57
    Æthelred marries Emma of
        Normandy   60–1, 70
    Æthelred's exile in Normandy   119–20,
        124–5
    Æthelings Edward and Alfred in
        Normandy   142
    chronological analysis of
        Heimskringla   156–60
Normans   64, 70, 135
Northampton   90, 115, 116
Northamptonshire   91, 116
Northman, son of Ealdorman
    Leofwine   142
Northumbria   2, 12, 13, 43, 44, 102, 108,
    109, 120, 137, 141, 145
Northumbrians   62, 103, 104, 106, 107,
    108, 129
Norway
    Earl Hákon   9, 50
    Olaf Tryggvason becomes king   48, 50,
        98, 103
    Swein Forkbeard's involvement and
        influence   9, 10, 66, 73, 95, 125, 133
    chronological analysis of
        Heimskringla   94, 120–1, 128,
        148–60
Norwegians   11, 32, 38, 48, 135
Norwich   22, 66, 67, 68, 101, 117

Offa, king of Mercia   110
Olaf *helgi*, king of Norway *see* St Olaf
Olaf Tryggvason, king of Norway
    journey to England   23, 35
    probably not at battle of Maldon   36
    leads Scandinavian army   37–8, 44,
        45–8
    attack on London: September 993   25,
        46–7
    treaty, *II Æthelred*, and friendship with
        King Æthelred   25, 44, 46–7, 48–9,
        57, 78, 98, 145
    return to Norway: 995   49–50, 51, 54,
        103
    battle of Svold: c.1000   10, 29, 63, 67,
        99, 103
    chronological analysis of
        Heimskringla   94, 152–61
Ólafsdrápa   127
Olof Skotkonung, king of Sweden   63, 133

Ordulf 71
Oswig 87, 88
Ottar the Black, skald 120, 121, 122, 127, 130
Otto the Great 24, 26
Ouse, River 88
Oxford 61, 86, 106, 115, 116, 117, 118, 122, 132
Oxfordshire 88, 91

Pallig 47, 51, 58–9, 61, 62–3, 68, 78
Penda, king of Mercia 110
Peterborough 114, 115
  monastery (also known as 'Burgh') 110, 111–12, 115
Pinhoe 57–8
Pomerania 9, 38, 66, 67
Pope John 55

Rani 157
Richard I, duke of Normandy 55
Richard II, duke of Normandy 55–6, 60, 61, 109
Ringmere 88
Rochester 96
Roger of Wendover's Chronicle 56
Rouen 55
Russia 17, 23, 35, 38, 147, 156, 157, 160

Salisbury 63, 65
Sandwich 35, 38, 72, 76, 79, 81, 82, 90, 104, 109, 120, 136
Saxo Grammaticus 8, 133
Saxons 26, 48
Saxony 23, 25, 26, 32, 33, 34, 35, 48, 66
Scandinavian army *see* Scandinavians
Scandinavians: definition 11
Scilly Isles 154
scipfyrd 17–18, 32
sciphere 58
Scotland 43
Severn Estuary 57
Sheppey, isle of 38
Shropshire 75
Siegfried, Saxon margrave 48
Sigeferth 104, 107, 127, 131, 132, 133, 134
Sigeferth's widow 133, 140
Sigeric, archbishop of Canterbury 37, 38, 46, 46 n.74
Sigrid, dowager queen of Sweden, wife of Swein Forkbeard 9, 10, 63, 67, 101, 156
Sigtuna 157
Sigurd, earl of Lade 154
Sigvaldi Strut-Haraldsson 9, 93

Sigvat the Skald
  skaldic verses as historical evidence 93, 106, 121–2, 127
  narrative explanation of verses 93, 127–8
  companion of St Olaf 93, 120–1, 127
  St Olaf's battles 93, 120
  St Olaf and Thorkell the Tall 84, 93, 95
  chronological analysis of *Heimskringla* 121, 128, 147–58
Silchester 116, 117, 118
Silvester II, Pope *see* Gerbert d'Aurillac
Sjæland 8
skaldic verses 7, 93, 106, 148, 149, 150, 151, 152, 153
Skuli, duke 151
Slavs 11, 25, 26, 33, 38
Snorri Sturluson
  author of *Heimskringla*, sagas of the kings of Norway 7, 127–8
  access to earlier writers and skaldic verses 7, 127–8
  Snorri's knowledge of skaldic verse 93
  Snorri's account of the battle of Svold 42
  Olaf Tryggvason's Irish Sea campaign 49
  St Olaf and Thorkell the Tall raid Viking shipping in c. 1011 93–4, 125
  King Swein's death 126–7
  Æthelred and St Olaf re-capture London and other towns 121–2, 129–30
  Campbell's 'interpretation' 94, 128, 147–9
  chronological analysis of *Heimskringla* 94, 128, 147–62
Somerset 57, 136
Søndervig *see* Suthrvik
Sons of Eric 153, 154
Sota Skerry 157
Southampton 46, 49, 55, 90
Southwark 121, 129
Spalding 110
St Brice's Day massacre 13, 22, 61–2, 70, 132
St Dunstan, *see* Dunstan, archbishop of Canterbury
St Edmund 126
St Mildrith's abbey 96
St Olaf, king of Norway
  skalds, Ottar and Sigvat, knew him personally 120–1, 127
  length of his reign 121
  said to have campaigned in England: 1009–12 94

campaigns off Jutland with Thorkell the
 Tall   77, 93–4, 125
helps King Æthelred re-conquer
 England   94, 119, 121–3, 124–5,
 126, 129–30, 133, 145
leaves England   136
chronological analysis of
 Heimskringla   94, 121, 147–62
St Oswald's arm   115
St Paul's minster   96
St Pega's monastery   111, 115
Stade   48
Staines   86, 117
Stamford   22, 115
Strathclyde *see also* Cumberland   48, 52,
 57
Strut-Harald, earl of Zealand   83, 84, 94
Suderwick *see* Suthrvik
Surrey   86, 91
Sussex   46, 56, 58, 82, 84, 91
Suthrvik   93, 94, 158
Sven Aggesen   8
Svold, battle of   10, 29, 42, 63, 67, 99, 103,
 155, 156, 157, 160
Sweden   17, 38, 50, 66, 73, 95, 133, 156,
 157, 158, 160
Swein Forkbeard
 synopsis of his life   7–11
 rebellion and accession   13, 32–3
 wars against Slavs and Norwegians   33
 driven into exile   13, 32–3
 invasion of England and Maldon
  campaign   33–4, 36
 raids eastern England   42, 43–4
 attacks London: September 993   25, 43,
  44, 46
 peace accord with Æthelred; raids Irish
  Sea locations   25, 46, 47, 48–9, 51,
  57
 returns to Denmark; re-establishes
  authority   34, 48, 49–51, 99–100
 marriages   67
 battle of Svold; hegemony over
  Scandinavia   42, 73, 99
 Swein's children   67, 100–2
 St Brice's Day massacre   13, 62, 63–4
 invasions of England: 1003–1005   13,
  63–6, 67, 68–70, 101
 supports invasions of England
  1006–1011   72–4, 83–4, 93, 95
 Thorkell makes peace with Æthelred:
  Swein's reaction   92, 98, 100, 102–3
 diplomatic offensive; support of northern
  and eastern England   13, 103,
  104–6, 107–8, 109–10, 111, 122,
  125–6, 145

conquest of England   1, 13, 27, 31–2,
 49, 85, 104, 111–18, 119, 120, 122–3,
 124, 125
garrisons London and other towns   121,
 122, 127, 128
death   119, 126–7, 128, 129
tranfer of authority to Cnut   123, 128,
 133–4
chronological analysis of
 Heimskringla   94, 155–62
Swein, brother of Erik of Lade   147, 156
Swein Estrithssson   151
Swein, son of Cnut and Ælfgifu of
 Northampton, grandson of Swein
 Forkbeard   137
Swein, son of Earl Godwine   73

Tees, River   108
Teignton   58
Tempsford   88
Thames, River   46, 85–6, 88, 90, 91,109,
 117, 121, 125, 129, 140
Thames Valley   2, 84, 86, 88, 102, 121, 127
Thanet, isle of   38, 82
Thangbrand the priest   156
Thetford   22, 66, 68, 88, 117
Thietmar, bishop of Merseburg   48, 99,
 131, 138, 150, 159
Thietmar of Merseburg's Chronicle   9,
 32–3, 34, 97, 131, 135, 138
Thingmen   122, 130
Thored, earl   39
Thorkell the Tall Strut-Haraldsson
 attempted invasion of Norway   9
 Thorkell: a subject of King Swein
  Forkbeard   83–4, 94–5
 invades England in 1009   76, 82–3, 84
 joins forces with Heming and Eglaf   76,
  82–3
 attacks Viking ships off Jutland, with St
  Olaf: c. 1011   77, 93–4, 125
 death of his brother, Heming, in
  England   92–3
 returns to England: c. 1011   77, 84, 93
 sack of Canterbury; murder of
  Archbishop Ælfheah   97
 'Thorkell's geld' paid to Ulf of Borresta:
  1012   73
 employed as mercenary by King
  Æthelred   47, 97–8, 100, 103
 King Swein's reaction   92, 98, 100,
  102–3, 109
 King Swein invades England; Thorkell
  remains loyal to King Æthelred   97,
  98, 117, 122, 145
 Thorkell at Greenwich   118, 124

Isle of Wight controlled by forces loyal
  to Thorkell 85, 122, 125
remains in England during Æthelred's
  exile; joined by St Olaf 125–6
helps Æthelred recover his throne 119,
  120, 129–31
disputed English succession 131–2
returns to Denmark; submits to King
  Cnut 133
helps Cnut conquer England 135–8
friendship with Queen Emma 135–6,
  138, 139, 141, 142
marriage of Emma and Cnut 141
made earl of East Anglia 141
effectively regent during Cnut's absences
  from England 142
outlawed by Cnut and removed from the
  scene 142–3
chronological analysis of
  Heimskringla 94, 149, 158–60
Thorketil *see* Thorkell the Tall
Thorney monastery 115
Thurcytel Mare's Head 87
Thurcytel *miles, see also* Thorkell the
  Tall 98
Tidings-Skofti 154
Toste *see* Tostig
Tostig 73, 76, 83, 124
Tostig, son of Earl Godwine 73
Towcester 116
Trent, river 104, 107, 124, 128
Tryggvi Olafsson 50, 153, 154
Turgar, abbot of Croyland 111

Ufegeat 70–1, 107
Uhtred, earl
  family background 108
  attends Æthelred's court in 1013 109
  changes allegiance and acknowledges
    Swein Forkbeard as king 104, 107,
    108, 113, 120, 127
  returns to King Æthelred 131, 134
  supports Edmund (Ironside) 104, 132,
    133, 137
  submits to Cnut 104, 137
  death 137, 137 n. 81, 139
Ulf of Borresta 73
Ulfcytel
  political background 67–8
  commands East Anglian *fyrd* in battle
    against King Swein: 1004 66, 67–8
  battle against Scandinavian invaders:
    1010 86–8
  changes of allegiance 104–6
  supports King Swein 120, 121–2, 127

fights against Æthelred's army:
  1014 106, 129
returns to King Æthelred 131, 134
death 106
unfriðhere see here
Unstrut, battle of 25
Uppland 73, 156

Valdamar, king of Garda 23
Vendland 154, 155

Wallingford 106, 116, 117–18, 122
Waltheof, earl 108
Wantage 52
Wantsum Channel 38
Watling Street 13, 104, 107, 110, 116, 117,
  120, 121
Weser, River 48
Wessex 21, 55, 72, 74, 76, 90, 91, 102,
  127, 135, 136, 139, 140, 141, 145
Wight, isle of
  Scandinavian army's winter quarters:
    993 46
  base for Scandinavian army: 998 52
  base for Scandinavian army: 1001 57–9
  possible winter quarters: 1003 67
  Scandinavian army's winter quarters:
    1006 74–5
  base for Scandinavian army:
    1007–1009 76, 77–8, 81, 83
  base for Scandinavian army after
    campaigning in Kent:
    1009–1013 82, 84, 85, 102
  controlled by Scandinavians loyal to
    Thorkell: 1013 85, 122, 125, 129
  Thorkell's likely place of refuge:
    1021–1022 142
*William of Malmesbury's Chronicle (Gesta
  Regum)* 6, 39, 62–3, 103
William of Jumièges's Chronicle 56, 62,
  109
William the Conqueror 29
Wilton 63–4, 65
Wiltshire 63–4, 65, 90, 91, 136
Winchester 59, 75, 106, 116, 117, 118,
  122, 129, 134
witan 19, 28, 32, 75, 89, 91, 96, 97, 119,
  129
witan of East Anglia 66
Woodstock 52
Worcester 3, 168
Wulf, son of Leofwine 87
Wulfgeat 70–1
Wulfheah 70–1, 107
Wulfnoth, son of Earl Godwine 73

Wulfnoth *cild* 79–81
Wulfric (Spott) 108
Wulfstan, archbishop of York
  an outstanding scholar 16
  disapproves of foreign mercenaries 47
  sponsor of the Æthelredian
    Exemplar 3–5, 47, 167–8

homilies 3,
laws 3, 79, 81
changes of political allegiance 3, 106,
  120, 127, 129, 131

York 3, 22, 106, 117, 128, 137, 141, 168
Yorkshire 43, 108

Warfare in History

The Battle of Hastings: Sources and Interpretations
edited and introduced by Stephen Morillo

Infantry Warfare in the Early Fourteenth Century:
Discipline, Tactics, and Technology
Kelly DeVries

The Art of Warfare in Western Europe during
the Middle Ages, from the Eighth Century to 1340 (second edition)
J. F. Verbruggen

Knights and Peasants:
The Hundred Years War in the French Countryside
Nicholas Wright

Society at War:
The Experience of England and France during the Hundred Years War
edited by Christopher Allmand

The Circle of War in the Middle Ages:
Essays on Medieval Military and Naval History
edited by Donald J. Kagay and L. J. Andrew Villalon

The Anglo-Scots Wars, 1513–1550: A Military History
Gervase Phillips

The Norwegian Invasion of England in 1066
Kelly DeVries

The Wars of Edward III: Sources and Interpretations
edited and introduced by Clifford J. Rogers

War Cruel and Sharp:
English Strategy under Edward III, 1327–1360
Clifford J. Rogers

The Normans and their Adversaries at War:
Essays in Memory of C. Warren Hollister
edited by Richard P. Abels and Bernard S. Bachrach

The Battle of the Golden Spurs (Courtrai, 11 July 1302)
A Contribution to the History of Flanders' War of Liberation
J.F. Verbruggen

War at Sea in the Middle Ages and Renaissance
edited by John B. Hattendorf and Richard W. Unger